Walter ||||W9-CFZ-359|||| Jr.
Collection / 1996

WINE
and
CONVERSATION

Adrienne Lehrer

Wine
and
Conversation

WINE
and
CONVERSATION

Adrienne Lehrer

INDIANA UNIVERSITY PRESS

Bloomington

This book was brought to publication with the assistance of a grant from the Andrew W. Mellon Foundation.

Manufactured in the United States of America

Library of Congress Cataloging in Publication Data

Lehrer, Adrienne.
    Wine and conversation.

    Bibliography: p.
    Includes index.
    1. Semantics. 2. Pragmatics. 3. Wine tasting—
Language. 4. Conversation. I. Title.
P325.L368 1983   412   82-48538
ISBN 0-253-36550-3
1 2 3 4 5 87 86 85 84 83

To Keith, Mark, and David

Contents

Acknowledgments   ix

Introduction   xi

Part I: The Semantics of Wine

1. Wine Words   3
2. Extending the Vocabulary   16
3. There Are Intensions and Intentions:
   An Exercise in Applied Philosophy   30

Part II: Wine Experiments

4. Remarks on Methodology   57
5. Experiments and Subjects   61
6. The Stanford Subjects   70
7. The Tucson Subjects   86
8. Wine Scientists—The Davis Subjects   113

Part III: Wine Talk in a Communicative Framework

9. Functions of Language   143
10. The Development of Scientific Language   152
11. Nonscientific Uses of Language   168

Part IV: The Semantics of Personality

12. Describing People; Or, Where Angels Fear to Tread   189

Conclusion   217

Notes   221

Bibliography   227

Index   235

Acknowledgments

I am grateful to the many people who have helped me at various stages of my work. I would like to thank the fellows and staff of the Center for Advanced Studies in the Behavioral Sciences, Stanford, California, where I began these studies. The opportunity to learn from social scientists in fields other than linguistics was a major impetus in my venturing beyond the traditional limits of the discipline. I also wish to thank the Arizona Foundation for supporting the experiments described in chapter 8.

I am also indebted to many individuals who read the manuscript in part or whole and made valuable suggestions. They include Adrian Akmajian, Richard Demers, Eva Kittay, Bill Labov, Tom Larson, Keith Lehrer, Sally McConnell-Ginet, Eugene Mielke, Richard Oehrle, Susan Philips, John Reid, Philip Rubin, Stephan Shanfield, Andrew Sihler, Susan Steele, Christine Tanz, and other colleagues at the University of Arizona and in Philosophy at the University of Illinois at Chicago Circle, where I was a visiting professor in the fall of 1979. The remaining errors must be blamed solely on me. I also want to thank Lin Hall, Patty Destafano, and Elisa Diaz for help in preparing the manuscript. Above all, I am indebted to my subjects for their cooperation and encouragement.

Chapter 1 is an expanded and revised version of my article 'Talking about wine', *Language* 51 (1975), and some of chapter 6 first appeared in that article. This material is used by permission of the Linguistic Society of America. Chapter 2 is partly based on my 'Structures of the lexicon and transfer of meaning', *Lingua* 45 (1978):95–123, and is used by permission of the North-Holland Publishing Company. The material in chapter 6 was reported in 'We drank wine, we talked, and a good time was had by all', which appeared in *Semiotica 23*, and is used with permission of Mouton Publishers. A German translation of chapter 8 appeared in *Zeitschrift für Semiotik 4* and is reprinted with the permission of the editor. Table 40 is from 'The development of a vocabulary and profile assessment procedure for evaluating the flavour contribution of cider and perry aroma constituents' by A. A. Williams, which appeared in the *Journal of the Sciences of Food and Agriculture 26*, and is reprinted by permission of the author. Portions of chapters 11 and 12 originally appeared in Adrienne Lehrer, 'Critical communication: wine and therapy', in *Exceptional Language and Linguistics*, edited by L. Obler and L. Menn (New York: Academic Press, 1982), and are reprinted by permission of the publisher. Lengthy quotations in chapter 12 are taken from *Diagnostic and Statistical Manual of Mental Disorders,* 2nd and 3rd editions, and reprinted by permission of the American Psychiatric Association; and from Carl Rogers, *Client-Centered Therapy* (copyright © 1951, renewed 1979) and Rogers, *On Becoming a Person* (copyright © 1961) and reprinted by permission of the publishers, Houghton Mifflin Company.

Tucson, Arizona
August 1982

Introduction

This book is not about wine, but about talking about wine. I use this semantic domain to explore problems of lexical meaning, denotation, semantic extension, and a variety of communicative and social functions that are served by language. Wine talk provides a rich corpus to work with since it occurs naturally in many settings—from convivial dinner party conversation to critical discussion and evaluation by connoisseurs to published research by enologists and other professional scientists.

One point that will be emphasized and empirically supported is that language is a dynamic, fluid, and versatile instrument. The idea that every word has a precise meaning and a fixed denotation is a myth. Indeed, the vocabulary of a language, though large, is finite, but the world, including the world of human perception, thought, and experience, is astronomically large in scope and does not divide itself neatly into categories that necessarily correspond to our vocabulary items. As a result, the words we have must make do for infinitely many things and experiences. Of course, we can always modify and qualify what we say, but it is not efficient to add a dozen modifying clauses to every utterance to gain greater precision, and, as I shall argue in chapter 11, it also is not necessary most of the time. Sometimes it is important to have precise meaning, as in scientific writing, and I shall discuss the social and linguistic processes that are used to sharpen up word meaning.

The first part of the book investigates the vocabulary for wine description. Lexical structure and interlinguistic relationships play a crucial role in permitting speakers to use words in novel and original ways, while still allowing hearers to figure out what the speaker's intentions are. Chapter 3 is a technical chapter which is concerned with formal theories of semantics, and which presupposes familiarity with the issues and the literature in the field. Readers who are interested primarily in wine or in conversation will probably want to skip this chapter.

The second part describes wine experiments that I have carried out—to find out to what extent speakers of English describe wines in the same or similar ways. Three groups of subjects took part in my experiments: two groups of ordinary wine drinkers and one group of experts. The actual linguistic behavior of speakers who are asked to describe the same wines shows that there is great variation and inconsistency in language use; there is also more miscommunication than most people may realize. At the same time, speakers exhibit originality and imagination in their descriptions and evaluations.

Part III looks at wine talk in a general framework. It is concerned with the special linguistics needs for scientific communication. But it also looks at the use of wine conversation in a variety of nonscientific settings: for asthetic purposes, for phatic communion, and in humor.

The last section, Part IV, is not about wine. In it I argue that wine conversation is not unusual or esoteric—rather, it is characteristic of language use in many areas of human concern—and demonstrate the parallels between talking about wine and talking about people. Finding adequate words to describe one's feelings is analogous to finding the right words to describe the taste of wine. Finding linguistically accurate characterizations of people—of their personalities, behavior, and moods—is also parallel in ways to describing wine, but it is of course a much greater problem.

Wine
and
Conversation

PART I

The Semantics of Wine

You can talk about wine as if it were a bunch of flowers (fragrant, heavily perfumed); a packet of razor blades (steely); a navy (robust, powerful); a troupe of acrobats (elegant and well-balanced); a successful industrialist (distinguished and rich); a virgin in a bordello (immature and giving promise of pleasure to come); Brighton beach (clean and pebbly); even a potato (earthy) or a Christmas pudding (plump, sweet and round).

—Derek Cooper, quoted in A. Bespaloff, ed., *The Fireside Book of Wine*.

Chapter 1
Wine Words

I originally became interested in the topic of wine vocabulary out of sheer curiosity. At a typical dinner party, some person, usually a man, would hold up a glass of wine to let the candlelight shine through, swirl it around, and make some pronouncement such as: "This is soft and sensuous—quite an improvement over the 67's, which were unstylish and flabby." Another diner might reply: "Yes, it's soft, but I would say that it's graceful rather than sensuous." A brief discussion might then follow on which adjective, *sensuous* or *graceful*, best fit the wine. I used to assume that the words had little or no meaning, and that such a verbal display served largely to amuse or impress other people, allowing the speaker to show off his knowledge, experience, and expertise. Thurber has parodied such conversation in one of his cartoons with the caption, "It's a naive domestic Burgundy, without any breeding, but I think you'll be amused by its presumption."

I was concerned with two questions. First, assuming that some of the wine words mean something, even if they are to be interpreted subjectively and evaluatively, what is the structure of this vocabulary? Second, how do speakers use these words and what do they understand when they hear them?

There is an immense literature on wines—books about wine and winemaking, regular newspaper and magazine columns by writers who tell you what to buy and what to drink with what food, and of

3

course wine advertisements and labels. There is general agreement among various writers on the internal structure of the vocabulary, and there is considerable self-consciousness in the choice of terms used by such writers. A wine book typically has a glossary, and the wine industry, through ads and labels, tries to educate the public about the use of some terms. This chapter is devoted to a structural analysis of wine words.

I have heard people complain that there are few words in English to describe tastes. Though it may be true that only a small number of words are used exclusively or primarily for tastes, there are in fact dozens of terms that can be and have been used to describe and evaluate wines. The words listed below are those that I have found in the wine literature. Many are from glossaries and are defined, but many have only been used to describe one particular wine. Therefore, all terms are attested. However, the set is not a closed one; the wine vocabulary can be indefinitely extended in ways described in chapter 2.

In addition to the wine descriptors listed, there are a number of technical terms used to describe and classify wines. There are two primary groups of expressions in this class. The first contains the names of the grapes used for the wine: *Cabernet Sauvignon, Johannisberg Riesling,* etc. These are an important part of the description of California wines, since in California the finest wines have traditionally been made from a single varietal (kind of grape); they are not so widely used in describing European wines.[1] The other group of expressions contains chemical terms for specific properties, often for defects. Examples in this category are *hydrogen sulfide, mercaptan, butyric, malolactic, fusel,* and *acetaldehyde.* This latter group of terms is found primarily in the literature and speech of winemakers and wine scientists.

The wine vocabulary is more than a mere list, however, for it possesses a lexical structure as well. The terms can be analyzed in terms of various dimensions: acidity, sweetness, body, balance, feel, age, nose, finish, activity, and quality. Some of these dimensions are interrelated. The analysis below is based on the commonest wine terms—those that turn up in most glossaries and are frequently used by wine writers. A few words refer to complex properties, and so they appear on more than one dimension. The technical-chemical terms will be dealt with in chapters 3 and 10.

Wine Descriptors Encountered in the Literature—Preliminary List

acetic	clean	ethereal	full-bodied	humble	nutty	redolent	smooth	tannic
acidic	cloying	empty	full-flavored	immature	oaky	refreshing	soft	tart
acrid	coarse	evolved	gassy	insipid	oily	respectable	solid	taut
aged	common	exhilerating	gay	has legs	odd	rich	sophisticated	tender
alcoholic	has come on	faded	gentle	light	off	ripe	sound	thick
aloof	complex	fat	generous	lingering (finish)	old	robust	sour	thin
aromatic	cooked	feminine	gorgeous	little	ordinary	roguish	spicy	tough
astringent	corked	fermenting	grapy	lively	original	round	has stamina	transcendental
attenuated	corky	fierce	graceful	luscious	ostentatious	rounded	stalky	twiggy
austere	creamy	fiery	grandiose	maderized	overripe	rough	steely	unbalanced
baked	crisp	fine	great	has majesty	oxidized	rugged	stemmy	unharmonious
balanced	dead	finesse	has grip	manly	pebbly	salty	stiff	unripe
beery	decrepit	finish	green	mature	penetrating	sappy	stony	vegy (vegetably)
big	delicate	firm	gun flint	meager	peppery	savory	sturdy	velvety
has bite	developed	flabby	hale	mealy	perfumed	scented	strong	vigorous
bitter	deep	flamboyant	hard	meaty	piquant	semisweet	stylish	vinous
bouquet	disciplined	flat	harmonious	medium	plump	senile	suave	vulgar
bland	discreet	flattering	harsh	mellow	has poise	sensuous	succulent	warm
blurred	distinctive	fleshy	heady	mettlesome	positive	serious	subtle	watery
has body	distinguished	flinty	hearty	mineral	powerful	sharp	sugary	weak
breed	dry	flowery	heavy	moldy	pretentious	short (finish)	superficial	wild
brisk	dull	foxy	herby	mossy	pricked	silky	supple	withered
buttery	dumb	fragile	herbaceous	musky	prickly	silly	sweet	woody
caramel	durable	fragrant	hollow	musty	puckery	simple	swallowable	yeasty
chalky	dusty	fresh	honest	neutral	pungent	skunky	syrupy	young
has character	early	frolicsome	hot	noble	racy	small	tangy	zestful
charming	elegant	fruity	huge	nose	rare	smoky		

Wine drinking is an aesthetic experience, or at least it is for people who write wine books, and possibly for those who read them; so naturally, the evaluative dimension is the most important. The evaluative dimension permeates every other dimension, even "descriptive" ones. The principal semantic configuration is that shown in Figure 1, and most of the dimensions conform to this structure.

Too much X	Right amount of X	Too little X
NEGATIVE	POSITIVE	NEGATIVE

FIGURE 1: Dimension X

The experience of tasting is a complex one in which taste, smell, and feel are intermingled; and one of the things that differentiates experts from others is their ability to separate and decompose the sensory experience. *Flavor* is usually used to describe tasting and smelling, and occasionally feeling as well (Broadbent 1977:14; Amerine & Singleton 1965:305). Many of the terms are found on more than one dimension. *Flabby*, e.g., means 'having too little of something', such as acid, tannin, or body.

Acidity.—The dimension of acidity, which affects taste, smell, and feeling in the mouth, is represented by Figure 2. *Sour* appears twice in Figure 2 because it has two meanings: (1) sour in taste, and (2) acetic, on the way to becoming vinegar—hence spoiled (like sour milk). *Crisp, piquant*, and the words below them may apply to tactile sensations as well as taste. (In addition, a number of other terms are used to describe particular flavors of wine: thus *steely, metallic, stony*, and *mineral* may refer to acidity or to a certain kind of acidity.)

Too much			Positive	Too little
NEGATIVE			POSITIVE	NEGATIVE
acetic	pricked	sour	tart	flat
sour		acidic	crisp	bland
		sharp	piquant	flabby
		hard	lively	
		biting	zestful	
			tangy	

FIGURE 2: Acidity

Sweetness.—Another dimension is sweetness, shown in Figure 3. Here words meaning 'too dry' are lacking, apparently because wine writers do not dislike dry wines. *'Bone dry'* is used to mean 'having no sweetness whatsoever'.

Too much NEGATIVE	POSITIVE	*Too little* NEGATIVE
syrupy cloying sugary	sweet semisweet dry	

FIGURE 3: Sweetness

Balance.—The next dimension is a function of both sugar and acid: balance. A balanced wine has a pleasant proportion of sugar, acid, and other constituents. A wine may be unbalanced because it has either too much sugar or too much acid; but generally, if someone merely labels a wine as unbalanced, he is likely to mean that the wine is too acidic. The terms are shown in Figure 4.

Too much *(acid or sugar)* NEGATIVE	POSITIVE	*Too little* *(acid)* NEGATIVE
unbalanced unharmonious acidic sour cloying etc.	balanced harmonious round	unbalanced unharmonious flat etc.

FIGURE 4: Balance

Since balance interacts with the dimensions of acidity and sweetness, a three-dimensional representation of these would be desirable; but Figure 5 will serve as an approximation.

	Too much NEGATIVE	POSITIVE	*Too little* NEGATIVE
SWEETNESS	cloying	sweet dry	
ACIDITY	sour	tart	flat
	unbalanced	balanced	unbalanced

FIGURE 5: Interaction of Balance, Acidity, and Sweetness

Astringency. —Another dimension is astringency, which is largely a tactile sensation, caused by the tannin in red grape skins. Too much astringency produces a mild feeling of pain, often described as harshness or sharpness. The words in this subset are mainly applicable to red wines, since white wines do not have tannin; but in fact, the terms are frequently applied to white and dessert wines to characterize the texture.[2] The terms are given in Figure 6. Many of the terms in the 'too much' column are used for excess acidity as well as tannin, since either can produce the tactile sensation. *Bitter* does not easily fit into this category, but a bitter aftertaste may result from excess tannin. *Puckery* is not a completely negative term. Whereas *hard* is negative, *firm* is positive; and though *soft* is positive, *flabby* is not.

Too much NEGATIVE		POSITIVE
hard	firm	soft
harsh	puckery	smooth
sharp		velvety
rough		silky
bitter		gentle
		tender
		mellow

FIGURE 6: Feel (Astringency)

Age. —Another dimension is age, which is an assessment based on taste and feel, particularly of those properties of acidity and astringency; see Figure 7. The connotative value of *young* and *old* depends on the particular wine, since some wines, such as clarets and ports, are highly regarded if old. But others are preferred young: an

Too young NEGATIVE		POSITIVE		Too old NEGATIVE	
green	young	mature	old	withered	dead
unripe	fresh	ripe		dying	
immature		mellow		decrepit	
		developed		senile	
		evolved			
		aged			

FIGURE 7: Age

old Moselle or an old Beaujolais might be considered undesirable. *Green* often just means 'young', but some writers apply it primarily to wines made from unripe grapes (Broadbent 1977; *Lexique* 1963).

The scales of acidity, astringency, and age can be correlated, to some extent, as shown in Figure 8. The term *flat* occasionally means "too old," especially for certain wines that are intended to be drunk young, and for sparkling wines that have lost their bubbles; but a wine can be flat from its beginning by never having had enough acid.

	Too young		*Too old*
AGE	NEGATIVE	POSITIVE	NEGATIVE
	unripe	mature	withered
ACIDITY			
ASTRINGENCY	sharp	crisp	flat acetic
	rough harsh	soft smooth	

FIGURE 8: Correlation of Age, Acidity, and Astringency

Body. — The dimension of body has perhaps more terms than any other. This is a complex concept, referring to the viscosity or weight of wine in the mouth. Its physical correlates are the percentage of alcohol and dissolved solids. Some writers use *body* for one correlate, others for both. The terms are given in Figure 9. Some of the terms in each column can perhaps be further scaled according to degree of fullness or degree of desirability, but I doubt that there would be very much consistency on this point. Schoonmaker (1965) defines *sturdy* as less favorable than *robust,* but more favorable than *coarse.* *Rich* seems to be a completely positive term, while *heavy* can be either positive or negative, depending on the wine. Heavy Burgundies are good; heavy Moselles, not so good. *Strong* may apply more to alcoholic content than to viscosity.

A visual phenomenon associated with body is known as *legs:* "the trails that slide down the inside of the glass after you have swivelled the wine round" (Vandyke Price 1975:182). Legs are related to the glycerine content, although not all writers are convinced that glycerine adds much viscosity to the wine (e.g., see Broadbent 1977:24).

Too much NEGATIVE		POSITIVE			Too little NEGATIVE
coarse	heavy		full	light	watery
	strong	big	rich	delicate	thin
?alcoholic	chewy	fat	deep	fragile	weak
		thick	powerful		meager
		solid	forceful		small
		sturdy	robust		flabby
		hearty	round		little
		meaty			

FIGURE 9: Body

The dimension of smell—of nose, in the wine vocabulary—has a number of terms. They are more easily categorized than scaled, although some words are positive, some neutral, some negative. Wine experts agree on a distinction between *aroma* and *bouquet;* aroma is the smell from the grape, while bouquet is that from the wine—i.e., the odors arising from the fermentation process. However, experts disagree about which terms apply to aroma and which to bouquet, and many are applied to both. Figure 10 shows the terms used. In addition to *fruity,* which is sometimes contrasted with *grapy,* writers mention specific fruits—apples, cherries, raspberries—to suggest aroma and bouquet. Other terms referring to specific odors, like *smoky* or *woody,* may be favorable—depending on the wine and the expert.

POSITIVE		NEGATIVE
fruity	grapy	specific undesirable smells
flowery	?sappy	(musty, yeasty), or
perfumed		comparisons, like burnt
scented		rubber, leather, ect.
fragrant		

FIGURE 10: Nose

A time dimension can be added in order to deal with aftertaste phenomena (Fig. 11). *Lingering* is a positive term, *short* and *hollow* are negative. Broadbent defines *finish* as "the end-taste." "A wine cannot be considered well-balanced without a good finish by which is understood a firm, crisp and distinctive end. The opposite, a short or poor finish, will be watery, the flavour not sustained and tailing off inclusively. The correct degree of the right sort of acidity is a decisive factor." A *hollow* wine has a foretaste and some aftertaste "but without sustaining middle flavour" (Broadbent 1977:96).

Foretaste	*Beginning of taste sensation* *Middle Flavor*	*End of taste sensation* *Aftertaste (finish)*
	hollow	lingering short

FIGURE 11. Finish

An activity dimension is presented in Figure 12. Many of the terms mentioned in the acid scale, such as *lively* or *zestful,* could be used to characterize the feel of the carbon dioxide in the wine. *Gassy* is sometimes used negatively, generally for wines that are supposed to be still but that are not.[3]

still	gassy	sparkling bubbling

FIGURE 12: Activity

Finally, there are terms whose meanings are largely evaluative. Pure evaluative terms, very common in the wine domain *(good, excellent, bad, terrible)* have not been listed. Evaluative terms (Figure 13) can be divided into terms of high praise, low praise, mild derogation,

HIGH PRAISE	LOW PRAISE	MILDLY DEROGATORY	STRONGLY DEROGATORY
complex	clean	insipid	off
breed	sound	bland	(general terms of
character	simple	common	disapproval: awful,
distinguished	refreshing	ordinary	ghastly, etc.)
great			
fine			
elegant			
delicate			
subtle			
finesse			

FIGURE 13: Evaluative

and strong derogation. Some of the words interact with other scales. *Delicate*, for example, would be more likely to be used for a light wine than a heavy one.

The term *complex* is a special one with a special almost-technical meaning, "many-faceted smell and taste, the hallmark of a developing fine wine" (Broadbent 1977:95). Machamer, who includes *complexity* as a parameter in his wine evaluation system, writes,

> Complexity . . . is an evaluative parameter. Its contrast term is simple. Complexity is the measure for the degree of intensity with which all the factors in the wine assault your senses in harmonious fashion. Complex wines . . . burst forth in the mouth in manifold dimensions providing the wine with an unmistakable depth and intra-connection of components. . . . Simple wines are just that—one taste and flavor of the wine dominates and not much else happens; there are no overtones played upon its basic note. (Machamer 1977:6)

As we have seen, most other words in the wine vocabulary are value laden as well, but they label wine as desirable or undesirable in certain ways. Neutral terms such as *woody* or *spicy* or even *sweet* may be positive or negative for some wine drinkers with respect to certain wines.

Clarity and Appearance.—Two other dimensions are important in wine description and evaluation: clarity and appearance (the latter includes color). The degrees of clarity given by Broadbent (1975:24) are *brilliant, star-bright, bright, clear* (all positive and arranged in order of desirability) to *dull, bitty* ('having particulate matter'), *hazy*, and *cloudy* (negative, arranged from bad to worse).

Appearance includes color, both hue and depth (saturation). Wines are grouped into red, rosé, and white categories. However, red wines vary from deep purple and reddish brown to shades of orange and pink, sometimes overlapping in color with the rosés. (To some extent the label classification may depend on the intention of the winemaker.) White wines vary from colorless to shades of pale yellow green, straw yellow, gold, and brown.

It is interesting from a semantic standpoint that in the wine context the terms *red* and *white* never literally refer to the prototypical colors (Berlin & Kay 1972), which would be exemplified by tomato juice and cream, for instance. In some languages the term *black* is used in lieu of *red* to describe wines of a dark hue. In Croatian, for example, such a wine is *crn*, 'black'.

Not all the terms on the list on have been accounted for. Many words refer to more or less specific flavors that do not fall into a neat structure, although some can be subgrouped: *okay* and *woody;* *chalky* and *earthy; metallic, mineral,* and *steely; smoky, nutty, spicy, herby, herbacious; stony* and *pebbly.* Two words can be singled out as having rather technical and specific meanings for wine experts where nonexperts might be misled: *foxy* and *sophisticated. Foxy* refers to the flavor that Fox, Concord, and other Vitis Labrusca varietals have. A *sophisticated* wine is one that is adulterated by the addition of a foreign substance (Amerine, Roessler, & Filipello 1959:498).

The list of specific tastes that can be attributed to wines is large and open. The following additional terms, not included above, are from Broadbent's glossary alone (1975): *bitter almonds, apples, asbestos, banana, bad eggs, boiled beetroot, black currants, caramel, cedarwood, filter pads, geranium, wild garlic, goaty, honeyed, mushroomy, mousey, peach-like, peardrops, rubbery, sulfury, vanilla.* Many of these terms can be correlated with specific physical properties, such as *apples* with malic acid and *wild garlic* with sorbic acid.[4]

I want to call attention to the terminology of one particular wine writer, Pamela Vandyke Price, in *The Taste of Wine,* because it is so unusual—or perhaps personal, as she might prefer to describe it. The following words, which are taken from her glossary, are items that I have not found elsewhere: *straightforward, assertive, broad, crunchy, dirty, forthcoming, limpid, pinched* ("mean in character"), *reserved, sensitive, sick, shaded, sloppy, soggy, turned in* ("withdrawn"), *uncoordinated,* and *vivacious.*

The white wines are classified by Vandyke Price in an ordinary enough way: first by sweetness *(bone dry, dry to medium dry, implicitly sweet, intensely sweet),* and then each of these is subdivided according to body. The red wines, however, are classified at the highest level into *straightforward, medium personality,* and *weighty.* This division is one of quality, with *weighty* being the best. *Straightforward* wines are further divided into *crisp* and *slightly assertive* wines as opposed to *firm, fruity,* and *robust* ones. *Medium personality* wines are either *fruity, assertive,* and *moderately robust* or *firm and fruity with a certain elegance.* Finally, the *weighty* wines are divided into three subcategories: wines that are *moderately fruity* and *robust;* wines with *assertive fruit* and *character;* and *elegant* and *profound* wines usually with *charm.* The subclassifications seem to refer to body, fruitiness, and quality.

Vandyke Price's glossary defines these terms, and often one can see that they are like other, commoner words. *Assertive* is defined as "possessing one particular, outstanding attribute, such as smell or taste, resulting from the grape, climate, soil, etc., which makes an immediate appeal. The term should not be confused with *aggressive*, which is usually undesirable" (180). The first sentence of the definition makes *assertive* similar to the meaning of *simple*. *Aggressive* is not defined, but one can infer that it refers to a wine with too much of some single property.

My favorite definition in Vandyke Price's glossary is for *round*:

> Many people find it helpful to think of wines as having a shape. Some immature wines often seem to be angular, others seem straight up and down in slightly unripe vintages. A round wine has its skeleton (the alcohol) adequately and pleasantly covered with flesh (the fruit) and is enhanced by a good skin (the fragrance). Excess rotundity shows a lack of proportion, but many young wines possess a type of puppy fat which they shed later. How round a wine ought to be depends on the quality it should ideally attain; a great wine at its peak should be only gracefully curved, a good youngish wine in the medium ranges can be rather more curvacious. Roundness is something felt as the wine passes over the palate and is held momentarily in the mouth. (183)[5]

Vandyke Price takes the concept of shape more literally than the definition for *round* might suggest. For example, one of her innovative suggestions for noting and remembering the taste of wine consists of diagramming their "profiles," where the horizontal axis represents the foretaste-taste-aftertaste dimension and the vertical axis represents a combination of flavor, complexity, and quality. Compare the profiles in Figure 14.

Great wine at its peak   Dull wine

FIGURE 14: Two Sample Wine "Profiles" (Vandyke Price 1975:44)

We have looked at the wine vocabulary. It is not just a list but rather a set of expressions that can be analyzed in terms of several dimensions. Many dimensions are interrelated, such as balance with acidity and sweetness. The evaluative dimension interacts with most of the other dimensions, and most of the words have both a descriptive and evaluative aspect of meaning. The wine vocabulary is an open set, moreover, and there are conventional ways of creating new wine descriptors to extend this vocabulary even further. Such linguistic devices and processes are the subject of the next chapter.

Chapter 2
Extending the Vocabulary

The first thing to do in tasting a wine is to see if it has a good nose. A good nose is very important since it allows the wine to breathe.

—Funky
Arizona Star
March 5, 1979

All languages have resources that enable speakers to increase their vocabulary—by adding new words and by extending the meanings of existing words. The wine vocabulary illustrates these processes very clearly, and this chapter will explore some of the common linguistic devices used.

Morphological processes, particularly suffixation, provide a rich source of new words in the wine vocabulary. Many words listed in chapter 1 can be broken down into a stem+suffix. The commonest suffix is -*y* added to concrete nouns (count or mass) to produce adjectives. The -*y* in these words means either 'having' or 'resembling', and sometimes the word can mean either. Wine tasters often use equivalent expressions with 'having' + noun, such as "This wine has good fruit, some wood, and no sugar." However, 'resembling' is the commoner meaning.

Not all wine words ending in -*y* have this meaning, of course. *Foxy* (in wine terminology), *meaty, racy, hearty, heady,* and possibly *fleshy* do not mean 'resembling'—their meanings have drifted from that of the noun stem.

The -*y* suffix can be productively applied to new items, subject to the semantic-pragmatic restriction that a wine could have or resemble the item mentioned: *muddy, sandy, coppery, barky, apply, pickly, chickeny, leafy, walnuty,* or *olivy,* are possible. There may be some phonological restrictions, in that /iy/ does not sound good when added to nouns already ending in /iy/. So *turkeyey* and *berryey* are out.

16

Some noun +y forms are possible, but perhaps somewhat unlikely to be used as wine descriptors.[1] Examples would be *crabby, rocky,* and perhaps *fishy.* These words already have highly salient meanings ('ill-tempered', 'full of rocks', and 'suspicious'), which might interfere with an intented 'resembling N' meaning. However, were they to be defined when introduced, problems of interpretation would not arise.

Wine Words Taking a −y Suffix

beery	mealy	spicy
buttery	moldy	stalky
chalky	mossy	steely
corky	musky	stemmy
creamy	nutty	stony
dusty	oaky	sugary
earthy	oily	syrupy
fleshy	pebbly	tangy
flinty	peppery	twiggy
flowery	salty	vegy
fruity	sappy	velvety
gassy	silky	woody
grapy	skunky	yeasty
herby	smoky	

Although there are no examples in the list on p. 5, the suffix *-like* is highly productive in the wine vocabulary. It can be added to concrete noun stems, and carries its meaning straightforwardly. Possibilities are *pearlike, applelike,* and *carrotlike.* Although *-like* could also be added to the nouns listed above, *fruitlike, grapelike, woodlike,* these latter are not so likely, since well-established adjectival forms already exist which would preempt the *-like* form. (See Esau 1973).[2]

Other suffixes are also found in the wine word list, but they are less frequent and less productive in this domain: *-ish (roguish, stylish), -ic (acidic, alcoholic, aromatic, metallic),* meaning 'having' or 'resembling'. The suffixes *-ful (graceful, forceful, powerful, zestful), -ous (harmonious, pretentious, sensuous, vigorous),* mean 'having' and are added to nouns (Ljung 1970). The list also includes past participles *(disciplined, distinguished, evolved, balanced)* and present participles *(lingering, fermenting, refreshing)* which are of course based on verb stems.

Most new words do not enter the wine domain via morphological rules, however, but via semantic extension. I recently heard a wine described as *raunchy*, but the meaning cannot be processed as 'having or resembling raunch'. The same wine was described by another taster as *having a kick*, an expression that I had not previously encountered for wine. To understand better how word meanings become extended, it is necessary to look at the organization of the lexicon. A structural analysis of the lexicon of a language must show two kinds of relationships—the relations between all the senses of a lexical item (a task which conventional dictionaries perform) and the relationships of related senses of different lexical items (Nida 1975). One prominent model for dealing with the latter—different lexemes that share some aspect of meaning—is the concept of the semantic field. The theory of semantic fields has been developed by Trier, Porzig, Coseriu, Lyons, and others and has served as a good working model for describing lexical structures, although no completely satisfactory definition of a semantic field can be given. A semantic field is roughly a subject matter or conceptual sphere, such as kinship, motion, personality traits, or furniture. A lexical set is a set of lexemes (or words) in a language which encode some or all of a semantic field and which bear certain specifiable relationships to one another.

In principle, every different conceptual field could be encoded by a completely disjoint set of lexical items. Semantic analysis would be easier than it now is, since there would be an isomorphism between fields and sets. However, almost all of the lexemes in a language belong to more than one field. This is not equivalent to saying that most words have more than one meaning, since a word can have more than one sense in the same field. For instance, *dog* meaning 'canine animal' and *dog* meaning 'male canine animal' presumably belong to the same field. However, a word like *head* belongs to the domains of body parts, shapes, spatial orientation, position of power, etc.

A major theoretical weakness of field theory, somewhat embarrassing to those who work in it, is that no adequate formulation has been given of the notion of semantic field, and no adequate criteria have been found that will help the semanticist conclusively decide how to delimit fields or how to decide whether a particular lexical item definitely is or is not associated with a particular field. Moreover, there is no reason to believe that the organization of semantic fields is rigid or fixed. Rather we can construct fields (and connect them to the appropriate lexical items) as we wish. Some fields are highly salient and easily identifiable, such as kinship, color, some animal and plant taxonomies, motion, and possession. Other less salient categories can be formed, however, such as instruments for cutting. The lexical set associated with such a domain would include *scissors, shears, saw, knife, paper cutter,* and *guillotine.* Lyons writes,

> Vaguely formulated though it has been, field-theory has proved its worth as a general guide for research in descriptive semantics over the last forty years; and it has undoubtedly increased our understanding of the way the lexemes of a language are interrelated in sense. The fact that it has not been, and perhaps cannot be, formalized would be a more damaging criticism, if there were available some alternative theory of the structure of vocabulary which had been formalized and which had been tested against an equal amount of empirical evidence; and this is not yet the case. (1977:267–68)

The field theory may be applicable to only part of the vocabulary of a language, but for that part it provides important insights. In a semantic theory such as that of Lyons (1977), the meaning of each lexeme *is* its relationship to other lexemes in that semantic field. There are a small number of these relationships, the most important of which (for wine talk) are synonymy, antonymy, and various kinds of terms that can be arranged in a scalar order (such as *hot warm cool cold*), and hyponymy (the 'kind of' relationship). What is especially interesting about this conception of lexical relations is that the same relationship between words in a field holds across different conceptual domains (see Kittay & Lehrer 1981).

> If there is a set of words that have semantic relationships in a semantic field, and if one or more items pattern in another semantic field, then the other items in the first field are available for extension to the second field. The semantic relationships will remain the same: synonyms will remain synonyms, antonyms will remain antonyms, etc. Perceived similarity is not a necessary condition for semantic extension. (Lehrer 1978a:96)

To show how semantic extension works, we will examine a number of semantic fields that have contributed vocabulary to the wine domain. First of all there are the taste words (*sweet, sour, bitter, tart, salty,* and *dry*), but their use in the wine domain is straightforward, and they are used to denote a specific taste. (The problem of the interpretation of scalar terms and their norms is discussed in later chapters).

There are two sets of words (not completely distinct) that come from the domain of touch and feel. The first of these consists of items that apply to both taste and feel. In the wine domain they are used to describe acidity (Fig. 2), since acid can be tasted (producing a tart or sour taste) and felt (producing a sharp or biting feeling). The general class can be characterized by the antonyms *sharp* and *flat*.

Let us begin with the set of descriptors that are used for acidity. Some of the terms are straightforward, and their meanings are used in highly conventional ways, although they have been derived (historically) from earlier senses of the word (Williams 1976). *Sharp*, for example, conventionally means 'causes intense sensation'. Since sharp objects can cause such a sensation, there is a natural extension to foods and beverages which produce this sensation. *Flat*, the antonym of *sharp*, means 'lacking sensation'.[3]

Terms like *peppery, spicy, biting, prickly,* and other words that are synonyms or partial synonyms of *sharp* can be used in a fairly straightforward manner. What needs explaining is the presence of items like *zestful, crisp,* and *lively*. See Table 1. (A wine cannot be crisp in the way that a cucumber is, that is, 'brittle'.) These words occur in a semantic domain that we can roughly gloss as 'animated' or 'full of life and activity', giving rise to expressions like *sharp mind* and *flat voice*, 'monotonous'. A possible link between the domains of flavorfulness and animation is provided by *zestful*. Zest is the outer part of a lemon or orange rind, used to give flavor. However, a much commoner meaning is 'spirited enjoyment, added interest, or charm, gusto', as in *zestful spirit*. *Lively* and *crisp*, as in phrases like *lively party* and *crisp walk* illustrate the 'animated' sense, and, via their semantic link to *zestful* and *sharp*, can be extended to flavor domains. In other words, because *zestful* is partially synonymous with *crisp* and *lively* in the semantic field of animation, and moreover because *zestful* is a taste word and can naturally be applied to wine, *crisp* and *lively* can also be extended to describe wine tastes by virtue of their partial synonomy with *zestful*.

The second set of touch or feel words among the wine descriptors correspond to tannin. Some of these can be found in Figure 6. The

TABLE 1: The Taste-Feel Vocabulary—
Lexical Items Connected with Sharpness or Flatness

Semantic Domain	SHARP											FLAT
	sour	*tart*	*acid*	*tangy*	*pungent*	*spicy*	*peppery*	*savory*	*zestful*	*crisp*	*lively*	*bland*
Taste: strong flavor	X	X	X	X	X	X	X	X	X			X 'lacking taste'
Feel: biting	X	X	X	X	X	X	X	X	X			X 'lacking feeling'
Animation									X →	X →	X →	X 'stale, dead'
Wine	X	X	X	X	X	X	X	X	X	X	X	X

NOTE: X denotes a conventional meaning in the semantic field.

whole set can be roughly divided into *soft-smooth* on one hand and *hard-rough* on the other. There are several antonyms: *smooth* vs. *rough, soft* vs. *hard, flabby* vs. *firm. Flat* vs. *sharp* might also be included here as well as the previous set, although they can denote spatial dimension as well as touch. (Table 2 shows the semantic fields in which these words pattern.)

One of the subfields of touch has to do with pleasantness and regularity of surface. Several words denote this sense, resulting in expressions like *smooth road, soft fur, gentle slope, flat surface* on the one hand, and *sharp point, rough road,* and *rugged landscape* on the other.

The other subfield has to do with yielding to pressure, as in *soft chair, hard seat, flabby body,* and *firm body.* These two subfields are related and linked by *soft.* Something can be soft in the sense of easily yielding to pressure, but *soft* also overlaps with *smooth.* This sense of *soft* is found in expressions like *soft skin.* It is not contradictory to say *he has baby-soft skin over his firm muscles.* According to the principle presented above, words in a lexical set may be transferred to a new domain whenever there is at least one word providing a link, that is, one word having meanings in both fields.

In the wine (and liquor) domain *smooth* and *hard* have standard meanings. Therefore, other words are available for transfer, and one finds *firm, flabby, velvety, silky,* and *gentle.*[4]

The wine words used to describe body are drawn largely from the lexical sets for spatial dimension, especially those for size, weight, and strength. (The semantic extension of *body* is itself interesting.) The dimension terms include words for size *(big, little, small, fat, thin, thick)* and also for other dimensions, *deep, high, shallow,* and *low. (High* and *low* are used in the expressions *high body* and *low body.)* Size words can be freely added to describe body. *Plump* must be interpreted as 'a little fat' or 'moderately big'. Asher (1974) has used *huge* and *massive* to describe particular wines, and the meaning can only be interpreted as 'very big'. One could even speak of a wine as *gigantic* or *elephantine.*

Closely connected to size words are words denoting substance—having body. *Meaty* and *fleshy* enter the wine vocabulary in this way, along with *hearty,* perhaps an expansion of *hearty meal.*

Size words are related to weight words, *heavy* and *light,* since, with concentration held constant, large things tend to be heavy and small

Table 2: Lexical Items Dealing with Texture

Touch Words Domain	Soft & Smooth							Hard & Rough					
	smooth	soft	gentle	silky	velvety	flat	flabby	rough	coarse	rugged	hard	firm	flat
Pleasantness & Regularity of Surface	X	X	?	X	X	X		X	X	X			X
Resistance to Pressure		X					X				X	X	
Wine	X	X	X	X	X	X	X	X	X	X	X	X	X

NOTE: X = conventional use in domains

things tend to be light. However, *heavy* and *light* are used in many semantic domains. When applied to wines and other liquids, they refer to the concentration of nonliquid ingredients, possibly dissolved, as in *heavy stew* or *light broth*. They can also be used simply for intensity of flavor. In this sense, the weight words are linked with the strength words.

The size words are linked with the strength words more directly. *Thin* and *thick* provide that link. *Thin* means (1) 'little, narrow in size' and (2) 'little or less in consistency or concentration'. *Thick* is the antonym in both domains. This is an additional link which permits size words to be used for strength. *Strong* and *weak* are the most general terms here, and they apply in many domains: concentration of (dissolved) ingredients in liquids, strength to do something, and strength to withstand. Some terms are used to describe states of health, but this could perhaps be subsumed under the strength to withstand (disease, stress) category. Table 3 summarizes the words from the *strong-weak* set. Although *weak* has a negative connotation, *fragile* and *delicate*, from the nonstrong side of the domain, are positive. Except for *strong*, which may be positive or negative, all of the words subsumed under *strong* are more or less positive: *rich, powerful, vigorous, forceful, robust, solid, sturdy*.

To summarize, since *strong* and *weak* have one meaning referring to concentration, these words can naturally be used for wine. Other words in different semantic domains which are semantically related to *strong* and *weak* are available for semantic extension to wine. Their meaning in the wine domain will depend on the relationship to *strong* or *weak* in whatever semantic domain they occur in. A synonym of *strong* in some other semantic field will be interpreted as a synonym of *strong* in the wine domain.

The domain of balance contributes a few items to the wine domain. *Balance* denotes the proportion and combination of elements (acid, sweetness, etc.). Other words from this domain are *unbalanced, harmonious, unharmonious,* and *graceful,* all of which are used in many aesthetic fields.

Although only a few wine descriptors come from the domain of shape, a few are worth mentioning because they are important descriptors, and because Vandyke Price describes wine in terms of shape (1975:44). *Sharp* and *flat* have already been mentioned. They

Table 3: Lexical Items Connected to Strength/Weakness

Domain	STRONG								WEAK		
	strong	rich	powerful	vigorous	forceful	robust	solid	sturdy	weak	fragile	delicate
Concentration of in liquid	x	x							x		
Ability to do something	x		x	x	x						
Ability to withstand	x					x	x	x	x	x	x
Health	x			x		x			x	x	x
Wine	x		x	x	x	x	x	x	x	x	x

Firm could be added here. (*Solid* could be listed in Table 4 as well, resistent to pressure) have standard meanings in the taste and touch domains, too. *Round* is an important shape word; in wine it denotes a properly balanced wine. Other shape words that might be extended to wine could be *angular, pointed,* or *curved.* A *curved* wine might be 'balanced', while a *pointed* or *angular* wine would be 'sharp'.

The domain of age is an important source of wine words. Since many wine writers describe wine as a living thing that goes through a succession of natural stages, we may not even be dealing with metaphor or semantic extension in describing wines as young or old. However, at least some of the terms, particularly those dealing with attributes of youth or old age, are semantic extensions into the wine vocabulary, like *decrepit* or *senile.* Other expressions dealing with age are also frequently used, such as *over the hill* for wines that are too old (see Table 4).

Flexibility provides another source, with expressions such as *stiff, supple, taut.* A *supple* wine is defined as "smooth and pleasant to drink" (*Lexique* 1963), and as "a combination of sap, vigor, and amenable texture" (Broadbent 1977:99). I have not found any definitions for *taut* or *stiff,* but they must denote whatever the opposite of *supple* is, perhaps 'rough.'

Terms for complexity provide another source for wine descriptors. *Complex* and *simple* are the basic antonyms. *Complicated* enters the wine domain as a partial synonym of *complex.* *Naive* may enter as a partial synonym of *simple,* although it could also come in through the domains used for personality.

The domains of personality, behavior, and character contribute a great many words to the wine vocabulary, and perhaps it is in this area that there is the greatest lexical innovation. There is overlap here with some of the domains that have already been mentioned, since domains like strength and balance are applied to personality as well: *strong willed, weak person, unbalanced mind, rounded personality.*

First of all, there are the terms that apply to breed or class. Thus a wine can be said to be of noble grapes or have *breed.* These expressions apply to a small number of famous wines that are carefully made and are noted for their high quality. A distinguished wine would fall into this class. *Ordinary* and *common* are the other end of the scale, with *vulgar* as the end point for low class. *Respectable* would fall somewhere in the middle of the breed scale.

TABLE 4: Lexical Items Dealing with Age

LIFE CYCLE — YOUNG (*fresh, green, unripe, immature, ripe*) / OLD (*overripe, dying, decrepit, senile, dead*)

Domain	fresh	green	unripe	immature	ripe	mellow	evolved	developed	mature	aged	withered	overripe	dying	decrepit	senile	dead
Period of life or growth			X	X	X		X	X	X	X	X	X	X		X	X
Attributes of age vigor or lack of vigor	X	X								X			X	X	X	X
freshness	X	X									X	X				X
maturity & experience				X	X	X			X	X						
Wine	X	X	X	X	X	X	X	X	X	X	X	X	X	X	X	X

Terms denoting character are also used, as is the term *character* itself, although as a wine descriptor, *character* applies to complexity as well as quality. In interpreting these words in the wine context, since there is no obvious relationship between the word and any physical quality of the wine, some sort of projection is necessary, and it is likely that several interpretations are possible and reasonable. A case in point is the term *pretentious*. A pretentious person is one who pretends to have a background, pedigree, education, or other qualities that he does not have. It should be possible to interpret a *pretentious* wine as one that looked, tasted, smelled, and felt like an aged Chateau Lafite, but was really a jug wine from the San Joaquin Valley selling for $1.89 a gallon—truly a winebuyer's fantasy. However, the connotation of *pretentious* is negative, so that a pretentious wine could not be really as good as a fine one. An expert would be able to tell that the noble qualities were lacking. Therefore a pretentious wine would probably have to be fairly expensive and be labeled to imitate a wine which was better. Another possible interpretation for a pretentious wine is one that tries to surpass the noble wines in certain ways. Since many great wines are heavy and rich, a pretentious wine would be even heavier and richer.[5]

Another term from this domain is *honest*. There is an obsolete meaning for this term when predicated of things—'commendable, worthy of honor, respectable', a meaning that exists in *an honest day's work* or *make an honest woman of her*. For hearers not aware of this meaning, other interpretations based on current meanings are possible. One possibility is that an honest wine is one in which there is no attempt to mask defects, e.g., by adding sugar to hide the excessive acidity. Moreover, the wine must be labeled so that the drinker will not expect it to be better. In this sense, *honest* would contrast with *pretentious*. Since *honest* is a term of low praise, it must be acceptable in quality. There may be some link between *honest* and Vandyke Price's term *straightforward*. Both terms are linked to notions like truthfulness and forthrightness.

One set of personality terms applies to seriousness: *serious, disciplined, austere, severe;* and *nonserious, frolicsome, gay, silly*. Other wine descriptors used apply to a variety of behavioral or personality types: *naive, roguish, wild, racy, poised, suave, redolent*. These latter terms are hard to process. The reader or listener must search through lexical networks until he finds another word that has some meaning in the wine domain. The words for seriousness can be indirectly linked to *heavy* and *light* via their use in the domain of seriousness. Compare a *heavy novel* or *heavy reading* with *light music*, a *light movie*. There are other possible interpretations as well, via other links. They might also be linked to tannin. An *austere* or *severe* wine is too *harsh*, i.e., too tannic or possibly too acidic.

In some cases the semantic link is so loose that it is not clear what semantic relationship exists. The link is a weakly associative or connotative one. The terms *feminine* and *masculine* are good examples of this type of association. *Feminine* connotes *soft, smooth, light, round, perfumed,* possibly *sweet,* and these words do have definite meanings in the wine domain. Hence a feminine wine will be understood as one having those properties. A masculine wine is *big* and perhaps a bit *rough.*

The presence of personality and character terms in the wine vocabulary provides the possibility for many other words to be transferred into the domain. Potentialities are *sincere, furtive, frank, well-intentioned,* and *villainous.* Whatever interpretation they may have will depend on whatever links can be found between some feature of their meaning and some semantic feature of a word that already has an interpretation in the wine domain.

Chapter 3
There Are Intensions and Intentions

An Exercise in Applied Philosophy

In Vino Veritas

A complete account of meaning must include the relationship between language and the world and the relationships among linguistic entities within a language. Some semantic theories have been concerned mostly with the first of these relationships and other theories mostly with the second. In the first two chapters I have considered only intralinguistic relationships, and I will present a more formal account of such relationships in this chapter.

The other aspect of meaning—the connection between language and the world—raises many interesting problems, some of which are investigated in this and later chapters. To what extent do speakers of the same language apply words to things, properties, events, and situations in the same way? (The experiments reported in Part II show that there is considerable variation in how the same wine is described by different people.) If there is disagreement on word-world connections (denotation), can we decide that some people are right and others are wrong? Who makes (or should make) such decisons? In talking about 'correct' or 'incorrect' descriptions, we are appealing to a notion of truth—the relationship between sentences (or utterances) and the world, and I shall also discuss truth with respect to sentences containing wine descriptors.

My major purpose in this chapter is to provide an account of the wine words.[1] Therefore, I have eclectically borrowed from any semantic theories that provide a promising analysis of any part of

30

the wine corpus. I do not wish to imply that there is no single theory that can in principle take care of the whole set of descriptors, but I have found that each theory so far developed provides an illuminating analysis of some word and sentence types and less illuminating analyses of other types. Even if the words and sentence types can be forced into a procrustean bed, such analyses fail to show what is most interesting and significant about the linguistic expressions which are inappropriately handled. Although a semantic theory cannot satisfactorily account for everything, it may be useful in certain domains, and it may be perfectly adequate for that part of the vocabulary or for the sentence types for which it was proposed.

The wine corpus could also be looked at as a challenge for semantic theories or as a way of testing semantic theories. Any theory that fails to account for part of this corpus is deficient to that extent. However, this is a different enterprise and one which I shall leave for another time. Readers are invited to test their own favorite semantic theory using the wine descriptors.

NATURAL KIND TERMS

One way in which words can be hooked up to the world is by treating the meaning of a word in terms of its reference (or denotation). There are standard arguments against this theory as a general account of meaning, since it is not clear what words like *not, and,* or *if* refer to. However, it is certainly the case that a large part of the vocabulary denotes things, properties, actions, processes, and events. Words that are amenable to such analyses would include names for certain properties, such as colors, and names for many types of physical objects, such as animals and plants, artifacts, and some geographical features. Moreover, the objects, properties, etc., denoted by a word usually have something in common—that is, they all share some property or feature.

We are faced with the problem of accounting for how a particular word is connected to something or some set of things. How is it that *grape,* for example, denotes a set of green or purple globular objects that grow on vines? An account of proper names by Kripke (1972) and one of natural kind terms by Putnam (1975) and extended by Teller (1977) provide a plausible account for fixing the relationship between some of the wine descriptors and their denotation—names for specific grapes, certain chemicals found in wine, and wines named for certain regions.

According to Kripke's analysis of proper names, a name is applied to an individual; the reference is fixed by some initial baptism, either by ostension or description, and it is handed down by a historical chain from speaker to speaker (Kripke 1972:328). These terms are called rigid designators, and they designate the same object in any possible world (269–70). In extending the analysis to natural kind terms, in addition to the initial baptism,[2] the objects in question have certain essential properties, and experts (typically scientists) determine what these essential properties are. They may be different from the perceptual properties which nonscientists use to pick out the object. The essential property of water, for example, is that it is H_2O, not that it is wet and colorless. Putnam (1975) has elaborated the facet of expert opinion, and has proposed a "hypothesis of the universality of the division of linguistic labor":

> Every linguistic community exemplifies the sort of division of linguistic labor . . . that is, possesses at least some terms whose associated 'criteria' are known only to a subset of speakers who acquire the terms, and whose use by the other speakers depends upon a structured cooperation between them and the speakers in relevant subsets. (146)

Even though people identify instances of these terms by certain properties, such as a lemon by its color and taste, or a tiger by its size and stripes, or water by its wetness and colorlessness, yet if there were other objects in the universe with the same perceptual qualities, experts (scientists in these cases) might discover that such things were not really lemons, tigers, or water. A substance that was like water but not composed of H_2O or a tigerlike animal that had a radically different DNA structure in its genes would not be classified as water or tiger.[3] The thesis that experts are the final judge is a separate one from the thesis that natural kind terms are to be analyzed the way that proper names are.

The part of the wine vocabulary for which this analysis is most appropriate is that which denotes varietal wines, terms for specific chemicals, and wines derived from particular places. Since varietals are paradigm natural kinds, there is no problem with a Kripke-

Putnam analysis. A Cabernet Sauvignon wine is one that is made from Cabernet Sauvignon grapes. An expression like "Cabernet Sauvignon-type wine"[4] is more complicated, because it means that the wine is like a Cabernet Sauvignon, but could have other, even different, ingredients. However, even here we can rely on experts to fix the designation and make the appropriate judgments. These experts will probably be different from those experts who fix the designation of the natural kind terms. Those fixing natural kind terms would be botanists, while those fixing wine types would be enologists or possibly shippers in the wine trade. An additional complication is that in some places, for example California, a wine can be called by a varietal name only if the wine is made mostly from that grape. Before January 1981, according to California law, a wine made from as little as 51 percent of a grape could be called by the name of that varietal. Since then, the minimum must be 75 percent. This could be handled as a case of exaggerated impurities, perhaps, just as we use the term *water* for the stuff that is in Lake Erie. Alternatively, we could insist on more precision and say that the right way to describe a wine with 51 percent Zinfandel and 49 percent other things is a *Zinfandel-based wine*.

Wines made from certain varietals have a number of stereotypic properties (Putnam 1975), and it is these perceptual properties that enable trained wine drinkers to identify the wine by tasting it. However, these stereotypic properties are not a necessary part of the denotation, since a varietal grown in an unusual soil in an unusual region may well taste and smell different. There are, in addition, typical ways of making wines from certain grapes which further help wine experts to identify the varietals. Although Cabernet Sauvignons are almost always made into dry red wine and are often aged in oak, if a wine maker decided to make a white wine out of Cabernet Sauvignon, leave 7 percent residual sugar, and age it in cedarwood, it would still be a Cabernet Sauvignon wine, though, ironically, no longer a Cabernet Sauvignon type.

A second class of terms for which the Kripke-Putnam analysis is plausible consists of words denoting specific chemical substances or effects of certain chemical processes: *sulfur, vinegar, fusel oil, malolactic*, etc. These terms rigidly designate certain substances, and their proper application depends on the presence of the necessary chemicals. Adjectival forms, *sulfury, vinegary, alcoholic,* are a little trickier, since they mean either 'having the properties of' or 'resembling', and something can resemble vinegar without being vinegar. On the other hand, if someone says, "This wine is vinegary," when in fact there is no vinegar but rather a different acid, an expert might correct him and say that though the wine tasted vinegary, it in fact was not.

To the third class for which a Kripke-Putnam analysis has some plausibility belong names for wines that are derived from the place where the grapes are grown. The clearest examples would be those wines that have *Appellation Contrôlée* referents. According to French law, wines with certain names must come from a prescribed region, and, more specifically, from certain named vineyards. Examples are Champagne, Sauternes, Graves, and Burgundy. But these wines must also be made from prescribed grape varietals, and it is the latter requirement that gives each of these wines their specific characteristics. I suppose that if the people who make Mouton Rothschild were to tear out their current vines, replace them with Thompson seedless grapes, and make wine from that, they would lose their privilege of calling their new wine a classified Bordeaux. However, since in at least some areas there are several grape varietals allowed, and since different winemakers use different amounts and different combinations of these grapes for their wines, the resulting wines differ significantly from natural kinds.

The situation is more complicated when we look at the use of terms such as *Bordeaux, Burgundy,* and *Sauterne* in the California wine industry, which has shown no respect for French laws. California generics are supposed to resemble the European prototypes for which they are named more or less, but they do not. About the only thing that California Sauterne has in common with French Sauternes is the color. (The spelling difference hardly compensates for the lack of other similarities.) Since California generics do not have the properties of their prototypes and do not come from that area, by what right can they be called by those names? The Kripke-Putnam analysis of names is especially apt here. Although objects designated by a term such as *Claret* or *Rhine* do not have any particular essential properties (except color, but color would not distinguish them from other generics of the same color), California Clarets and Rhines may be called that because their winemakers have baptized them as such.

For communicative purposes and probably semantic purposes as well, it is necessary to distinguish California Sauterne from *real* Sauternes.[5] Wine experts are not likely even to use *Sauterne* for the California liquid.

An adequate semantic analysis shows the intralinguistic relationships among words. The relationships among the words we have looked at so far (those for natural kinds and for wines named after places) are quite simple—synonymy, hyponymy, and incompatibility. They can either be shown by statements of semantic entailments (meaning postulates) or they can be derived from their extensions (denotations):

Claret	→	Red Bordeaux
and		
Red Bordeaux	→	Claret
or Chenin Blanc	←→	Pineau Blanc de la Loire.

Hyponymy can be expressed as entailment:

Medoc	→	Bordeaux
Concord	→	Vitis Labrusca

To derive these relationships via their extensions, we can say that terms that necessarily denote the same things in all possible worlds are synonyms. If one term A denotes a set of objects, and another term B denotes a proper subset of those in all possible worlds, then B is a hyponym of A. Incompatible terms denote different, nonoverlapping sets of objects. For example, Rhine ≠ (is incompatible with) Burgundy. There are standard objections to deriving intralinguistic relationships from extension, and expressions like *necessarily* and in *all possible worlds* attempt to remedy them, so that *creature with a heart* and *creature with a liver* do not turn out to be synonymous. However, meaning postulates are always available to express the intralinguistic relationships.[6] In any case, deriving the intralinguistic relationships from extension works for only a small proportion of the words in the domain. As we shall see in the next three classes, the use of extension is inadequate.

GRADABLE ADJECTIVES

When we turn to descriptors like *heavy, light, smooth, rough, young,* or *old,* we encounter new difficulties and complexities. What property does something have to have to be heavy or old? Is it the same thing for wines as for people? Is a five-year-old wine an old one? Who decides? One major difference between these scalar words, often called gradable terms, is that they admit of degrees, whereas natural kind terms do not.[7] We can say, *Wine X is heavier than wine Y.* But a question such as, *Is this wine more of a Zinfandel than that?* is odd. The hearer is required to reinterpret the question to make sense of it. The gradable antonyms (*heavy-light, sweet-dry, old-young*) are defined as those antonyms that do not divide the semantic domain sharply into two parts but rather admit of intermediate cases. So we can say, *This wine is neither heavy nor light, but in between.* There are many syntactic and semantic complexities connected with these words: I will mention only some of the problems connected with their interpretations in sentences about wine.

Terms like *heavy* and *light* are characterized by dictionaries as having many senses, but their most salient meaning is in the field of weight. An alternative treatment would be to say that they are neutral with respect to domain, and leave to the pragmatics of a theory of language their interpretation. They denote weight in some contexts, body in others, saturation in still others. Even if one does not take this route and rather sticks with the standard treatment, the most significant thing about them in terms of their intralinguistic relationship is that they are scalar antonyms, and I am inclined to believe that this intralinguistic fact may be more important than the denotation of such terms. To say that context is important is true but inadequate, even if the context can be narrowed to wine. One of the problems for semantics is that entailments which work for expressions when not modified by such descriptors, such as terms that are related taxonomically, do not work when such modifiers are present. Imagine a situation with four wines: A and B are Rhines and C and D are Moselles. The Rhines are heavier than the Moselles, and also A is heavier than B. Now it might be true that wine B is heavy for a wine but light for a Rhine. Even though *B is a Rhine* entails *B is a wine,* it is not the case that *B is a light Rhine* entails *B is a light wine.*

Therefore, the context must be narrowed even further—to heavy for a Rhine wine, or for a Rhine wine from a certain vineyard in a certain year. Although there are many treatments of these gradable adjectives, they can be grouped into those which analyze the positive (noncomparative) adjective in terms of the comparative and those analyses which do not.

Sapir (1944) perhaps best exemplifies the former approach. He writes,

> Such contrasts as *small* and *large, little* and *much, few* and *many,* give us a deceptive feeling of absolute values within the field of quantity comparable to such qualitative differences as *red* and *green* with the field of color perception. This feeling is an illusion, however, which is largely due to the linguistic fact that the grading which is implicit in these terms is not formally indicated, whereas it is made explicit in such judgments as 'There were *fewer* people there *than* here.' (122)

According to Sapir's approach, John is *tall* is to be analyzed as 'John is taller than some X' and X is some implied norm.

The other approach takes the positive as basic and derives the comparative from that. McConnell-Ginet (1973) has proposed such an account, and my treatment of the meaning of gradable adjectives is based on her work.[8] According to McConnell-Ginet's analysis, the domain to which a relative term can apply can be divided into two parts, one part to which the application of the term is true and one part to which it is false. Thus *John is tall* is to be analyzed as follows: There is a set of things to which *tall* could be applied. It would include people, houses, and trees, but exclude ideas, rivers, and money, since it makes sense to speak of tall people but not of tall money. This set of things is divided into the subset of things that are tall and the remainder—the subset of things that are not tall. John belongs to the former set. *John is taller than Bill* is to be analyzed as follows: "The set of delineations over which 'John is tall' is true (at some index i) over some delineations such that 'Bill is tall' is not true over that delineation" (McConnell-Ginet, 1973:110). The index has to pick out the dividing case, as well as the reference class. More informally, the set of things which can be tall may be divided into two proper nonoverlapping subsets, one of tall things and one of non-tall things. John belongs to the first subset while Bill belongs to the other. A delineation is a boundary-fixing function for a predicate which fixes the extension of that predicate. The index (or rather indices) must pick out two things: the reference class, such as tall for men, or tall for American men, or tall for American men in Southern California of Anglo parents, between the ages of 17 and 25 with incomes over $25,000 per year. An index also has to pick out the dividing point, that which separates tall from non-tall.

McConnell-Ginet provides a great deal of evidence for her analysis, including the morphological evidence. Apparently all languages with a comparative construction treat the positive as morphologically unmarked and the comparative as marked (96). Languages without a comparative construction express comparison with a positive assertion and a negative assertion, so that *John is taller than Bill* would be encoded something like 'John is tall and Bill is not tall' (Small, quoted in McConnell-Ginet, 78).

There are two important features in this analysis. First of all, the domain is partitioned into two parts—the part which is X and the remainder, which is not X. Second, the line between the two parts can be drawn in a multiplicity of ways, depending on the context. But after the line is drawn in that context, the language imposes restrictions. So, for example, if a wine is placed among the set of sweet things, it cannot be called *dry* in that context. Third, when these terms are used as simple predicates, as in *Wine X is light,* the relevant class is not specified. Of course, a speaker can provide this information by adding a phrase, such as *Wine X is light for a Burgundy,* but what is so interesting about wine talk is that speakers use gradable predicates very frequently and do not provide any clue to their reference class. And listeners ask for clarification even less often. This phenomenon is true of conversation in general.

A reference class might be wines in general, but it seems usually to be more specific: white table wines, red table wines, or dessert wines. It can become more and more specified: all (French) Burgundies, or Burgundies from Beaune, or Burgundies from a part of Beaune in a certain year. Wine experts appear to use a narrower reference class than nonexperts, probably because they know more about wine subclasses and are more familiar with the typical characteristics of each subclass. The experiments described in the next section show that the lack of specification of the relevant reference class is a cause of lack of consensus in describing wines and a source of miscommunication. A speaker may say *Wine X is light* and have in mind California Cabernet Sauvignons from Napa Valley, whereas the listener has as a reference class all red wines.

In the application of these gradable expressions, there may be some threshold conditions. A wine with 10 percent sugar will very likely be judged sweet by everyone, and a wine with no sugar will be judged dry.[9] Although wine with 10 percent sugar would be sweet for a wine in general, it would not necessarily be sweet for a dessert wine. (The question of whether such a wine would be *too sweet* is still another issue, taken up in the next section.) So we can see shifting even here. Presumably a wine with 50 percent sugar would be sweet with respect to every reference class. But in the intermediate cases, say a wine with 1 percent sugar, the McConnell-Ginet account shows how the domain can be divided into two parts in alternative ways. Similar examples can be found for other descriptors. There are some wines that are so light, they would be judged as such with respect to any wine reference class. A 200-year-old wine would be old even for a vintage Port.

Some wine descriptors straddle both classes we have discussed—natural kind terms and gradable predicates. Examples are *chalky, earthy, buttery, woody, oaky, maderized, oxydized,* and *tannic.* These terms denote rather specific properties and in this way they resemble natural kind terms. But they also admit of degrees. Wine A can be earthier than wine B. They are also vague in presupposing some reference classes. Wine A may be chalky for a white wine but not for a Chablis, while wine B is tannic, even for a Cabernet.

How are we to fix the denotation of these gradable terms in any given context? That is, who is to decide whether a wine is heavy for a 1978 Clos de Vougeot? The role of experts was already mentioned with regard to making judgments of class membership with respect to natural kind terms. The judgments and opinions of some members of the society—experts—are given more weight than those of other people, and appealing to the judgments of experts may also be reasonable in the case of gradable terms as well. Both wine experts and nonexperts are inclined to agree that the judgments by experts carry more weight than judgments by others. Of course, if experts disagree among themselves (and they often do), then we have not solved the problem. We can try to find a way of determining which experts are more expert or we can give up and say that we do not know who is right or we can say that a statement like *Wine X is heavy for a 1978 Clos de Vougeot* has no truth value—that is, it is neither true nor false.

In stating the semantic relationships among gradable expressions, synonyms and hyponyms can either be derived from denotation or stated in terms of meaning postulates. In either case, the context of relevant domain must be stated, since certain expressions that are synonyms or hyponyms in the wine domain are not necessarily so in other domains. Examples of synonyms using meaning postulates would be

$$
\begin{array}{ccc}
\text{rough} & \rightarrow & \text{harsh} \\
\text{harsh} & \rightarrow & \text{rough}
\end{array}
$$

or alternatively,

$$
\text{rough} \quad \longleftrightarrow \quad \text{harsh.}
$$

Examples of hyponyms would be

$$
\begin{array}{ccc}
\text{robust} & \rightarrow & \text{full-bodied} \\
\text{round} & \rightarrow & \text{balanced}
\end{array}
$$

Alternatively, one could derive synonyms from the denotata: any two expressions that denote the same set of wines in all possible worlds (according to a given delineation) are synonyms. If A denotes a set of wines, and B denotes a proper subset of those wines in all possible worlds (for a given delineation), then B is a hyponym of A.

When we turn to gradable antonyms, however, we must have meaning postulates, since it is not possible to derive this semantic relationship from denotation. Suppose we partition the domain of things to which *light* can apply according to some delineation into those things that are light (L) and those things that are not light ($\overline{\text{L}}$). We cannot conclude that *heavy* can be applied to all those things in the class that are not light ($\overline{\text{L}}$), because some things may be neither light nor heavy. In fact, the defining feature of gradable antonyms is that they do not divide the semantic domain sharply into two parts but rather admit of intermediate cases.

Therefore, we must use meaning postulates. As a start, let us begin with the following entailments:

$$\text{heavy} \quad \rightarrow \quad \text{not light}$$
$$\text{light} \quad \rightarrow \quad \text{not heavy}$$

These entailments, however, are not sufficient, since antonymy is not distinguished from ordinary incompatibility.[10] *Cat* and *dog* are incompatible but are not antonyms.

Gradable antonymy has not, as far as I can tell, been handled within logical semantics. Lyons (1977) takes antonymy as a basic semantic relationship; so does Katz, but Katz (1972) does not distinguish between gradable antonymy and other kinds of incompatibility; he calls all of them antonymous sets.

Lehrer and Lehrer (1982) propose the following characterization of gradable antonymy. First we must begin with the notion of a scale. "A and B are antonyms if everything that is A is not B and everything that is B is not A and if everything that is A is more (less) ϕ (on that scale) than anything that is B; but there are some things that are more (less) ϕ than anything that is B that are not A."[11] More on antonyms later.

EVALUATIVE WORDS

The third class of words with which we must deal is made up of evaluative words—words that contain an evaluative component. Philosophers have worried about the meaning of *good* in various contexts, but most current semantic theories, especially those based on extension, or those where intension is defined in terms of extension, have had little to say about these words.[12] One can always make trivial statements, of course, such as that *good* denotes anything that is good, but one expects a semantic analysis to be more enlightening. Whereas there is considerable agreement on picking out tigers, chairs, and lemons, how does one pick out heroes, villains, and fools? Klapp (1962) in his study of social typing shows that one individual may classify a person, say Franklin D. Roosevelt, as a hero while another would classify him as a villain. These evaluative words were of special concern to the general semanticists, Korzybski and others, but their remarks were embedded in such an implausible theory of language that their work has been largely ignored by contemporary semanticists.

To deal with the evaluative words in the wine domain, we need not solve all the problems with using *good*, however; we can select a treatment that will do for the more limited purposes at hand—the wine vocabulary. The most reasonable place to begin is with treatments of *good* in aesthetics. Now, wine is not a work of art, though it is interesting to speculate on what would be necessary for wine to be put in that class. But many of the problems involved in evaluating art are relevant to those of wine as well—selecting criteria for evaluation, accounting for differences of taste among people and changes from time to time and place to place, and justifying judgments.

The first thing to point out about *good* and related terms is that they are gradable terms, like those in the previous class of words (*heavy, sweet*), and some reference group is implied. Thus a wine made from Thompson seedless or Mission grapes may be good for its type, but ordinary for a wine in general, since the potential from these varietals is limited.

Another thing to point out is that the semantic relationships between *good* and *bad* must be stated in terms of meaning postulates, as was done with gradable antonyms like *heavy* and *light*. Many of the other purely evaluative wine descriptors (*fine, great, ordinary, common*) must also be related in terms of meaning postulates.

Dickie (1971) and Urmson (1953) survey a number of analyses of *good*. Subjectivism is the view that 'what is aesthetically good' is 'what is liked by me'. Therefore, to understand any utterance containing such expressions, we must index the utterance to the speaker (Dickie 1971:161). Emotivism is the view that evaluative sentences do not assert anything—they are merely expressive. To say *Wine X is good* is to invite or induce the hearer to hold a favorable attitude toward wine X. Although it often is the case that someone says "This wine is good" to express his or her liking or to commend it, neither subjectivism nor emotivism will do as a general account, since a speaker may say, "I know Mogen David isn't [considered] a good wine, but I like it anyway" or "I like ordinary wines best of all," or "This is a great Port, but I wouldn't recommend it to you, because you hate Port."

The most plausible account of evaluative words in the wine domain seems to be some combination of relativism and nonnatural intuition. Relativism is the view that aesthetic (and moral) judgments have a commending function (like emotivism), but that in addition there are criteria for making these judgments, such as Wine X is good because it has qualities A, B, and C, where such qualities are considered desirable in wine. However, these criteria cannot be further justified; the judges decide to accept them, and different judges may adopt different sets of criteria. A bit of relativism is necessary to account for the fact that experts with comparable credentials may disagree. Wine connoisseurs trained on European wines often fail to appreciate the characteristics of California wine, and vice versa.

Nonnatural intuitionism (which Dickie calls Platonism 2) is the view that all beautiful things have certain empirical properties and that one can discover what these properties are (Dickie 1971:169). Therefore, criteria are available on which judgments can be based. Allowing for differences of criteria among experts (such as whether blended wines are better than unblended wines), there are a number of general criteria that are widely accepted for judging all wines and some additional criteria for judging specific wines. (Botrytis is a virtue in Sauterne, and maderization is a necessary feature of Sherry, but these would be considered defects in Chardonnay.) With respect to general criteria, Beardsley has proposed that all works of art must have unity, complexity, and intensity (see Dickie 1971:150). For wine, these features are nearly right, but one speaks of *balance* rather than *unity*, and *intensity* might be included in something else — possibly *flavorfulness* (since the opposite would be *blandness* or *insipidness*).

After criteria are established, others can learn to judge according to these criteria. Urmson (1953) writes: "It should be clear that, whatever else there may be that is puzzling about grading, in ordinary typical cases, at least, there is no puzzle about or doubt that it is a business done in accordance with principles and which one can learn to do in the way other people do it" (162). Or, in the context of grading cheese,

It is a fact that there is a stable majority (we need not now settle among which people the majority will be) who prefer, like, choose, cheese with the characteristics A B C. Then A B C becomes the characteristics which are accepted even by the majority, for grading cheese. Thus, even if one happens to hate all cheese, one will still be able sensibly to distinguish good from bad cheese. (180)

Finally, how do we connect statements containing evaluative terms with the world? Does a statement such as *Wine X is good* (with respect to a given reference class) have a truth value? Perhaps we can answer this question affirmatively, subject to several caveats and qualifications. First, we have said that the judgments of certain people—experts—count most heavily, and secondly, that they can agree on criteria. Moreover, the criteria must be relativized to many things—types of wines, place, time, and possibly even groups of experts. The important question is whether a given group of experts at a given time and in a given place judges wines consistently—that is whether the responses of each individual expert are consistent over time and whether there is significant agreement among the experts in the group, within some reasonable margin of error. Although I believe that there are such experts, I do not yet have sufficient evidence, and therefore, the question is open. But I suggest that whether evaluative wine judgments have truth value is an open, empirical question.[13]

There are a number of evaluative terms besides *good* and *bad*. For example, there are degrees of goodness—fine and great wines, for example, are very good. There are two ways of looking at *fine* and *great* with respect to *good*. On one hand, *good* can be seen as a general term, with *fine* and *great* being hyponyms (Fig. 15). Alternatively, *fine* and *great* can be analyzed as extending the scale of *good* (Fig. 16).

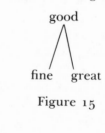

Figure 15

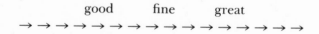

Figure 16

There are sentences that illustrate both of these possibilities:

That wine is not good, it's great.

or:

That wine is good—it's even great.
That wine is not only good, it's also great.

The feature of a term having both a general meaning to denote a scale and a more restricted meaning to denote all but the extreme end of the scale is such a common and pervasive feature of language that it would be uneconomical to establish two senses of *good* (compare also *large* with *huge*, *small* with *tiny*, or *cold* with *freezing*).

Sentences with *not only* provide a test for dealing with words having this semantic structure. The *not only* test produces bizarre results with words that are truly incompatible, such as *cat* and *dog*.

?That's not only a dog, it's a cat.
?That's not only a cat, it's a dog.

The strangeness of these sentences is not due to the nouns in it, since the test works for nouns that are hyponyms:

That's not only a car, that's a Cadillac.

The acceptability of

That wine is not only good, it's great.

shows that *great* can be a hyponym of *good*.

We can additionally establish a pragmatic function, as suggested by Nunberg (1978), where *good* may be contrasted with *great* (or *excellent*, *fine*, etc.) if *good* is negated, as in

The wine is not good, it's great.

The pragmatic function would state that whenever the context ruled out the interpretation of treating *fine*, *great*, or *excellent* as hyponyms of *good*, given by meaning postulates such as *fine* → *good* and *great* → *good*, then *good* would be interpreted as specifically meaning 'less good than great'.

Fine can be defined not only as 'good', but as 'very good', and *great* can be defined as 'very very good', where *very* is a proper subset indexer. That is, *very* functions to restrict the range of whatever it modifies (cf. Wheeler, 1972). To put it more technically,

> Some things that are very ϕ are better than some things that are ϕ; and there are things that are ϕ but not very ϕ [~(very ϕ)] that are more ϕ than things that are ϕ.

(*Very* must be pronounced with high pitch to convey the correct meaning; negation has wide scope.)

An example using *good* would be as follows:

> Things that are very good are better than some things that are (just) good. There are things that are good but are not (quite) very good, but they are better than other things that are good.

> Good things   Very good things
> a   b   c   d   e   f   g   h (things scaled for goodness)
> a, b, and c are good; f, g, and h are very good. d and e are better than a, b, or c, but still not very good.

Being better than some good things is a necessary but not sufficient condition for being very good.

An important part of the wine vocabulary consists of words that have both a descriptive and an evaluative component. They are words that involve classes two and three. Examples are *thin, coarse, sour, unbalanced* as negative descriptors, and *smooth, balanced,* and *delicate* as positive ones. As was emphasized in chapter 1, evaluation permeates the wine vocabulary. Some terms are generally neutral (*dry, light, young*), but they may take on evaluative force in certain contexts. In chapter 1 these were listed as positive, but perhaps the designation 'nonnegative' would be more appropriate.

The descriptive part of these words can be analyzed like the other gradable expressions in class two. For instance, a *thin* or *watery* wine is to be treated as a light wine—either relative to all wines or to a subset of wines. The same pragmatic function discussed with respect to *good* and *great* is operative here, since we can define *thin* either as a part of the lightness scale or as an extension of it. *Watery* seems to be a hyponym (or extension) of *thin*. This can be diagrammed as follows:

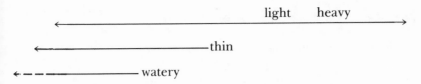

The *very* indexer will work here, since *thin* entails *very light,* and *watery* entails *very thin.* Since hyponymy is transitive, *watery* also entails *very light,* or in this case, perhaps *very, very light,* but my intuitions here are uncertain.

With respect to the evaluative part, *watery* is not only 'very light'—it is also 'too light', where *too* is a negative evaluation indexer. I can find no example where a positive word must contain a *too* indexer in its definition. It is, in fact, hard to imagine how something can be undesirably good. However, this is different from saying that a wine has too much of a property, where having a small amount of that property would be good. This is the difference between *sweet* and *cloying. Sweet* is neutral (though it may be used evaluatively in some contexts), but *cloying* is definitely 'too sweet'. Of course, we can say things like *This wine is too good to drink with pizza* or *This wine is too good for John,* but we are not predicating *too good* of the wine.

So to provide the semantics of *Wine A is watery,* we begin with the meaning postulate

$$\text{watery} \quad \rightarrow \quad \text{light}$$

In addition, we can say:

The set of things to which *light* can apply is for some delineation partitioned into those things that are *light* (L) and the remainder, not light ($\bar{\text{L}}$). Moreover, the set L is further partitioned into a proper subset of things that are very very L (vvL) and the remainder of L. Wine A belongs to the set vvL. In addition, wine A is judged (by experts), with respect to body, to be bad.

The analysis of *good* and other evaluative terms or words with an evaluative component proposed here are only intended to serve for wine discourse. I do not suggest (or deny) that such an analysis can be extended to other aesthetic realms. It is highly unlikely that it can be extended to ethics or picking out instances of heroes, villains, and fools.

PRAGMATICALLY INTERPRETED DESCRIPTORS

There are still some wine descriptors that have not been accounted for. These include *honest, pretentious, decrepit, charming,* and *taut.* One high-level theoretical decision is whether in fact any semantic theory should be required to deal with them. Many scholars working in the philosophy of language, for example, Kempson (1977), Katz (1977), Clark & Clark (1979), and others, argue for a distinction between semantics and pragmatic principles of interpretation, where the semantic component deals with conventional meaning (including conventional metaphors) and the pragmatics handles whatever the semantics cannot. We must assume a number of Gricean principles (Grice 1975), such as the presumption that the speaker wishes to communicate something, that what he says is relevant, etc.

A minimal pragmatic theory will say merely that hearers (or readers) have a way of computing speaker meaning when that diverges from sentence (conventional) meaning. However, a developed pragmatic theory will provide a list of strategies available for figuring out the intended meaning. For example, Clark & Clark look at denominal verbs in English. Conventional expressions such as *bicycle to work, bottle the wine, milk the cow,* or *butcher the cow* can be analyzed in terms of a limited number of relationships between actions and objects (or to put the matter linguistically, between verbs and thematic relations). The common relationship between nouns and verbs *(a bicycle* and *to bicycle, some milk* and *to milk)* provides a pattern for the formation of new verbs from nouns. Hence, Clark & Clark analyze how expressions like *porch the newspaper* and *Houdini one's way out of a closet* are interpreted by listeners. The set of relationships between the actions and objects will provide a limited number of possible alternatives, so that the actual interpretation of an utterance will depend on a variety of pragmatic factors, including mutually shared beliefs.

Returning to the wine domain, the means available for extending the vocabulary will also be available for interpreting novel uses of words. The notion of semantic relationships holding across many semantic fields seems to be one of the most important ones in the wine domain. For example, age expressions are easily interpreted in this way. They retain their place with respect to other age words in terms of the natural state of development or growth. *Decrepit* and *senile* can be paraphrased roughly as 'old, aged, having lost former powers and capabilities, approaching death'. (There are further features to distinguish the two from each other.) In wine, this would be interpreted as 'too old, approaching end of cycle of development', and perhaps 'no longer capable of providing satisfactory taste'. However, since we have moved beyond conventional meaning, we can expect different people to provide different interpretations. The discovery of interpretation strategies is a ripe area for explanation and research. Much of the work on metaphor is relevant (Kittay & Lehrer 1981, Levin 1977, and Lakoff & Johnson 1980).

The final question with respect to sentences containing metaphors or other kinds of semantic extensions is whether they have truth value.[14] A standard answer is 'no'. For example, Loewenberg (1975) writes, "Once identified as a metaphor, the statement is neither true nor false" (338). Yet there is another side. Consider the sentence

John traded in his hot car for a cold one.

and consider two situations: in one case John traded his sporty Porsche for a VW Beetle and in the second case he traded his VW Beetle for a Porsche. The sentence seems to accurately (though perhaps metaphorically) describe the first situation but not the second. Therefore, it seems incorrect to deny that sentences containing novel metaphors and other kinds of semantic transfers and extensions lack truth values. (Dead metaphors can be taken care of with machinery already established, since the meanings are conventional.)

Levin (1977) adopts a position where we reinterpret deviant (metaphorical, poetic) sentences in some way—that is, by literalizing them, and then determining their truth. Goodman (1968) also argues for the position that sentences with metaphor and transfer have truth value. He does not advocate going through a process of literalization. He also has little to say about the process.

> The question why predicates apply as they do metaphorically is much the same as the question why they apply as they do literally. And if we have no good answer in either case, perhaps that is because we have no real question. At any rate, the general question why things have the properties, literal and metaphorical, that they do have—why things are as they are—is a task I am content to leave to the cosmologists. (78)

The position I wish to suggest with respect to the truth of pragmatically interpreted wine words is an intermediate one. If there is consensus among a group of speakers that a predicate can be applied to a property (or complex of properties) either by direct denotation or mediated by a chain of intralinguistic connections, then a sentence with that expression may have a truth value. If there is no consensus, then the statement has no truth value. If *feminine* is consistently applied to wines that are soft, perfumed, light, and delicate and never to wines with contrasting properties, then we might say that *feminine* can be predicated truly or falsely. If in time *feminine* were frequently and standardly applied to wines, then of course it would develop a conventional meaning as a wine descriptor and would move out the category of pragmatically interpretable terms, probably into category two, those of gradable adjectives.

However, there is no reason to think that most of the predicates in this class—*taut, severe, honest, pretentious,* or *senile*—would be used consistently by speakers and consensually by groups, even of experts. I suppose that one could still try to apply a truth conditional theoretical semantic theory by talking about speaker meaning, idiolect, and other idiosyncratic aspects of language use. However, the fact that some nonanalytic, declarative, non-nonsensical sentences may have no truth value should not be disturbing. People talk for many reasons, only one of which is to describe states of the world.

SUMMARY

Although the wine vocabulary is only a small part of the English language, it contains a great variety of kinds of words. I have tried to show how some of these words can be fixed to denotation—to objects and properties in the world—and how relationships among the words can be stated. In the case of natural kind terms, a word denotes a class of objects that have some property, and certain members of the society—enologists or viticulturists in this case—are acknowledged to have special skills and knowedge concerning these objects. Their judgments in connecting words with the world are given a decisive role.[15] In Western societies, where science and scientists are highly regarded, if all the scientists agree on a denotation, the rest of the population will go along. If an expert says that *Wine A is a Zinfandel,* and all other experts confirm this, then that statement is true.

Some descriptors, such as *light* or *young,* admit of degrees, of more or less. The interpretation of sentences with these words requires a reference class, which can be explicitly stated but often is not. We may appeal to experts to assess the truth of statements using these words, and these experts will probably be wine connoisseurs.

The words in the third group are evaluative. They are also gradable, and they admit of more or less. But the most important aspect of these words is that they are tied up with human preferences. How these words are hooked up to the world is not at all clear, and there is great disagreement about how to apply them to wines. Many people in our society are willing to trust experts—again wine connoisseurs—to decide on the connection, but there is much less willingness to do so than in the case of natural kind terms. In addition, the experts may disagree among themselves in trying to decide whether a wine is good. In such cases, some people may conclude that no one is right or wrong—it's just a matter of opinion.

Finally, we have looked at words that do not have any conventional connection to wine or to any properties found in wine. In such cases the hearer or listener must figure out what a reasonable interpretation would be, drawing on his or her knowledge of interlinguistic relationships and shared knowledge of all sorts. We can expect considerable disagreement in the interpretation of sentences. For example, if someone says *Wine X is aloof,* it could mean 'Wine X is hard to get to know and appreciate', or 'Wine X is unusual and hard to classify' as well as many other things.

We have also looked at the intralinguistic relationships—synonymy, hyponymy, antonymy, incompatibility, etc. These relationships provide a way of interpreting sentences with words that are not used in conventional ways. If a speaker says *Wine X is huge,* a hearer can relate *huge* to a phrase that does have a conventional meaning in the wine domain—*very big.* Then the hearer can interpret the sentence as 'Wine X is very big'. In fact, since intralinguistic links are stable and shared, they provide a method of communicating, even when referential links are weak.

POSTSCRIPT: *SWEET* AS A NATURAL KIND TERM

Does *sweet* share properties with natural kind terms? Before discussing *sweet* I will mention Kripke's description of light and heat. Kripke (1972) argues that light and heat cannot be a matter of human sensations, since even if we were blind and could not feel or even if we did not exist, light and heat would exist. Light is a stream of photons and heat is molecular motion. The perception of these things is a different matter (325–27). Pain, however, belongs to a different category; it would not exist if animate beings did not feel it. Kripke says (327),

> My argument implicitly concludes that certain general terms, those for natural kinds, have a greater kinship with proper names than is generally realized. . . . It also applies to certain terms for natural phenomena, such as 'heat', 'light', 'sound', 'lightning', and presumably, suitably elaborated, to corresponding adjectives—'hot', 'loud', 'red'.

Of course, since the analysis of adjectives is not yet elaborated, we cannot know what Kripke would do. But first it must be noted that *hot* is gradable. It is simply misleading to say that anything with heat, that is, anything with molecular motion, is hot. Cold things like ice or water at 4°C have molecular motion, and may in a technical sense be 'hot', but of course to say that cold things are hot is a semantic contradiction.

Turning to *sweet,* now, the perception of sweetness is correlated with a chemical class of sugars (as well as other substances such as saccharin). Some individuals and some species are apparently taste-blind. However, the fact that other individuals and species are not enables us to label those with taste-blindness as deficient, as lacking a perceptual ability. The sweetness of kinds of sugars differs, and this is measured and calibrated by human judges. Sucrose and fructose are two of the sweetest of sugars and xylose is one of the least sweet (Moskowitz 1970). Now, it is conceivable that there is some physical property of sugars that correlates with sweetness, so that the more (or fewer) atoms a sugar molecule has, the sweeter it is. If this were all there was to say, then sweetness would be similar to heat.

But the problem is complicated by the fact that, when tastes are combined, their properties are not necessarily additive. Sometimes one taste masks another taste, and sometimes it enhances it. Acids like lemon tend to mask sweetness. Suppose we have two solutions with 10 percent sugar; one of these solutions, however, is 50 percent water and 50 percent lemon juice. (We have already corrected for the sugar in the lemon juice and the kinds of sugars involved so that both solutions have the same percentage and the same kinds of sugars.) Perceptually they are not equally sweet—the solution without lemon is definitely sweeter than the lemon drink. Yet if sweetness is to be equated with amount of sugar, both solutions would have to be regarded as equally sweet.

My own view is that sweetness is more like pain than it is like light and that the correlation of perceived sweetness with physical phenomena is a contingent fact, not a definitional stipulation. Therefore, I would classify *sweet* as a gradable expression, rather than as a natural kind term.

Part II

Wine Experiments

Chapter 4
Remarks on Methodology

I have investigated wine talk from a variety of perspectives, and I have employed a variety of methods and tools in order to do so. Part II of this book could be entitled "experimental semantics," in that in it I have tried to investigate systematically how speakers actually describe and discuss wines when they are drinking them. Since there is no universally accepted paradigm for studying what I wanted to study, I have borrowed freely and eclectically from the various methods used in the different social sciences.

Interdisciplinary studies are valuable in many ways. They supply information from one field that may provide a solution to a problem in another. They may show how information from one discipline fits into a larger picture—for instance how a theory of language contributes to a general theory of communication. However, a less obvious value of interdisciplinary studies is that they provide an opportunity to question the basic assumptions of one discipline by examining those of other fields.

Each of the social sciences has its favorite methodologies and mathematical tools, taught by practitioners of that science and handed down to students. Professional journals may prescribe the format of articles, and this fact contributes to a standard way of investigating problems as well as of stating results. All this is part of what Kuhn (1962) has called normal science. At the same time social scientists are generally aware that practitioners in other fields often use very different methods, and even within a discipline there are often great theoretical and methodological disputes.

Contemporary generative-transformational grammarians, influenced by philosophers of language, have relied heavily on their own intuitions—judgments about whether a particular string of words is grammatical, meaningful, appropriate, or acceptable. Occasionally the investigators' intuitions are supplemented by those of other speakers, using elicitation or interview methods. The validity and reliability of intuitive data have been discussed (e.g., Spencer 1973; Botha 1973, 1979; Labov 1975; and McCawley 1979b), and there is a general recognition of the fallibility of intuitions as well as an awareness of the theory-laden nature of the concepts involved, especially of grammaticality. A further problem is that the relationship between intuition and actual behavior is not clear. Speakers will often label sentences presented to them as unacceptable or ungrammatical even though they themselves use such constructions in informal unguarded speech.

On the other hand, asking speakers if they could or would say certain things is such a convenient and efficient way of gathering data it would be foolish to reject such a source. In vocabulary studies especially, where the lexicon is vast, a linguist might wait years for certain words to be used in spontaneous conversation. (The use of computers for data processing and retrieval has helped this problem somewhat.)

The principal formalism in linguistics has been the algebralike system of phrase structure and transformational rules, and that is being rapidly supplemented with various versions of symbolic logic. Statistical statements have been useful in studies of language typology and dialectology.

The experimental method has been the paradigm for many branches of psychology (psychophysics, psycholinguistics, learning, social psychology) where a number of subjects are required to do something, such as memorize a list of words, solve a problem, or judge how sweet a substance is. The advantage of this method is that a situation or environment is devised in which the investigator can control for different variables that might influence the outcome. If the success rate in memorizing sentences varies with the length or complexity of words, the investigator can use stimuli which control for this. If the temperature of a stimulus affects taste perception, the investigator can discover this by giving subjects samples which differ only in temperature. In addition, the investigator can compare populations with respect to their performance on some task. If language learning ability varies with sex or handedness, the investigator would select an adequate sample of men and women or of left- as well as right-handed subjects. Of course, there are an enormous number of possible variables, so the investigator only controls for those known to be or likely to be relevant. In the psycholinguistic literature with which I am familiar, no one has tried to correlate the ability to remember sentences with eye color.

The limitation of the controlled experiment is that it is not clear to what extent the results obtained are influenced by the experimental setting and can therefore be projected outside the laboratory. D. Miller also points out that the kinds of things that can be studied experimentally are limited: "For ethical as well as economic reasons, the range of behavior which can be created in the social experiment is limited (by size of group, strength of sanction, time, etc.), so limited that experimentation must be classified as a very specialized method which cannot perform alone the same function for the social sciences as it has for some physical sciences" (1967:3).[1] The mathematical tools used include a variety of sophisticated statistical techniques, many of which can only be carried out by computer (e.g., multidimensional scaling).

Observational studies, where the investigator observes behavior in a natural setting, are used in cultural anthropology, language acquisition studies, and sociolinguistics. In linguistics this method includes the study of spontaneous speech in normal settings. The study of written texts might also be included in this class, although such material is more carefully constructed and edited than that which occurs in spontaneous speech. Sometimes simply observing behavior is not enough because the investigator cannot understand its meaning and significance, as, for example, in the case of the anthropologist who has just arrived in an unfamiliar place. Therefore, observation is often supplemented by interviewing those being studied. Such reports are of great value, but are subject to the same limitation as intuitions or any other sort of introspective behavior.

Another type of method is the case study, a special type of observational study. Miller observes that although one cannot make legitimate generalizations on the basis of one case, the study of many cases may result in cumulative knowledge. However, the main value of the case study is that it "is a process of generating hypotheses, not for testing them. If the achievement of systematic statements concerning sets of phenomena is a goal, then the first step will often be a case study" (1967:4). The comparative method, another type of method involving naturalistic observation, attempts to achieve what the experimental method tries for—the study of behavior under different conditions and in various settings (1967:6).

Survey data is widely used in sociology, economics, political science, and a few areas of linguistics, such as sociolinguistics. The advantage of surveys is that a very large sample of people can be questioned in order to provide a large enough population for correlating many variables and parameters. However, the kinds of things that can be studied in this way is limited. In addition, "in most surveys only operational definitions (in the form of the measuring instruments themselves) are employed" (1967:5). For example, when trying to determine whether religious people are more or less tolerant than nonreligious people, definitions of *religious* and *tolerant* are measured by responses to certain questions in the survey. Finally, survey methods are subject to the same weaknesses as introspective data acquired in other ways. Respondents may inaccurately report what they do or believe. A variety of statistical tools are used in the analysis of survey data.

The studies reported in the following chapters utilize a combination of the methods: experiments, observations, surveys, and the introspections of the subjects and participants. The various methods prcduce converging results, which reinforce each other and strengthen the conclusions.

Chapter 5
Experiments and Subjects

If meaning consists of the relationship among lexical items *and* the relationship between lexical items and denotata, then one aspect of a wine words study should be the way in which speakers apply words to samples of wine. Since linguists rarely study this sort of behavior, and since philosophers hardly ever do empirical studies, and since experimental psychologists who deal with naming behavior have generally used rather simple stimuli (plastic chips of various colors, for example), there has been no accepted set of experimental paradigms to use, and I have had to devise some.

When I first began my investigation of how people apply words to actual samples of wine, I planned to do only one set of experiments with a single group of subjects. Because the results suggested new questions to be asked, further experiments were done with two other groups of subjects. I selected tasks for the latter two groups similar to those used with the first in order to be able to compare the performance of all groups of subjects. However, in carrying out the experiments, questions and problems arose concerning the experimental methods themselves and the way in which subjects interpreted the instructions, so that the methodology and instructions were modified.

It is difficult to carry out wine-tasting experiments in a naturalistic setting. There are too many variables to be controlled for. Subjects' perceptions of the wines they drink change during the course of the sessions. As they drink wine, some sensory fatigue occurs, and moreover the alcohol sometimes impairs subjects' ability to discriminate. The wines also change after they are opened and aerate; white wines, if served chilled, change as they warm up to room temperature. Replication studies, i.e., serving the same wine on different occasions, involve various difficulties. Subjects' perceptions are affected by such things as how recently they brushed their teeth and the brand of toothpaste used, or whether they recently smoked a cigarette or chewed gum. Wines, too, change over time. Even if two bottles are from the same cask, the cork on one bottle might be denser than the other and let in less air. A period of six months may give a wine time to age; the sediment from a red wine may settle in a bottle which has stood upright for two days, whereas an 'identical' bottle served immediately after a journey from the wine store might have the sediment thoroughly homogenized. Subjects, too, change over time. As they become more experienced and knowledgeable, they learn to notice and appreciate many subtle characteristics of wines, and their preferences change.

Many of these factors can be controlled for, and are controlled for in tasting laboratories in large wineries and institutes of enology. Studies in technical journals of enology on wine tasting are based on carefully controlled experiments. However, speakers of languages do not learn to use most of their vocabulary in a carefully controlled setting. Words are learned in uncontrolled and unique contexts, and my goal in studying the first two groups of subjects was to discover how people actually applied words to wines under normal conditions. (Of course, experimental tasks, especially paper and pencil ones, do not take place in normal conversations, but the results provide useful data that can be analyzed statistically.) Casual wine drinkers—nonexperts or semiexperts—learn to talk about wine in uncontrolled settings. They may read books, but books only provide an inventory of words and make a few general suggestions as to which kinds of wines might have the relevant qualities. The reader has no way of checking whether he or she is applying the words correctly. People also take wine courses, which often consist of six or eight lectures with a variety of wines to taste. Buy my experience with such courses suggest that very little time is given to carefully teaching the use and application of words, and students are not tested on their use of terms. The subjects in the third group, in contrast to the first two, were wine experts—more precisely, wine scientists—for whom the careful use of words was very important.

The basic question in the wine experiments was this: do speakers of English apply words to wines in the same way? Do they mean (denote) the same things when they use the same words? An affirmative answer, an instance of "success," was measured by consensus within the group. When I describe one group of subjects as performing "better" than another or of performing "better" at one time than another, I mean that there was higher intragroup agreement. A second question was: can speakers improve? That is, can a group of speakers increase their intragroup agreement in describing wines?

THE SUBJECTS: THEIR PREFERENCES AND KNOWLEDGE

The first group of subjects consisted of twenty-two fellows and staff of the Center for Advanced Study in the Behavioral Sciences in Stanford, California (eight women and fourteen men) who participated in five experimental sessions. This group will be referred to as the Stanford group. These subjects had neither drunk nor discussed wine together as a group before the experiments, so that their responses provide some information on how a diverse group of speakers of English drawn from all over the United States apply words to a set of complex stimuli—wine.

Two questionnaires were given to the Stanford subjects before any wine tasting was carried out—one to elicit information on the subjects' wine preferences and experience and the other on their wine knowledge. Of the twenty-two subjects, twenty reported drinking wine at least weekly. Fourteen reported having read one to three books or articles on wine, three subjects had read more than three items, and five had read nothing about wine. With respect to preferences, subjects overwhelmingly reported preferring dry wine to sweet, red and/or white to rosé, table wine to dessert wine, and still wine to sparkling wine. Ten of the twenty-two subjects said that they did not like sweet wines. See Table 5.

The responses to the questions on wine knowledge varied from 1 to 10 correct with an average of 5. Two of the subjects were highly

TABLE 5: Wine Preference and Experience Questionnaire Results

	Stanford (N=22)	Tucson (N=16)	Davis (N=10)
How often do you drink wines?			
At least once a week	20	8	
One or more times a month but less than weekly	2	7	
Less than once a month	0	1	
Almost every day			7
At least weekly but not every day			3
Have you read about wine?			
Three or more books or an equivalent number of articles	3	3	
One to three books or articles	14	7	
Never	5	7	
What are your wine preferences?			
Sweet or dry			
Sweet	1	1	0
Dry	19	15	5
Red, white, or rosé*			
Red	15	5	8
White	10	10	4
Rosé	0	1	0
Still or sparkling			
Still	14	14	8
Champagne	4	0	0
Table or dessert			
Table	19	14	6
Dessert	2	0	0
*Are there any types of wines that you dislike?**			
(Very) sweet	10	9	1
Sherry	2	3	
Port		1	
Pop wines, fruit wines			2
Native American varieties			1

*Some subjects checked red and white.
**Responses were free; no categories were suggested in the questionnaire.

knowledgeable about wine: one was an amateur winemaker and one had been collecting wine as a hobby for many years. Table 6 presents the questions on the wine knowledge questionnaire and the subjects' scores.

The subjects in the second group were also ordinary wine drinkers (nonexperts) for the most part. There were originally eighteen members in this group (ten women and eight men), but two dropped out after three sessions, leaving nine women and seven men. A total of thirteen sessions were held: twelve experimental sessions plus a

TABLE 6: Wine Knowledge Questionnaire

| Question | Number Correct* | |
	Stanford Subjects (N=18)	Tucson Subjects (N=17)
1. What color is most German wine?	17	17
2. What is the principal grape used in Rhine wine?	6	2
3. How does (natural) Champagne get its bubbles?	12	4
4. List three sweet wines. (Give generic, not brand names.)	11	9
5. What kind of wine is Chablis? (Color, country, dry or sweet.)	14	11
6. What wine is made with Flor yeast?	2	0
7. How does rosé wine get its color?	10	3
8. What is the principal grape in Brodeaux (type) wine?	6	2
9. What is the difference between aroma and bouquet in a wine?	0	0
10. Name two classified first growths of Bordeaux.	3	½
11. What is the relationship between the color of wine and tannin?	9	0

*Part scores were given for questions 4, 5, and 10.

Answers: 1) white 2) Riesling 3) sugar is added to wine in the bottle 4) eg. Port, Sauternes, Marsala, Madeira, Tokay, some Sherry 5) dry white from France 6) Sherry 7) red grape skins remain for a short time during fermentation 8) Cabernet Sauvignon 9) aroma involves smells from the grape and bouquet those from the wine 10) Lafite, Margaux, Latour, Haut Brion, Mouton-Rothschild 11) tannin deepens the color.

party. This group will be referred to as the Tucson group. The central question that I wished to investigate with the Tucson group was to what extent wine-describing performance would improve over time if a group of people met together regularly and frequently to discuss wine. By "improve" I mean that there would be greater consensus in describing wines at the later sessions as compared to the earlier sessions. Because I wanted to maintain a casual setting, I invited subjects to my home over a period of eight months.

The Tucson subjects were given the same questionnaires on preference, experience, and knowledge as were given to the Stanford subjects (see Tables 5 and 6). Of the sixteen subjects who remained for the duration of the experiments, eight reported that they drank wine at least weekly, seven at least monthly, and the remaining one less than monthly. Only one subject had read more than three books or articles on wine, seven had read between one and three items, and the rest had never read anything. The wine preferences were similar to those of the first group. All but one subject preferred dry wines to sweet ones, and all but one preferred red and/or white to rosé. Subjects mentioned sweet wines or heavy dessert wines such as cream sherry or port as wines they disliked. The range of correct answers to the quiz was 0 to 5, with an average of 3, so it can be seen that the Tucson subjects knew less about wine than the Stanford ones. (The most knowledgeable Tucson subject did not take the wine quiz.)

The third group of subjects—the Davis subjects, consisted of ten wine scientists (eight men and two women) connected with the Department of Enology at the University of California at Davis. This would be as favorable a group as one would expect to find to determine to what extent speakers might share and apply terms in the same way. The Davis subjects were either students in enology or members of the winery research staff. All subjects knew each other and some had belonged to the same wine tasting group or had taken courses together, but not all subjects had in fact drunk wine and talked about it with one another. Moreover, the professor who had been in charge of training students in sensory evaluation and description of wine had retired so that not all subjects had been trained by the same expert. The Davis subjects were concerned with the problems of using words in the same way and agreed that consensus in word application was necessary and important for enologists.

A questionnaire to elicit information on the subjects' preference and experience was given to the Davis subjects, but I revised the questionnaire to make it more appropriate to this particular group. Seven of the ten subjects reported drinking wine almost every day, and the other three drank wine at least once a week. Subjects were asked to rate themselves as wine experts compared to other wine experts and compared to average wine drinkers. Nine of the ten rated themselves as average with respect to other wine experts and one rated himself as above average; nine of the ten rated themselves as above average compared to average wine drinkers and one rated himself as average. Davis subjects were more reluctant than the other groups to express preferences. They tended to qualify their responses, indicating a wide range of tastes. To the extent that they stated their preferences, they preferred red wines to white or rosés, dry wines to sweet ones, still wines to sparkling wines, and table wines to dessert wines.

It would have been insulting (as well as ridiculous) to give the Davis subjects the knowledge questionnaire (Table 6), and it was obvious to me in talking to the Davis subjects that they were not only wine experts, but wine scientists. Their knowledge and experience exceeded that of all subjects in the first two groups.

THE EXPERIMENTS

Several experimental paradigms were used with the three groups of subjects, some of which involved paper and pencil tasks and others of which involved talking to one or more other subjects. At all of the sessions three wines of the same class were served—either three white table wines or three red table wines.[1] However, all three wines at each session were perceptually distinct; they were drawn from different classes. At a typical session subjects might be served a German Riesling, a French Graves, and a California Chenin Blanc. No subject ever reported that any wines at the same session tasted alike. At all sessions the wines were served blind; either the bottles were covered, so that the subjects could not see the label and the shape and color of the bottle when the wine was poured, or else the wine was served already poured into glasses, with bottles out of view. Wines were coded by letter or number. At all sessions subjects were instructed to taste all three wines before performing any of the tasks. Occasionally the order of tasting was randomized by the experimenter, but usually the subjects were free to choose the order. Subjects could also taste any wine as often as necessary, so that a good wine memory was not necessary.[2] Water was provided so that subjects could rinse out their mouths or clean their palates between wines, and spittoons or empty glasses were provided in case subjects did not wish to swallow the wine. Only the Davis subjects made use of the spittoons.

With the Stanford subjects there were five experimental sessions which took place at weekly intervals (with two weeks between sessions 3 and 4). The sessions were held in a large room during the day. Subjects performed some tasks individually and some in pairs. Sessions typically lasted for thirty minutes although there was some variation in the amount of time each subject required. At the first four sessions subjects wrote out all their responses. At the fifth session, pairs of subjects met to describe wines together, and the conversation was tape-recorded.

Testing with the Tucson subjects took place at twelve experimental sessions and a Christmas party over an eight-month period, with sessions held in my living room in the evening, usually at two-week intervals, but with two intervals of four weeks. At one session subjects worked in pairs, but at all other sessions the whole group met together. At each session there were one or more experiments followed by informal discussion. The experiments usually lasted for thirty minutes and the discussions from a half hour to an hour. A tape recorder was placed on a coffee table in the middle of the living room to record the conversation during the experimental sessions (unless they were strictly pencil and paper tasks) and during the discussions.

Testing with the Davis subjects took place over a period of three days at the University winery. Three sessions were held, each lasting about an hour. At sessions 1 and 3 all subjects assembled together for paper and pencil tasks; at the second session, subjects met in pairs to describe wines to each other, and their conversations were tape-recorded.

Even though it would be desirable to be able to provide some information on the physical and chemical properties of the wines that were served to subjects, unfortunately I did not have the means to do so. But then, the correlation between chemical properties of wine and sensory perception is not one to one (Amerine, Panghorn, & Roessler 1965:494–97). However, I measured sugar content roughly with Tes-Tape, a yellow paper that turns greener with increasing sugar. Beyond 2 percent the tape is as green as it gets. In some cases the wineries supplied me with the information on sugar content. The percentage of alcohol was taken from the label on the bottle.

Chapter 6
The Stanford Subjects

CONSENSUS EXPERIMENTS—SESSIONS 1 AND 2

The first two test sessions with the Stanford subjects attempted to provide information on how much consensus there is among speakers when they describe wine. Since these individuals had never discussed wine with the other participants, consensus in describing wines would be less likely than with the other groups of subjects. On the other hand, if significant consensus *could* be found with such a group, this would provide very strong evidence that a group of speakers who shared a vocabulary and grammar did in fact apply words to things and properties in the same way.

The experimental tasks given to the subjects at sessions 1 and 2 were the same. The only difference between them was that red wines were served at session 1 and whites at session 2. Subjects worked alone in these experiments and wrote down their responses. At the first session each subject was given three glasses, each with one of the wines in Table 7. The subjects were to taste each wine in any order and to state whether they liked it.

Wine F was a noncommercial Zinfandel with less than 0.25 percent sugar, probably not a perceptible amount, since the threshold for tasting sweetness is between 0.75 and 1.5 percent (Amerine & Singleton 1965:302). One of the most salient characteristics of F was its strong aroma, a feature which virtually all subjects commented on,

TABLE 7: Red Wines Served at Session 1—Stanford (N = 15)

				Preferences		
Code	Wine	% Sugar	% Alcohol	Like	Neutral	Dislike
F	Zinfandel	>0.1,< 0.25	14*	5	5	5
R	California Burgundy	>1.0,< 2.0	13½	10	3	2
T	Petite Sirah	< 0.1	12½	6	3	6

*Reported by winemaker

either positively or negatively. This wine was the most controversial of the three. Wine R was a popular California Burgundy made for wide distribution, with a perceptible amount of sugar, and wine T was a California Petite Sirah with barely a trace of sugar.

The subjects' first task was to describe the taste, smell, and feel in the mouth of each wine and to write its description on a blank sheet of paper provided. Subjects commented that the task was fairly difficult, but everyone was able to describe all the wines, and some individuals gave rather long, detailed descriptions and comparisons, occasionally after protesting that they didn't know any wine words.

The most striking result on all the tasks, especially this one, was that descriptions (not just evaluations) varied enormously depending on whether or not the tester liked the wine. Wine F was described by one person as "sweet, bubbly . . . flowery, light fizzy feeling in the mouth" and as "quite dry, quite tangy" by another (both liked the wine). The same wine was described as "harsh odor, pungent, unpleasant; taste is bitter, sharp" by one who did not like it. The only consensus on wine F was that it had a strong aroma. Many subjects also commented that F was sweet. But since this wine had very little sugar, the strong aroma was probably responsible for this judgment. *Sweet* can of course be applied to smell as well as taste. Wine R was described in a variety of ways, but no general patterns seemed to emerge. Wine T was often characterized as *full, heavy, robust, chewy,* or *thick* with respect to body, and *sour, acid* or *astringent* with respect to taste and feel.

After completing the first task, each subject was given three copies of a list of 145 wine descriptors. These terms were selected from wine descriptors found in the published literature on wine, and those selected were the most frequently used and those for which definitions or characterizations could be found (see Fig. 17). For each wine, subjects were asked to circle any and all words that aptly described that wine. This task was designed to provide information on consensus of description, and in addition, it would provide some information on which words subjects knew and which words were common descriptors. The list of words was also intended to help subjects who claimed "they did not know any wine words" on the assumption that they would recognize many words even if they could not recall them.[1]

FIGURE 17: List of 145 Wine Descriptors

acidic	fat	hot	puckery	strong
aged	feminine	insipid	pungent	sturdy
alcoholic	fierce	light	racy	stylish
aromatic	fiery	little	rare	succulent
astringent	fine	lively	refreshing	sugary
austere	finesse	maderized	rich	supple
baked	firm	manly	ripe	sweet
balanced	flabby	mature	robust	syrupy
big	flat	meager	rough	tangy
bitter	flowery	mealy	round	tannic
bland	forceful	medium	rugged	tart
bouquet	foxy	mellow	salty	tender
chalky	fragile	metallic	sappy	thin
character	fragrant	mineral	savory	unbalanced
clean	fresh	moldy	scented	unharmonious
cloying	fruity	mossy	semisweet	unripe
common	full-bodied	musky	sensuous	velvety
complex	gassy	noble	sharp	vigorous
corky	gay	nutty	simple	watery
creamy	gentle	oaky	small	weak
crisp	graceful	odd	smoky	wild
deep	grapy	off	smooth	withered
delicate	great	old	soft	woody
developed	green	ordinary	solid	young
disciplined	hard	overripe	sound	zestful
dry	harmonious	peppery	sour	
earthy	harsh	perfumed	spicy	
elegant	hearty	positive	steely	
empty	heavy	powerful	stiff	
evolved	honest	prickly	stony	

Table 8 lists words that were most frequently circled by the subjects. The figure in parentheses shows the number of subjects who circled that word.

TABLE 8: Most Frequently Circled Words, Session 1—Stanford
(N=15)

Wine F		Wine R		Wine T	
fragrant	(7)	dry	(6)	dry	(11)
fruity	(7)	smooth	(6)	acidic	(7)
semisweet	(7)			full-bodied	(7)
grapy	(6)			puckery	(7)
perfumed	(5)			astringent	(6)
aromatic	(5)			hearty	(6)
astringent	(5)			robust	(6)
flowery	(5)				

For the third task, subjects were given a list of twenty common adjectives (see Table 9 column 1) and asked to decide for each wine whether a term applied or not.

The results are presented in Table 9.[2] Chi square was used to analyze the data. With a binary choice, if twelve of the fifteen subjects provide the same response, the result is significantly above chance ($p < 0.05$). There was much greater agreement on what characteristics a wine does *not* have than what it does have. Statistical significance was reached largely because tasters agreed that a wine did not have a particular quality.

Some interesting correlations were found between a subject's responses on task 3 and his evaluation of the wine. For example, subjects who liked wine F indicated by checking the 'yes' column that *clean* and *lively* were appropriate descriptors, while subjects who disliked F or were neutral checked the 'no' column ($p < 0.05$).

Most tasters agreed that wine R was *clean,* but there was a complete split in judgment as to whether it was *dry, fruity, full-bodied, light, lively,* or *semisweet.* Though everyone checked the 'no' column for *sweet,* this wine in fact had a perceptible amount of sugar. (I argued in chapter 3 that *sweet* is a relative term and that the presence of sugar does not require that we call that wine *sweet.* According to some implicit reference class, subjects did not consider wine R *sweet.*) When responses to the term *dry* for wines F and R were pooled and plotted against preference, there was a significant correlation ($p < 0.05$), such that those who liked a wine described it as *dry,* while those who disliked it tended to say that it was *sweet.* Recall that almost all subjects mentioned that they preferred dry wines, and several

Table 9: Agreement/Disagreement on Characteristics of Red Wines
Served at Session 1 (N = 15)

Adjective	Yes	No	Yes	No	Yes	No
bitter	2	13**	2	13**	5	10
bland	3	12*	5	10	2	13**
chalky	0	15***	0	15***	4	11
clean	10	5	11	4	6	9
complex	2	13**	5	10	6	9
dry	7	7	8	7	0	15**
earthy	2	13**	2	11*	7	8
flat	2	13**	2	13**	3	12*
fruity	11	4	9	6	4	11
full-bodied	5	10	5	9	12	3*
light	10	4	7	7	3	11*
lively	8	7	8	7	4	11
metallic	2	13**	2	13**	0	15***
off	2	13**	4	11	5	10
semisweet	10	5	6	9	1	14
sour	3	12*	3	12*	7	8
spicy	7	8	2	13**	2	13**
sweet	4	11	0	15***	0	15***
tart	8	7	4	11	9	5
woody	1	14***	3	12*	5	10

*p < 0.05, **p < 0.01, ***p < 0.001

said that they disliked sweet ones. Moreover, people may believe they should prefer dry wines. "Wine connoisseurs tend to 'look down their noses' at sweet wines" (Amerine & Singleton 1965:303). "Traditionally the mark of a cultured person has been his or her appreciation of the low-sugar wines as an integral part of enjoyable wines" (Filipello, Berg, & Webb 1958:509). Thus it appears that *sweet* and *dry* are evaluative as well as descriptive words. This conclusion was further confirmed by a clustering task in which subjects were given words and asked to group them according to similarity of meaning. *Dry* was generally grouped with positive terms like *elegant, rich,* and *balanced,* while *sweet* was put either with *fruity* and *grapy,* or with negative terms like *rough* or *flabby. Sweet* and *dry* are not purely evaluative, and a wine such as T was unanimously judged to be *dry* by everyone. For *sweet* to be used there must be some physical correlate—some sugar or perhaps just a strong, perfumed aroma.

On wine T besides significant agreement on *dry*, subjects agreed that the wine was *full-bodied*, but disagreed on whether the wine was *bitter, clean, complex, earthy, off, sour,* and *tart.* Further analysis showed that tasters who liked wine T described it as *fruity,* and neither *sour,* nor *bitter,* nor *off.* Those who disliked it described T as *off, not fruity,* and either *sour* or *bitter* or both (p < 0.05). (The evaluative aspect of *sour* and *bitter* are quite obvious.) The response to *earthy* was interesting. There was a split between subjects, with seven 'yes' and eight 'no' judgments, whereas only two subjects found wines F or R *earthy. Earthy* is a technical term that applies to a special odor and taste, and, according to Professor Maynard Amerine, no commercially available California wine has (or at least at that time had) an earthy quality. However, ordinary wine drinkers frequently do not know of this technical meaning and apparently interpret earthy as "hearty, down-to-earth, pleasant, or robust," in opposition to "delicate or elegant." (A similar problem arose for the Tucson subjects in using this word.) At any rate wine T had something that half the Stanford subjects thought might be appropriately described as *earthy.*

The same three tasks in the same order were carried out a week later. The white wines listed in Table 10 were served, slightly chilled.[3]

TABLE 10: White Wines Served at Session 2—Stanford (N = 15)

				Preferences		
Code	Wine	% Sugar	% Alcohol	Like	Neutral	Dislike
B	California Chablis	<0.1	12	4	5	6
N	Chenin Blanc	1.6	11½	10	5	0
W	Emerald Riesling	1.2	11½	9	4	2

On the first task, the free description, wine B, the driest of the three, elicited mostly evaluative comments. The most salient feature noticed was the acidity of the wine, described as *sour, acid,* or *sharp.* With wine N, many speakers noted its slight sweetness. Although as little as 0.7 percent sugar can be perceived, and both N and W had over 1 percent, sugar alone will not necessarily determine whether a wine will be judged sweet, since high acidity will mask the sweetness. In addition to noticing the sweetness, many subjects made evaluative comments. In general, N was not thought to be a great wine. The responses to those who liked it were terms of low praise: *clean, pleas-*

ant, sound, mild. Those who were neutral described N as *bland, not exciting, lacking in strength, character,* and *personality,* or *somewhat mediocre.* The most frequently mentioned feature of wine W was its fruity aroma. Whereas the two who disliked this wine and three of the four who were neutral mentioned its sweetness, only one of the nine who liked it mentioned sweetness.[4] Subjects giving favorable or neutral responses also commented on its mild acidic feel: *tangy, tingling feel, bites gently, slight pinch.*

The word-circling task was carried out next. The responses to the list of 145 wine descriptors is presented in Table 11. The number of subjects circling a word is given in parentheses.

TABLE 11: Most Frequently Circled Words, Session 2—Stanford (N = 15)

Wine B		Wine N		Wine W	
dry	(9)	light	(7)	fruity	(7)
acidic	(6)	fruity	(6)	light	(6)
bland	(6)	semisweet	(6)	tangy	(6)
common	(5)	smooth	(6)	dry	(6)
empty	(5)	acidic	(5)	aromatic	(5)
light	(5)	soft	(5)	clean	(5)
sour	(5)	clean	(5)	fragrant	(5)
thin	(5)	gentle	(5)	refreshing	(5)
weak	(5)			sweet	(5)

Although wine N had the most sugar of the three, 1.6 percent, it was described as *dry* by four subjects, all of whom like the wine. Both *sweet* and *dry* were used significantly often for wine W, but no subject used both terms for that wine.

The results of the third task, requiring subjects to make a 'yes' or 'no' choice on whether a word was applicable to a wine, are presented in Table 12. There was consensus that wine B was *dry, light,* and *not fruity.* (It is not clear why some subjects on task 2 did not circle *dry;* perhaps it was too obvious.) Although disliking the wine and finding it *sour* and/or *bitter* did not correlate significantly, the use or nonuse of *sour* and *bitter* did correlate with one another (p < 0.01). Thirteen of the fifteen subjects either circled both words or neither.

TABLE 12: Agreement/Disagreement on Characteristics of White Wines Served at Session 2 (N = 15)

Adjective	Yes	No	Yes	No	Yes	No
bitter	5	10	3	12*	1	14***
bland	9	6	5	10	1	14***
chalky	0	15***	1	14***	0	15***
clean	7	8	8	7	11	4
complex	2	13	6	9	6	9
dry	14	1***	6	9	9	6
earthy	1	14***	4	11	3	12*
flat	6	9	2	13**	0	15***
fruity	0	15***	10	5	9	6
full-bodied	2	13**	7	8	8	7
light	4	11	7	8	9	6
lively	3	12*	4	11	8	7
metallic	4	11	1	14***	0	15***
off	5	10	1	14***	0	15***
semisweet	0	15***	8	7	5	10
sour	7	8	2	13**	0	15***
spicy	1	14***	2	13**	4	11
sweet	0	15***	0	15***	3	12*
tart	7	8	3	12*	6	9
woody	1	14***	1	14***	1	14***

*$p < 0.05$, **$p < 0.01$, ***$p < 0.001$

Theoretically, a white wine should not be perceived as bitter, because the agent which makes wine bitter is the tannin from the skins, and skins are discarded before making white wine.[5] However, studies have shown that untrained tasters frequently confuse sour and bitter tastes (Robinson 1970; Amerine, Panghorn, & Roessler 1965:108). Perhaps something is perceived as sharp (or possibly unpleasant), and the further distinction as to whether that taste is sourness or bitterness is of less importance. Although nine of the fifteen tasters judged wine B as either *sour* or *tart* or both, six found it to be *flat*, and two checked 'yes' for both *sour* and *flat*. Since sourness is the result of too much acidity and flatness the result of too little, there seems to be a considerable division of opinion. The two subjects who applied both would seem to be contradicting themselves. However, *flat* may also mean "insipid" or "dull," and these subjects may have intended *flat* as a negative evaluative term. There was no consensus on the qualities present in wine N. Subjects did agree that it was not

bitter, woody, spicy, metallic, chalky, off, sweet, flat, sour, or *tart.* But subjects split on whether N was *semisweet* or *dry, light* or *full-bodied,* and
on various evaluative terms, *clean, complex,* and *bland.*

Subjects agreed that wine W was not *sweet,* but they disagreed as to
whether it was *dry* or *semisweet.* Three subjects said it was both, which
is probably interpretable as "dry, but not bone-dry." Subjects did not
agree on whether W was *full-bodied* or *light,* and three said it was
both. (I do know how to interpret this.) Eleven tasters called the wine
clean, and more than half found it *fruity* and *lively.* Those who liked
W were more likely to give a 'yes' response for these terms than
those who did not.

Two of the six wines were served again at two additional sessions,
approximately eight weeks later. Wine T, the Petite Sirah, was
served along with a shipper's Bordeaux and a California Gamay.
Wine N, the Chenin Blanc, was served with a Liebfraumilch and a
white Bordeaux (both inexpensive shipper's wines). The problem of
reliability studies has already been discussed, and in this case there
was a further problem, since the wines being repeated were served
with different wines for comparison. Just as a sample of chartreuse
will look yellow if placed on a green mat and green if placed on a
yellow mat, so a wine may taste sweeter or drier, heavier or lighter, if
placed with different wines. Hence, the results of the reliability tests
must be evaluated with caution.

Task 2, circling words from the 145-word descriptor list, was presented to six subjects. I had to judge whether the tasters picked out
the same features, using synonyms or other words with similar
meanings, as well as choosing the same words that they had previously chosen, since one could not expect them to pick out identical
words for the wines, even if their judgments were the same.

On the Petite Sirah, T, the preferences of three of the six subjects
remained the same, and the adjectives circled by two of them were
similar to those circled at session 1—that is, the tasters chose items
from the same semantic classes and same ends of the scales. One
subject showed the same preference but gave descriptions that were
different from his earlier ones. Another subject changed his preference from 'like' at the first session to 'neutral' at the later session, but
the adjectives he chose were similar on both occasions. The other
two subjects reversed their preferences from 'dislike' to 'like', and
their choices were very different at the two sessions.

Three subjects showed the same preferences for wine N, the Chenin Blanc, at both sessions, and two of those described the wine in roughly the same way. The third one described it very differently. A fourth subject, who was neutral to N when it was first served but who like it later, characterized it the same both times. The other two subjects changed both their evaluations and their selection of words.

In general there was no striking consensus on the three tasks presented at the first two sessions. Although subjects sometimes agreed that some feature of a wine was salient, such as the aroma of wine F or the acid in wine W, they usually found different ways of expressing their reactions. In many cases, however, the descriptions were more than different—they were inconsistent. If one looks at subjects' responses in terms of their preferences, then clearer patterns can be seen in the data. We have already seen how the vocabulary itself is value-laden, where many descriptive words like *thin* and even *dry* have an evaluative aspect of their meaning. This fact is strongly reflected in the tasters' descriptions. These descriptions, though variable, were not random but were strongly biased by preferences.

The word-circling task was also designed to find out which wine descriptors are known and used by ordinary wine drinkers. Table 13 provides some information on the most salient items, based on the frequency of use in describing the six wines. (A different selection of wines may have elicited somewhat different words, or course.)

TABLE 13: Frequency of Word Use, Sessions 1 and 2—Stanford
(Possible maximum = 90: 15 subjects, 6 wines)

More than 30 Times	More than 20 Times	More than 10 Times	
dry	acidic	astringent	lively
	aromatic	balanced	ordinary
	clean	bitter	perfumed
	fruity	bland	pungent
	light	bouquet	scented
	refreshing	common	soft
	smooth	delicate	sour
		developed	sweet
		flowery	tangy
		fragrant	tart
		full-bodied	young
		gentle	

COMMUNICATION EXPERIMENTS—SESSIONS 3 AND 4

Various versions of a communication task were used with all three groups of subjects. Typically there are two subjects, each of whom receives three different wines. One subject must describe and differentiate the wines so that the second subject can match the same three wines with the first taster's descriptions. Subjects may not refer to the color or appearance of the wines, but any other descriptions are permitted: comparative statements (*wine X is sweeter than wine Y*), noncomparative descriptions (*wine X is sweet, fruity, and light*), or evaluative statements (*wine X is ghastly*). The wines given to one taster have letter codes, and the same wines for the other subject have numbers, so that the subjects can refer to the wines. Several variations of this experiment were used over the course of the study.

At the third session of the Stanford subjects, a written version of this problem was performed. Seven pairs of subjects were tested one pair at a time. Each subject sat at a different table so that he or she could not see the wines that the other subject was drinking. Both tasters received three red wines and three white wines. One member of the pair described the red wines for his or her partner to match and the second described the whites. Table 14 gives the list of wines. Subjects wrote their descriptions for each of the three wines on a separate card (with the letter or number code). The cards were then given to the other member of the pair, who tried to match the same wines with the first taster's descriptions.

The only wine that was correctly matched more often than chance (p <.05) was the Riesling, the sweetest of the three, with five correct matches out of seven. Moreover, all five who communicated suc-

TABLE 14: Wines Served at Session 3—Stanford (N = 14)

Whites	% Sugar	% Alcohol
Riesling	2.25	12
California Chablis	0.2	12
California Rhine Wine	0.6	11½
Reds		
Zinfandel	<0.1	12½
California Burgundy	<0.1	12
Petite Sirah	0.75	14

cessfully mentioned sweetness in their descriptions. I was not able to find any consistent pattern with respect to other correct matches. One problem—probably the reason for there being so many failures—was that different subjects found different aspects of the wine salient: one taster noticed bouquet, another commented on astringency, a third discussed sweetness, and a fourth talked about body. The only pair of subjects that matched all six wines correctly ($p = 1/36$) consisted of the two subjects who scored highest on the wine-knowledge test. The probability for three correct matches is 1/6 and for any single correct match is 1/3.

For both the reds and the whites, there were ten correct matches out of a possible twenty-one (7 subjects × 3 wines), which is not above the .05 level of significance.

A second version of the communication task was carried out at session 4. In this version, the message-sender consisted of a committee of three—two wine drinkers whom I judged to have sensitive palates and myself. (One of the others had been a subject at the first three sessions.) Prior to session 4 we devised two sets of characterizations: a straightforward one and a far-fetched one. To reduce the possibility of matching correctly by chance, a fourth description, a fake, was added, but one using words that were different from those in the three actual descriptions and one that we thought did not appropriately describe any of the three wines. Table 15 gives the three white wines and the four descriptions.

Fourteen subjects participated in this communication task at session 4. Half of the subjects received the straightforward descriptions first, and after they matched the descriptions with their wine samples, they were given the far-fetched descriptions to match with the same wines. The other seven subjects received the two sets of descriptions in the opposite order.

Wine Z was described as *perfumed, fruity,* and *smooth* for the straightforward description. Since this wine tasted the sweetest, we were going to add *sweet,* but it had less sugar than K,[6] a wine whose acidity masked the sweetness, so I decided to omit *sweet* from the description of Z. However, when subjects were asked which wine tasted sweetest to them, eleven of the fourteen picked Z.

The communication attempt was unsuccessful. The only characterization that achieved better than chance results, with seven out

TABLE 15: Wines Served at Session 4—Stanford with
2 Sets of Descriptions

Wine	Straightforward Description	Far-Fetched Description
A Chenin Blanc <0.1% sugar 12½% alcohol	acidic, light, very dry, faint bouquet	hollow, hard, stony, austere
K Chenin Blanc 1.8% sugar 12% alcohol	tart, tangy, balanced light; pleasant light bouquet	savory, fresh, delicate, tantalizing bouquet—like a rain forest
Z Blanc de Blancs 1.5% sugar 12% alcohol	perfumed, fruity, smooth	round, feminine, graceful, ripe
Fake description	thin, flat, woody, a bit bitter	metallic, spicy, earthy, flabby

of fourteen correct responses,[7] was *round, feminine, graceful, ripe* for
wine Z. The group which received the straightforward description
first did better than the other group. Three mistakes became apparent in the post-test analysis. First of all, omitting *sweet* from the description of Z deprived subjects of an important clue. Secondly, the
fake description was often confused with that for wine A, characterized as *acidic*. Since sourness and bitterness are often confused,
the *bit bitter* phrase caused some subjects to match wine A with the
fourth description. The committee had carefully debated as to
whether A was bitter or sour and concluded that the wine was
definitely not bitter. At any rate, seven subjects matched wine A with
thin, flat, woody, a bit bitter, and ten matched it with *metallic, spicy,
earthy, flabby.* A third source of miscommunication was due to the fact
that the committee liked wines K and Z better than A, something
reflected in the descriptions. However, some subjects preferred A,
and some of them matched it with a favorable characterization, especially *tart, tangy, balanced* and *savory, fresh, delicate.*

In looking at the correlation between the two sets of descriptions,
only one subject matched up all four of the straightforward descriptions and the far-fetched descriptions as the committee intended by
applying them to the same three wines. (However, he did not match
descriptions with wines as the group of senders intended.) Four sub-

jects matched up two descriptions correctly, three matched one, and six paired the far-fetched descriptions with one wine and the straightforward one with a different wine. In looking at the descriptions themselves, two subjects gave the description of *acidic, light, very dry, faint bouquet* to the same wine as to *hollow, hard, stony, austere;* four described the same wine as *tart, tangy, balanced, light,* etc. with *savory, fresh, delicate . . . like a rain forest!* Four matched *perfumed, fruity, smooth* with *round, feminine, graceful, ripe;* and five paired the two fake descriptions. There were in all, fifteen pairings of straightforward descriptions with far-fetched ones out of a possible fifty-six (as intended by the senders).

At the end of the experimental session, subjects were asked to rate the quality of the descriptions on a five-point scale: very good, good, okay, poor, very poor. There was no significant preference for the straightforward characterizations over the far-fetched ones. The descriptions correctly matched were not rated significantly different from those incorrectly matched. On the whole, subjects found the wine characterizations adequate, with an average evaluation just below 'good.'

EXPERIMENT THREE: CONSENSUS THROUGH CONVERSATION

At the last experimental session with the Stanford subjects, tasters met in pairs and were served three red wines, a Cabernet Sauvignon and two California Burgundies (which were, however, distinct). All wines contained 12 percent alcohol and all were dry (0.2% sugar or less). Subjects sat at a table facing each other, and their task was to agree on a characterization by discussing the wines as they tasted them together. In this experiment I wanted to see whether pairs of subjects could agree, and if so, whether subjects working in pairs produced greater consensus than those working individually. I also wanted more information on the process of communication—how one person points out features of a wine to another—and also, if no agreement is reached on a point, whether the discussion would reveal if the disagreement is due to different perceptual judgment or different linguistic usage.

Each pair was able to agree on a characterization on most wines, but there was no group consensus. That is, each pair came up with different, often inconsistent, descriptions. Preferences, among other things, influenced the results.

In the case of disagreement, further discussion revealed that the difference was sometimes one of applying terminology, as illustrated by the following transcription from the tape:

A: It's bitter to me.

B: It doesn't seem bitter to me.

A: . . . I think it's less bitter than the others but I tend not to like dry wine, so I would probably say that all dry wines are bitter.
[A was the only taster who preferred sweet wines to dry ones.]

A: . . . perfumy?

B: Not quite perfumy—that's a little bit too sweet. A faint aroma. You know—drier than the other we tasted—and it doesn't have as much of a fruity flavor.

A: I don't think it's fruity . . . but I tend to think it smells perfumy.

B: I don't think the smell is sweet enough to be called perfumy.

A: So perfumy is sweet to you.

B: Yes.

Two processes are revealed in this conversation. First, there is an attempt to agree in applying terms to actual referents in the environment. But secondly, when there is disagreement, the individuals explore the meaning postulates or other kinds of intralinguistic associations to see if the trouble is located there. For speaker B, *perfumy* → *sweet* is a semantic entailment, whereas it is not one for A. The association of *bitter* and *dry* for A may be weaker than a semantic entailment. Speakers have various options at this point. They can both adopt the usage of one speaker, or they can both continue to speak as before, but try to keep in mind the other's meaning when interpreting his or her utterance, or they can cease using the word. As we will see in the following chapter on the Tucson subjects, speakers used all three strategies.

The experiments requiring subjects to talk to each other produced another effect which was revealed more clearly by later experiments. When speakers work out wine descriptions together and come to a consensus, they usually show a high degree of satisfaction with their results. However, the descriptions of one pair or group of speakers may have little in common with those of other speakers, who have an equally high degree of satisfaction with *their* descriptions.

The overall results of the consensus experiment showed that a group of speakers, all of whom are native speakers of English and seem to use the same lexical items, do indeed apply words quite differently from each other. In some cases there is evidence of different intralinguistic relationships, although this does not seem to be the primary cause of miscommunication when that occurs. One source of disagreement is largely tied to the implicit norm of scalar terms, so that a wine that is sweet for one subject is dry for another. Another source of disagreement results from different preferences, since the wine vocabulary is heavily value-laden; the words selected will reflect the tasters' preferences.

Chapter 7
The Tucson Subjects

Most experiments raise new questions in the process of answering the original questions. The consensus experiments with the Stanford subjects showed that there was a large amount of variation in how speakers describe wines, and considerable miscommunication as well. The question raised, however, was whether speakers who drink wine together and discuss these wines will improve—that is, develop greater consensus—over time. My hypothesis was that speakers will come to apply words to wines with greater consensus under such conditions.

The sixteen Tucson subjects who remained with the project were comparable in wine preferences and wine knowledge to the Stanford subjects. They liked wine and drank it frequently, but most of them did not know a great deal about wine. All subjects attended at least seven of the thirteen sessions, the average being nine.

At each session at least three wines were served blind. Bread or crackers and cheese as well as water were available during the experimental sessions so that subjects could rest their palates between wines. Some paper and pencil tasks were performed during part of the session, but most of the time was spent in conversation to provide the opportunity for agreement in word use to develop. The paper and pencil tasks provided data that could be treated statistically, and they also elicited responses from people who did not talk much during the sessions. All sessions were tape-recorded on a cassette recorder placed within view of the subjects. I tried to make the setting as casual and natural as possible, within the limitations imposed by the experiments and the paper and pencil tasks.

Most of our vocabulary, at least most of our nonscientific vocabulary, is learned in casual, perhaps even haphazard ways. We learn new words or new meanings for old words in new contexts. Someone might be corrected if he misuses a word or uses it differently from other participants in the conversation, but frequently there will be no comments. And unless drastic miscommunication does occur, there will be no attempt to determine whether or not speakers are using a word in the same way. To try to make such a determination would be too inefficient. Conversation could never get started if speakers first had to find out whether they meant the same things by the words they used. I wanted to avoid a setting in which there was a strong leader who would proceed to teach the others how to use words "correctly" and make sure that the others did as instructed. (That may be how experts learn, however.)

Some of the tasks were similar to those performed with the Stanford subjects—for instance, the word-circling task and the communication problem, and new tasks were added to elicit more data and different kinds of information. Greater use was made of getting subjects to agree on a wine characterization by letting them discuss the wines freely. The list of wine descriptors (see Figure 18) was shortened to 117 words, mostly by deleting some words that the Stanford subjects never or rarely used, but a few new words were added that the Stanford subjects found useful.

Before turning to the experiments and the results, however, it may be helpful to look at the wine descriptors that the subject used or said they used. First of all, Figure 18 presents the revised list of wine descriptors used with the Tucson subjects. The selection of words would reflect something about the nature of the wine as well as the vocabulary of the subjects.

At the sixth session, in preparation for another experiment, subjects were given the revised list of words and asked to circle those they thought were good wine terms—that is, words that were informative and that the subjects themselves would use and understand—and to cross out those that they thought were bad— words that they would not use and would not understand. Words in

FIGURE 18: Revised List of 117 Wine Descriptors

acidic (45)	elegant (6)	harsh (14)	powerful (1)	spicy (7)
aged (10)	empty (7)	hearty (5)	prickly (7)	sturdy (8)
alcoholic (20)	fat (2)	heavy (5)	puckery (24)	strong (9)
aromatic (24)	feminine (10)	honest (10)	pungent (15)	succulent (2)
astringent (42)	fine (5)	insipid (6)	refreshing (17)	subtle (9)
austere (23)	finesse (5)	light (37)	rich (5)	sugary (6)
balanced (33)	firm (8)	little (9)	ripe (15)	sweet (15)
big (5)	flabby (1)	lively (12)	robust (6)	syrupy (9)
bitter (18)	flat (9)	maderized (1)	round (10)	tangy (26)
bouquet (19)	flowery (5)	manly (4)	rough (9)	tannic (37)
bland (8)	forceful (13)	mellow (18)	rugged (5)	tart (28)
buttery (5)	foxy (1)	metallic (20)	salty (8)	taut (12)
chalky (3)	fragrant (11)	mineral (8)	savory (4)	thin (19)
character (15)	fresh (19)	musky (9)	scented (9)	unripe (18)
clean (25)	fruity (30)	nutty (5)	semisweet (22)	unbalanced (21)
cloying (1)	full-bodied (7)	oaky (1)	sharp (18)	velvety (8)
common (14)	gassy (4)	odd (12)	sensuous (17)	vigorous (10)
complex (10)	gentle (17)	off (10)	simple (18)	water (15)
crisp (15)	grapy (13)	old (2)	small (14)	weak (15)
delicate (16)	graceful (8)	ordinary (10)	smooth (21)	wild (1)
developed (16)	great (2)	peppery (1)	soft (9)	withered (5)
dry (49)	green (22)	perfumed (12)	solid (7)	woody (6)
earthy (7)	hard (13)	positive (7)	sound (3)	young (26)
			sour (18)	zestful (11)

Numbers in parentheses show the number of times a word was selected, from a maximum of 174 times (12 wines, 10 to 17 subjects, 4 sessions).

Preferred Words from Revised List (Session 6—Tucson)

acidic	fruity	simple
aged	full-bodied	smooth
alcoholic	lively	strong
astringent	mellow	spicy
bitter	nutty	subtle
bland	perfumed	sugary
bouquet	powerful	sweet
dry	puckery	syrupy
earthy	refreshing	tart
flat	robust	tangy
flowery	scented	watery
fragrant	semisweet	weak

neither of these categories were left unmarked. (Since the choice of good and bad descriptors involved multiple criteria, different subjects may have concentrated on different ones.) The words I call "preferred" were considered good wine descriptors by at least eight of the thirteen subjects present at the session. Those I have labeled "rejected" were crossed out by eight or more subjects.

Rejected Words from Revised List (Session 6 — Tucson)

big	feminine	positive
buttery	gassy	round
fat	honest	small
foxy	manly	sound
	maderized	

The experiments and the results will be discussed first, followed by an analysis of the tapes. However, the analyses of both kinds of data support each other.

Consensus in Applying Words and Selecting Points on Scales

At the first session subjects were given three red wines. Wines K and V were quite distinct, and no subject reported that they tasted alike. As in the previous experiments, subjects were to taste all three wines in any order and to decide if they liked, disliked, or were neutral to each wine. Next they were given the revised list of wine descriptors (see Fig. 18). Then they were asked to judge each wine along eight seven-point scales: sweetness, acidity, balance, tannin, quality, age, body, and nose, with some anchor point provided on each scale (see Fig. 19).

TABLE 16: Red Wines Served at Session 1 — Tucson

Code	Wine	% Sugar	% Alcohol
B	Zinfandel	0	12½
K	Bordeaux	<0.1	11
V	Shipper's Blend from Bordeaux	0	—

At the second session, the same tasks were performed with the white wines. The hypothesis being investigated in this series of experiments was whether subjects developed greater consensus over time. To check consistency and improved group reliability I wanted to measure the responses to the same wines at different times. Therefore, the red wines which were served at early sessions were again served six months later, at session 10, and two of the same whites were served at session 12, 6½ months later (the third white was unavailable), and subjects were asked to perform the same tasks.

There was one important difference when the red wines were retasted. The subjects were asked to talk about the words that were

	Bone dry						Very sweet
Sweetness	—	—	—	—	—	—	—
	1	2	3	4	5	6	7
	Acidic		Tart				Flat
Acidity	—	—	—	—	—	—	—
	1	2	3	4	5	6	7
	Unbalanced Too Acid			Balanced			Unbalanced Too sweet
Balance	—	—	—	—	—	—	—
	1	2	3	4	5	6	7
	Astringent						Soft, smooth
Tannin	—	—	—	—	—	—	—
	1	2	3	4	5	6	7
	Insipid						Complex
Quality	—	—	—	—	—	—	—
	1	2	3	4	5	6	7
	Young				Aged		Too old
Age	—	—	—	—	—	—	—
	1	2	3	4	5	6	7
	Thin		Light		Full		Coarse
Body	—	—	—	—	—	—	—
	1	2	3	4	5	6	7
	No smell						Big bouquet
Nose	—	—	—	—	—	—	—
	1	2	3	4	5	6	7

FIGURE 19: Seven-Point Scales Used at Sessions 1, 2, 10, and 12.

TABLE 17: White Wines Served at Session 2—Tucson

Code	Wine	% Sugar	% Alcohol
L	Chenin Blanc	>0.5,< 1.0	12
P	Côte de Bordeaux	<2.0	12
Q	Vouvray	0.1	—

used for the scales and to characterize the anchor points on the work sheet for Figure 19. The discussion revealed several cases in which different speakers meant different things by the same words and pointed out some difficulties with the scales themselves. For example, *complex* was given as an anchor point on 7 on the quality scale, reflecting the value judgments of wine experts. One subject, however, reported that she did not like complex wines. *Big bouquet* has decidedly positive connotations, but one subject asked what to do about a wine with a powerful, unpleasant smell. After discussing the words, subjects then rated the wines along the scales and then circled the words they thought appropriate.

In evaluating the results on the scales, it is not the arithmetical mean but rather the variation that is important. The hypothesis was that there would be more consensus, hence less variability, after six months of drinking and tasting, and that the group would come to share norms for sweetness, body, and aroma. With respect to the red wines, shown in Table 18, there was greater consensus in fifteen cases, less in eight, and the same in the remaining one. However, F-ratios show that the improvement in consensus reached significance ($p < 0.05$) in only two cases—one the dimension of body in two wines. Near significance was reached on the acidity scale of one wine.

TABLE 18: Consensus, Sessions 1 and 10—Tucson

	Zinfandel	Bordeaux	Shipper's Blend
More consensus (lower variance)	6 scales Body p <0.01	7 Body p <0.05 Acidity p <0.06	2
Less consensus (higher variance)	2	0	6
Same	0	1	0

The wine on which there was least consensus on retesting was a very light French country wine, and I believe that the taste of many of the subjects changed during the year. Whereas half liked it at the beginning of the sessions in October, by April only a third said they liked it. This wine may have seemed inoffensive at the beginning of the sessions, but by the end it seemed uninteresting.

The white wines were retasted at the last session, but there was no discussion of word meaning prior to tasting. There was greater consensus on nine items and less on seven; but when F-ratios were computed for the two identical wines, there was significantly greater consensus in only one case ($P < 0.05$)—the quality scale on the Chenin Blanc (see Table 19).

TABLE 19: Consensus, Wines at Sessions 2 and 12

	Chenin Blanc	Côte de Bordeaux	(Third Wine)*
More consensus	6	6	4
	Quality $p < 0.05$		
Less consensus	2	5	4

*The third wines were different.

The significant increments on the three scales (out of 48) are hardly impressive—in fact, one would expect this much variation by chance alone. I do not know whether the less than significant increments would continue if the experiments were to continue for another six months or for several years and would eventually add up to greater consensus, or whether the apparent improvements show just random fluctuation.

The results of the word-circling task are somewhat harder to assess. The words were provided in part to give subjects a vocabulary. We can look at the words used more frequently in the last sessions to learn which ones the subjects came to use as a result of the wine session, that is, those they learned to use as wine words, but it is also useful to look at words used less often, because these may be words that subjects felt were not as informative as they had previously thought. The total number of times a word was used in the first two sessions (six wines) was compared to the total used in the repetition tests. Since there were fewer subjects at the latter sessions, those totals were transformed before comparing them with the earlier use. (The transformation was a ratio of the number of subjects at the two sessions. For instance, there were 17 subjects at session 1 and 10 at session 10, where the same wines were retasted. If *dry* was circled 34 times at session 1, and 20 times at session 10, the 20 was multiplied by 17/10 and transformed to 34. Thus the use of *dry* was equivalent at both sessions.)

Words used at least twice as often in the latter sessions as in the first ones (based on the transformed numbers) were *buttery, crisp, fresh, grapy, positive, round, small, spicy,* and *sweet.* Words used only half as often at the end of the year were *bitter, earthy, flat, odd, off, scented, soft, strong, syrupy, subtle, unbalanced,* and *young.* As with the Stanford subjects, the Tucson group showed a strong bias based on preference. On the red wines, *acidic, astringent, puckery, tannic, harsh, thin,* and *weak* were frequently used by subjects who did not like the wines, whereas *gentle, bouquet, balanced, fresh, soft,* and *positive* were selected by those who liked them. On the whites, *off, green, bitter, hard,* and *young* were applied to wines not much liked. Other commonly used words, but ones that did not correlate with preference, were *austere, clean, crisp, dry, fragrant, fruity, light, perfumed, semisweet,* and *sweet.*

Individual consistency was checked to see whether subjects used the same word for identical wines. There is of course a problem in counting specific lexical items, since a person might select one word for a wine at the first session and a phonologically different but synonymous word at the retest. Ratios were calculated for each subject on each wine, where the numerator was the number of words used for the same wine both times (at the first tasting and the retasting), and the denominator was the total number of words used for that wine by a subject. The range was from 0 to 50 percent on a given wine (that is, on one wine there was no overlap of word choice and on another wine half of the words were used at both sessions with percentages in between on the rest). The overall average for all subjects and all wines was 12 percent. In looking at the consistency of individual subjects, the range was from 0 to 28 percent on all six wines. The significant factor seems to be whether a subject liked or disliked a wine on both occasions. The subjects who had a consistency ratio of 25 or better (that is, used the same words for the same wine at both sessions) were designated as high consistency subjects, and they were compared with those with a ratio of less than 10 percent—the low consistency subjects. A Chi square test comparing the two groups of subjects showed that subjects with a high consistency ratio expressed the same preference (like, dislike, neutral) for the wine on both occasions ($p < 0.05$), whereas those with low ratios did not.

THE MOST AND THE LEAST

Another experiment carried out with the Tucson subjects involved giving them three wines and asking them to decide which had the most and which the least of a particular property. The purpose of this task was to test a hypothesis suggested to me by Maynard Amerine (personal communication) that there would be more consensus on commonly used words than on unusual words. This hypothesis was then put together with the main one in this set of experiments to see if there was greater improvement on common words or on uncommon ones. (Recall that subjects had previously been asked to evaluate the wine descriptors in Figure 18.) Among the words most commonly selected as good descriptors were: *earthy, flat, grapy, light, perfumed, pungent, smooth,* and *tart;* and eight uncommon words: *big, buttery, feminine, honest, manly, positive, round,* and *small.* The questionnaire presented in Figure 20 was constructed, based on these words.

At the next session, two weeks later, subjects tasted three red wines (see Table 20) and were then asked to select the wine that had the most of each of the sixteen properties—the *biggest,* the *flattest,* the *roundest,* etc., and the wine that was the *least big,* the *least flat,* etc.

TABLE 20: Red Wines Served at Session 7—Tucson

Code	Wine	% Sugar	% Alcohol
C	Australian Cabernet Sauvignon	0	12
K	California Ruby Cabernet	>0.1	12½
N	California Burgundy	0	12

There was significantly greater than chance agreement in six cases: the *flattest,* the *least perfumed* ($p < 0.001$); the *least pungent* ($p <$

Opinion of each wine (like, dislike, neutral)

C _____ K _____ N _____

Please decide which wine has the most and the least of the following properties:

biggest wine_____	least big wine _____
most buttery _____	least buttery_____
earthiest _____	least earthy _____
most feminine_____	least feminine _____
flattest_____	least flat _____
grapiest_____	least grapy _____
most honest_____	least honest _____
lightest _____	least light _____
most manly _____	least manly_____
most perfumed_____	least perfumed _____
most positive_____	least positive _____
roundest_____	least round_____
smoothest_____	least smooth_____
smallest_____	least small_____
tartest _____	least tart _____

FIGURE 20: Questionnaire Used in 'Most and Least X' Experiment (Session 6—Tucson)

0.01); the *most pungent*, the *smallest*, and the *least flat* ($p < 0.05$).[1] Performance on the common words was better than for the uncommon ones in this experiment, there being significant agreement in five cases with common words and only one case with uncommon ones.

One month later the same task was repeated with white wines (Table 21). There was, however, one important change in the procedure. Before the wines were served, the subjects spent more than thirty minutes discussing the words on the list to agree on definitions or characterization. In all but a few cases, they reached a verbal consensus on intralinguistic relationships and exemplars. (The discus-

TABLE 21: White Wines Served at Session 9—Tucson

Code	Wine	% Sugar	% Alcohol
L	Emerald Riesling	>1.0,< 2.0	11
B	Chenin Blanc	>1.0,< 2.0	12½
Q	Shipper's Chablis	<.1	13

sion of word meanings is presented later.) After the wines were served and tasted, subjects were again asked to select the ones with the most and least of each of the sixteen properties.

There was significant agreement on a few more items than on the red wines: the *most pungent, least feminine, least flat, least honest, least round, least smooth* (p < 0.01); *earthiest, grapiest, least grapy,* and *least tart* (p < 0.05). There was a small improvement in performance at the second session over the first (significant agreement on 10 items as opposed to 6). As with the reds, there was greater consensus on common words (7) than uncommon ones (3). During the discussion of the words, most of the time was spent trying to provide useful characterizations for the uncommon terms (*manly, round, honest, feminine,* etc.), and this fact may account for the improved agreement on these words.

It may be recalled from the discussion of the word-circling task that certain words were used more frequently at the later sessions than at the beginning: *buttery, grapy, positive, round,* and *small,* all of which were on the *most and least X* questionnaire. It is reasonable to infer that the increased use of these terms was a result of the tasks in which subjects were forced to use them and of the discussions of their meanings. Two words were used less often: *earthy* and *flat.* The discussions about these words revealed to subjects that the terms were not as useful and meaningful as they had previously thought. The analysis of the tapes (presented below) confirms this.

The results of the *most and least X* experiment revealed one problem in the choice of items. Some words, in particular *buttery*[2] and *earthy,* denote rather specific properties in wines, which few wines possess. Therefore, one would not expect to find consensus among subjects when asked to pick the most buttery among three wines without this property.

COMMUNICATION EXPERIMENTS

In the communication tasks, with the Stanford group, it may be recalled, one person or team of people was given three wines to differentiate verbally and other subjects tried to match the descriptions with the same three wines. Various versions of this method were used with the Tucson subjects.

The first version, which was employed at the third session, used a

committee of four (three subjects and myself), who agreed on characterizations for three red wines (Table 22). To make the task harder
we added a fake description, but one which we felt did not fit any of
the three wines. It took us about half an hour to agree on the descriptions.

TABLE 22: Wines Served at Session 3 — Tucson, with Descriptions

Wine	Committee's Descriptions
B Valpolicella <0.1% sugar 12% alcohol	The lightest; simple, ordinary, some acidity but less than the others; pleasant.
F Rhône <0.1% sugar 12½% alcohol	Pungent odor, perhaps burnt; strange taste and odor: moldy or musty; slightly medicinal; unpleasant: has a bite.
O Cabernet <0.1% sugar 11½% alcohol	Spicy bouquet; spicy on the palate; tangy, intermediate in flavor and body; good character.
Fake	Semisweet, flowery, fruity, grapy, very weak.

The four descriptions were dictated to the thirteen other subjects
present, who wrote down the descriptions and then matched them to
the three red wines. Subjects were also asked to state whether they
liked, disliked, or were neutral toward each wine, to indicate how
certain they felt that they matched each wine with the descriptions
correctly, and to pick out the parts of the description that they found
the most helpful.

Only wine F was matched correctly more often than chance (p <
0.01). This correlated significantly with disliking F (p < 0.05). That
is, the tasters who disliked wine F matched it with the senders' description. Wines B and O were most often confused, and the description for the fake wine was most often incorrectly matched with
F.

The same words were picked out as useful by subjects who

matched correctly or incorrectly, although those who made correct matches mentioned more parts of the descriptions. The most frequently mentioned useful words were *pungent* for wine F, *simple* and *ordinary* for B, and *spicy* and *tangy* for O. There was no correlation between a subject's feeling certain that his or her match was correct and being correct.

The same task was repeated two weeks later at the fourth session with white wines. The same committee plus an additional subject constituted the senders. We had expected an improvement if the same senders were used, hypothesizing that the subjects who were to make the matches would have learned something about the senders' vocabulary and word application from the previous session. The wines and descriptions are presented in Table 23.

As at the previous session the descriptions were dictated to the other subjects to match with the wines.

Wine A was correctly matched more often than chance (p < 0.01) as was the fake description (p < 0.05). Wines M and Z were most

TABLE 23: Wines Served at Session 4—Tucson, with Descriptions

Wine	*Committee's Descriptions*
A Moselle >1.0, <2.0% sugar 10% alcohol	Fruity, soft, gentle, with a hint of sweetness.
M Green Hungarian 0% sugar 12½% alcohol	Not much flavor; rather harsh, even on the palate, that is, does not change.
Z Shipper's Chablis <0.1% sugar 13% alcohol	Dry, something distinctive about the first smell, reminiscent of something organic or of alcohol.
Fake	Rich, heavy, full-bodied, sweet, powerful; smoky smell.

often confused. Since all of the ten subjects liked A and either were neutral toward or disliked M and Z, no correlations could be made between preference and correct matches. There was significant *negative* correlation between feeling certain that the correct match was made and matching correctly. That is, subjects who felt certain of their matches tended to be wrong, and those who felt uncertain were correct. On the parts of the descriptions picked out as useful, for Z *first smell is distinctive* was noted. For M *rather harsh* was noted by three of the four subjects who matched this wine correctly. In all other cases, different subjects found different parts of the descriptions useful.

The matching task was presented a third time—at the second to last session. Two of the three wines were identical to those served at the first matching session. The senders' committee consisted of three subjects (none of whom had served as senders previously) and myself. Table 24 lists the wines and descriptions.

TABLE 24: Wines Served at Session 11—Tucson, with Descriptions

Wine	Committee's Descriptions
K Shipper's Burgundy <0.1% sugar 11½% alcohol	Puckery and metallic
O Cabernet Sauvignon (same as wine O at session 3) <0.1% sugar 11½% alcohol	Moldy and mossy, vegetably, especially the smell.
B Valpolicella (same as wine B at session 3) <0.1% sugar 12½% alcohol	Bitter, a bit thin, with medium odor; the least distinctive.
Fake	Sweet, fruity, feminine, and elegant.

Only the fake description was identified correctly more often than chance. Wines K and B were most often confused; these wines were also the most difficult for the senders to describe adequately. The six subjects were not asked to state their wine preferences or certainty feelings about the matches at this session.

The second version of the matching task (Session 5) consisted of four pairs of subjects and one trio who were served the same three red wines and were required to match them. Each subject sat at his or her own table and conversed with the other subjects(s). The participants could talk back and forth to characterize the taste, smell, and feel of the wine, but they could not refer to color or appearance. Two pairs of subjects matched all wines correctly, one pair matched one wine, and the fourth pair missed all. Of the trio, two subjects matched all wines correctly and the third made no matches.

There was no pattern with respect to which wines were matched first or what the salient characteristics were of the wines. The wines are presented in Table 25, and the descriptions of successful matches in Table 26.

TABLE 25: Wines Served at Session 5—Tucson for Matching Task

Code	Wine	% Sugar	% Alcohol
1	Zinfandel	0	12½
2	Cabernet Sauvignon	0	12
3	Petite Sirah	0	12

The first pair of subjects matched the Petite Sirah first and characterized it as *light*. The second wine to be identified was the Zinfandel, which was labeled *sweet*. The third, the Cabernet, was described as *acidic and medicinal*. The second pair of subjects matched the Cabernet first. One subject began the task by saying of this wine, *It's awful,* and both subjects characterized it as *harsh* and *acidic*. The Zinfandel was the second to be identified and this was characterized as *the sweeter of the two remaining ones*. The third was matched without any description.

There was a considerable amount of confusion with the trio. The subject who had no matches with the other two had descriptions which did not line up with the descriptions of the others. The two who matched successfully first identified the Zinfandel as *light, mel-*

TABLE 26: Descriptions Producing Correct Matches,
Session 5—Tucson

Pair	Zinfandel	Cabernet Sauvignon	Petite Sirah
1	sweet (2)*	acid and medicinal (3)	light (1)
2	sweeter than others (2)	awful, harsh and acidic (1)	(no description) (3)
3	light, mellow, ripe, almost sweet, but dry and fruity (1)	more bitter and biting, musky, pronounced pungent smell, tickling (2)	less pronounced smell, least bite, lingering aftertaste (3)
4		sulfur smell or smell of roses, sour aftertaste	

*Number in parentheses indicates the order in which the wines were matched.

low, ripe, almost sweet, but still dry and fruity. The next characterized the Cabernet as *more bitter and biting, musky, pronounced pungent smell, tickling.* The Petite Sirah was described as *less pronounced smell, least bite, lingering aftertaste.*

The next pair had one correct match on the Cabernet, which they agreed had a *sulfur smell or smell of roses, and a little sour aftertaste.* The second description was *least smell, not so complicated; dark and gloomy.* The third description was *salty.* The last pair, which missed all matches, described one wine as *fruity, with a dryness between the other two* (one subject chose the Zinfandel and the other the Cabernet). The second description was *less dry, more flat* (one subject selected the Petite Sirah and the other the Zinfandel). The third description was *dry, light, pleasant.*

The success rate overall was not better than chance ($p < 0.05$).[3] It is interesting to note that all subjects who correctly matched with the Zinfandel mentioned sweetness, although the wine did not contain any sugar. The two pairs who matched all three wines took the least time (less than ten minutes) and used the fewest words in their descriptions. In fact they decided to pick a single term if possible, whereas the other subjects needed at least half an hour and sometimes came up with lengthy descriptions.

The final version of the matching task involved the whole group together. Each of the ten subjects present was given the white wines listed in Table 27. (Each glass of wine had a different three-digit number so that subjects could refer to their wines.) Subjects had to match their wines with everyone else's by using verbal characterizations. The first description agreed on was *dry and sour*. The remaining two wines were thought to be sweeter. One of these was described as *sweeter than the previous one, tart, and grapefruity,* and the other was *soft, smooth, and the sweetest*. Subjects had some difficulty agreeing on how to differentiate the latter two, since not everyone agreed that one was sweeter than the other. However, when one subject suggested *grapefruity*, the rest of the group expressed great satisfaction with that term and believed that it fit one of the two sweeter wines.

TABLE 27: White Wines Served at Session 8—Tucson

Wines	% Sugar	% Alcohol
Australian Moselle	>2.0	12
Green Hungarian	0.25	12
Chenin Blanc	<.5	12

Twenty-two out of the thirty matches were correct, which is significantly better than chance ($p < 0.001$). The post-test discussion revealed that the dry and sour wine was the easiest to identify, and since the other two were sweet, the term *grapefruity* was very useful in distinguishing the two.

In summarizing the results on all the matching tests, the subjects performed better on the white wines than on the reds. The dimension of sweetness could account for the correct responses, and since there was a greater range of sweetness in the white wines, this was a likely reason for the subjects' doing better on the whites. Apparently degrees of sweetness are easier to distinguish than other properties. Given that the subjects did not do well at the second to the last session, it does not seem that performance improved during the year, or at least their performance did not improve on matching red wines.

SHORT-TERM RELIABILITY

The experiments just described provide some data on long-term reliability, where responses to the same wine served after an interval of several months are elicited. But what about short-term reliability, that is, responses to the same wine in a single evening? To investigate short-term reliability, thirteen subjects were served the three white wines listed in Table 28 and instructed to agree on a description for each one. Paper and pencils were provided for making notes. One subject argued that a large number of descriptive words tended to be confusing and that the group should try to agree on a single word. However, other subjects felt that it was too difficult to pick a single term. As a compromise, each wine was described fully, but a single property of each was noted as the most distinctive. Subjects who disagreed with the group consensus were told to write down any specific part or parts of the descriptions with which they disagreed. The descriptions are provided in Table 28, column 2, with the number of subjects disagreeing with parts of the characterizations in column 3.

After the subjects finished, I collected their glasses and comments and informed them that the experiment was only half over. Then three more white wines were served, two of which were virtually identical to the wines served earlier. Of course, the subjects were not told this, although some guessed that one or more wines might be the same. Wine J was a bottle from the same lot as F, a Portuguese white. R was the same varietal from the same vineyard as H but was one year older. However, I tasted the two and could not distinguish between them. The third wine, a Moselle, was in fact perceptually different and will not be discussed. Subjects were given a blank sheet of paper and asked to describe the second three wines in any order. The last three columns of Table 28 give their responses. Column 4 lists the words most frequently selected at the second presentation, column 5 gives the number of subjects who selected that word or a near synonym (such as *sourish* for *tart*), and column 6 gives the number of subjects who rejected a descriptor at the first presentation but selected it on the retaste. For the Portuguese white wine, only *light* or *thin* was selected by a majority of subjects. *Odorless* and *fruity* or *grapy* were selected by some subjects, and a new property, described as *tangy* or *bite* was also mentioned by four subjects. The fol-

TABLE 28: Short-Term Reliability Experiment, Session 6—Tucson (N = 13)

WINE	FIRST PRESENTATION Description Accepted by majority of S's	No disagreement	SECOND PRESENTATION Words selected by subject	No. selecting the word or a synonym	No. selecting word on retaste after disagreeing first time
B Moselle >1.0,<2.0% sugar 10% alcohol	organic-chemical smell	3	(No comparable wine served)		
	*green apples**				
	tart	2			
	puckery	3			
	light				
F = J Portuguese white >2.0% sugar 11% alcohol	semi-to fairly sweet				
	odorless	1	odorless	4	
	semisyrupy	3			
	fruity	5	fruity or grapy	5	2
	light, not heavy		light, thin	8	
	nonalcoholic		tangy, bite	4	
H = R	*fruity smell***	4	fruity, grapy, perfumy	4	
California Chablis 0.1% sugar 12% alcohol	very dry		dry	7	
	light to watery	5	thin, watery	7	2
	tart		tart, acidic	6	
	bite	1	astringent	5	1
	semibitter	3	bitter	2	1

*Most distinctive properties in italics.
**Subjects originally used 'perfumy'.

lowing new descriptors were used once: *alcoholic odor, bubbly, complicated scent, green, licorice aftertaste, lively, ripe, smooth,* and *unripe.* In retasting the California Chablis, eleven subjects commented on the smell, but only four described it as *fruity, grapy,* or *perfumy.* Other descriptors, each used only once were: *like crabmeat, like coconut, like hoarhound candy, minty, old, synthetic (i.e., chemical),* and one subject said that the wine was *odorless.* Other descriptors which were introduced in the retasting were: *alcoholic, pungent, semipungent, less than ripe, cloying,* and *smooth.* Slightly over half the tokens selected for the Portuguese white and two-thirds for the California Chablis were the same (or roughly synonymous) on the retaste, compared to the first presentation. There was some similarity in describing the same wines in the same evening, but the results were considerably short of identical and therefore the reliability of the subjects even in the short term was disappointing.

There are limitations on counting identical or synonymous words since some subjects used a large number of such words to describe a single property and other subjects might say nothing about that property. Therefore, to check the similarity of descriptions on identical wines, two people who did not participate in the wine experiments were given each subject's description for wines J and R and asked to judge their similarity to descriptions of F and H for that subject. A 1-to-5 scale was used, where 1 was 'almost identical, clearly the same wine' and 5 was 'totally different, no resemblance'. The average score for similarity between J and F was 2.5; for R and H it was 2.8.

LEARNING NEW WINE WORDS: ANALYSIS OF THE TAPES

All sessions with the full group of subjects were tape-recorded on a Sanyo M 4210 cassette recorder placed on the coffee table in the middle of the room. For the small committees that served as senders for the matching tasks, senders sat around a small table with the recorder nearby. Listening to these cassettes later, I gained some insights on how adult speakers learn to use new words or use old words in new ways.

Counting the number of times a particular word was used during a session proved to be of limited value. Such quantification does provide some indication of the basic words in a field and of which words most speakers are likely to know. But it does not tell us whether a word is used for a description or whether it is repeated in the conversation as affirmation, denial, question, or exclamation. However, it was possible to correlate the words used in free conversation with those which subjects circled in the experiments and listed as good descriptors. The following words were used by a large number of different speakers at many of the sessions to describe a variety of wines: *acidic, alcoholic, balanced, biting (bite), bitter, dry, distinctive, flat, fruity, full-bodied, grapy, harsh, interesting, light, perfumed, pleasant, puckery, pungent, semisweet, sour, smooth, spicy, strong, sweet, tart, thin, vinegar(y),* and *watery.* Other words used fairly often were *chemical, moldy, mossy, musty,* and *strange.*

More interesting than the frequently used words were the unusual ones. Wines were often described in comparison with other substances whose tastes and smells the hearer might know, for example, other wines or liquors *(Chianti, Mogen David, vodka)* or quite different substances: *burlap, cheese, crabapples, dill, fish, formaldehyde, Listerine, medicine, mutton, persimmons, quinine, raisins, rancid butter, soy sauce, turkey,* and *wheat.* Even more distant associations were observed, such as descriptions of wine as being *autumnal, sexy, opulent,* or *ragged.*

Some learning of wine words took place while the subjects were drinking particular wines, and so to some extent the definitions were ostensive. However, much defining was strictly intralinguistic; that is, the words were defined or characterized solely by other expressions. Even when ostensive definitions were used, linguistic means were necessary to focus attention on a particular property, since each wine has a complex variety of smells and tastes.

Although there is some information on definition for lexicographical purposes (Nida 1975, Weinreich 1962) and some material in anthropology on eliciting definitions from informants (Casagrande & Hale 1976, Metzger & Williams 1966), and a great deal of word association data (e.g., Deese 1965), I have not found much in print on how people define new words or sharpen definitions in normal speech situations where everyone in the group is a native speaker of the language.

The kinds of definitions that were used most frequently by the

Tucson subjects were the following (based on Casagrande & Hale's classification of semantic relationships):

Attribution. — 'X is defined with respect to one or more distinctive or characteristic attributes of Y': *buttery*, "kind of smooth," "kind of rich"; *manly*, "very acidic, strong," "robust, big, strong-flavored"; *astringency* or *tannin*, "tends to be an unpleasant sharpness."

Synonymy. — 'X is defined as being equivalent to Y': *big*, "full-bodied"; *small*, "tiny," "teeny-weeny," *earthy*, "down-to-earth, solid."

Exemplification. — 'Providing an example that typifies or illustrates the concept':[4] *big*, "a heavy Burgundy"; *grapy*, "Mogen David or Manischewitz."

Comparison. — 'X is compared or contrasted to Y': *Earthy*, "like moss," "makes you think of pebbles or stones," "basement-like," "like a cave"; *flinty*, "like a metal."

Negation of a property. — 'X is defined as the negation of Y': *honest*, "not complex"; *earthy*, "not fancy"; *round*, "not sharp."

Class inclusion. — 'X is defined with respect to its membership in a hierarchical class Y': *heavy* "refers to body"; *tannin*, "it's an acid."

Grading. — 'X is defined with respect to its placement in a series or spectrum that also includes Y': *positive*, "it's a half-way house between *honest* and *manly*" (these had been previously defined); *Insipid*, "worse than just *ordinary.*"

Operation. — 'X is defined with respect to an action Y of which it is a characteristic goal of recipient': *positive*, "something you like."

A considerable proportion of the conversation at many sessions was devoted to defining and characterizing wine words. These discussions served at least two functions: they helped to define words for speakers who were not familiar with them in wine contexts, and they served to show that some words were unexpectedly ambiguous and that some speakers used them with one meaning without realizing that other speakers had assigned quite different meanings.

Below are transcripts of parts of the discussion aimed at reaching agreement on the meaning of words. The excerpts are taken from sessions 7 and 9, in which the subjects were to select from three wines the wine with the most of each property and the least. The discussion, which preceded the serving of wines, is concerned only with the meaning of terms. I have edited the texts to eliminate repetitions and incomplete utterances that do not further the discussion.

Overlaps, where one speaker begins before the previous one finishes, are not shown. Adrienne is the author. All other names are false but correctly reveal the sex of the speaker.

Earthy was a term that subjects had previously claimed was a good wine descriptor, and *round* was listed as a poor one.

ADRIENNE: *Earthy!*
HENRY: Mossy—like moss smells and tastes.
EDWARD: Kind of flinty—that would be earthy—Chablis.
HENRY: Yeah.
EDWARD: Makes you think of pebbles or stones or something.
SAM: Minerally?
EDWARD: Mineral? What mineral? Stones in the mouth.
LINDA: That seems like a very unpositive quality for a wine to have.
EDWARD: Down to earth?
NED: Right.
HENRY: You mean proletarian sense?
ADRIENNE: Let's see if we can agree on a sense of it. . . . It would be useful if we all meant the same thing. Why don't we stick to the "like-earth" sense?
HENRY: But that's really hard.
EDWARD: Flinty.
IRENE: I don't know about flinty.
HENRY: It's like metal.
DONNA: Metallic? It's not metallic.
NED: It has corners?
EDWARD: Smell of an unburnt match?
HENRY: Smell of somebody's cellar, in a wet place.
DONNA: Musty or something?
HENRY: Musty. That's what I associate.
EDWARD: You can see how there's an awful lot of ambiguity. Why don't we agree on something?
HENRY: Do you want to stipulate something?
ADRIENNE: All right. Why don't we do it that way?
EDWARD: Well, flinty people can't identify, so there's not much point.
ADRIENNE: Minerallike. That's what you suggested.
EDWARD: I'd be at a loss.
LINDA: Basementlike.

EDWARD: Basementlike. Everybody's sniffed a basement—unless there are some native Tusconons here.

HENRY: What about a cave?

LINDA: That would be good.

HENRY: A wet cave.

LINDA: A damp cave, not a dry cave.

BETTY: I don't think that's very positive. *Earthy* would be more like the smell of good soil, not smelly, but humus, like grass. But it doesn't smell of moisture. That really offends me, like rot, damp, mold.

LINDA: Rotten, damp, moldy.

EDWARD: That is a negative connotation.

HENRY: We don't have any idea what it means.

ADRIENNE: And that was one of the commonest words, incidentally.

EDWARD: I bet it was used in the sense of "down-to-earth."

DONNA: Yeah.

HENRY: That means uninteresting to me.

DONNA: No.

EDWARD: That means solid, drinkable wine.

LINDA: Honest and practical.

BETTY: Honest or basic.

LINDA: Basic, maybe.

ADRIENNE: But the wine experts don't use it that way. They use it to mean "has the smell or taste of earth," whatever that is.

CAROL: Really?

ADRIENNE: Well, before we were talking about the possibility of the smell of a wet basement.

BETTY: I don't like that at all.

EDWARD: Well, just the fact that it makes you think of wine as planted in the earth, and somehow the grape and flavor and all reflect the character of the earth.

BETTY: Usually [grapes are] not planted in damp places . . . nice, sunny.

EDWARD: Nice, right.

A satisfactory definition of *earthy* was never agreed on, and it was one of the words which was used less often at the end of the year than at the beginning in the word-circling task. Apparently subjects became aware of the fact that it was ambiguous and hence less likely to communicate successfully. Moreover, subjects did not agree in picking out the most or least earthy wine.

The discussion for the meaning of *round,* in contrast to *earthy,* serves to illustrate agreement on a definition for a new word in the wine vocabulary.

ADRIENNE: *Round!*
HENRY: There's going to be no agreement.
EDWARD: That's how we're going to use it now, to get that idea.
LINDA: Not flat.
BETTY: Full?
HENRY: Balanced?
EDWARD: Balanced.
HENRY: Balanced. Like nothing really shoots out.
ADRIENNE: Not sharp.
NED: Not pungent.
EDWARD: It's not sharp and it's not flat.
HENRY: Nothing about it knocks you any more than anything else about it. That's what *balanced* means.
EDWARD: Balanced to me is compatible with it being partly acidic. Just that the acid shouldn't be out of whack with the other flavors. It can't have any sharp edges.
DONNA: It has to be a little on the sweet side, doesn't it?
ADRIENNE: No, I wouldn't say it has to be sweet.
DONNA: If it's acidic, I wouldn't call it round.
ADRIENNE: Not sharp.
EDWARD: If it was acidic, it would not be round. That's what I was getting at.
HENRY: Comes in a round shape.
EDWARD: No edges. Nothing that offends the palate. I think that's fair.
BETTY: Would you say that a dry wine can't be round?
EDWARD: Sure it can be round. Think of a Burgundy.
BETTY: I think so. Donna suggested that it had to be sweet, but a wine that's mellow would be round.
EDWARD: A flavorful wine that's mellow.
SAM: Would lightness or heaviness have anything to do with it?

HENRY: Can't be too much of either.
EDWARD: I don't think I would describe a really light wine as round.
There's not enough of it to have any shape. . . . I can see I'm a big
help. Do you want me to leave?

The group seemed to have reached a satisfactory characterization
of *round*. This word was used more often at the end of the year in
the word circling task, and subjects were able to agree on the least
round wine at the sessions during which the word was discussed.

CONCLUSION

What actually were the results of the months-long Tucson experiment? Did the way the subjects talked about wine and described actual wines really change?

There is evidence of vocabulary growth—either the acquisition of
new words or new meanings for old words. The tapes show that
some subjects were learning words and meanings, but I have no data
on their continued use of these words when the experiments were
ended. The increased use of some words in the paper and pencil
tasks further confirms that some learning took place.

There is no evidence to suggest that a stable set of norms was ever
established for the subjects, although the participants became aware
of the fact that there was a problem at times. Some linguistic criteria
were agreed on with respect to the definition of words, but subjects
did not necessarily apply the words more consistently thereafter.

What the experiments show is that in a friendly, casual social setting the requirements for precise communication are rather low,
even if people are motivated to use language carefully and thought-
fully. Subjects did not improve much on the objective tests during
the eight-month period in spite of the fact that they thought they
were doing better. It may be that over a five-year period in the same
casual setting, the small increments would add up and become
statistically significant. At any rate, a casual setting is not at all
efficient for producing consensus and precision.

The subjective responses of subjects, however, would rate the experiments as successful. The participants felt that they had learned a
lot and could use words more precisely and consistently. The follow-

ing testimonials, the first from a man and the second from a woman, taken from the tapes, are typical:

> I taste a lot more when I taste the wine now than I did before. Before, when I tasted them, I either liked them or didn't like them. Now I'm thinking of the body, or tartness, or astringency.

> I think some of the words are meaningful. Now I think I can recognize an honest wine.

Much of the satisfaction was expressed as people were leaving each session, when they mentioned to me how much they had enjoyed the session and how much they had learned. In fact, subjects were very surprised to learn that the results of the paper and pencil tests showed they had not greatly improved. Subjects were highly motivated to do well, partly for their own satisfaction and partly because they felt that I would be happier with the experimental results if they improved. Subjects sometimes apologized for not doing better, and one subject offered to withdraw from the experiments in order to improve the statistical results!

One thing many subjects learned was whose taste they shared. One subject remarked that if X liked a particular wine, he would like it too, but if Y liked that wine, he would hate it. So participants learned to trust the palates of some tasters more than others. This is not to say that some individuals were recognized by the rest as experts and trustworthy. Rather, subjects to some extent filtered descriptions on the basis of the speaker. If one subject preferred heavy tannic wines, those subjects who disliked that type of wine would apparently give less weight to the speaker's description.[5]

Throughout the experiments speakers continued to believe that their discussions were informative. This would explain why subjects decreased their use of words like *earthy* when they discovered that other people did not understand them or used them differently. Even at the last sessions, when subjects had become aware that their attempts to communicate were not always successful, the participants still tried hard to select words in a meaningful way, believing perhaps that more practice and concentration would produce communicative success. No one ever made a remark on the order of, "I'll describe this wine as cheesy and sullen, since none of these words means anything anyhow."

Chapter 8
Wine Scientists—
The Davis Subjects

Of the three groups, the Stanford subjects were the least likely to use words in a similar way: they had not drunk wine together before; they came from different parts of the country; and they had no way of developing a common terminology. What I wanted for comparison was the most favorable group of subjects—people who were not only very knowledgeable about wine but who frequently interacted together in wine-tasting settings—namely, a group of wine experts all located in the same place.

There are two kinds of wine experts, and some individuals may be both. First there are those who are very experienced in tasting wines but do not necessarily have any experience in making wines or have not studied the chemistry of wine. The other group of experts would be wine scientists—those who are primarily interested in the science of winemaking. For both groups, but especially for the second, it is very important that there be a common terminology that is applied with consistency. If a wine scientist publishes a paper in the *American Journal of Enology* and reports that a certain grape, vinified in a certain way, produced a *buttery* flavor, it is important that writer and readers apply *buttery* in the same way.

The Davis subjects consisted of ten wine scientists connected with the Department of Viticulture and Enology at the University of California at Davis, the leading research institute on winemaking in the United States. Subjects were either students in enology or members of the winery research staff. The subjects all knew each other, and some had belonged to the same wine-tasting group or had taken courses together, but not every subject had in fact drunk and discussed wine with every other subject. The Davis tasters were seriously concerned with the problems of using words in the same way, and all agreed that this was necessary for enologists.

Testing took place over three days, and the tasks selected were basically the same ones that had been used with the Tucson subjects in order to compare the performance of experts with nonexperts. Three tasks were performed on the first day. First, subjects were given three distinct white wines along with the list of common wine descriptors used with the Tucson group (Fig. 18) and asked to circle all the words that aptly described each wine. They were invited to add descriptors that were not on the list as well. For the second task, subjects were to rate each wine on the eight seven-point scales (Fig. 19). For the third task, subjects were presented with three distinct red wines and asked to select the one with the most and the least of sixteen properties (Fig. 20). The same tasks were repeated on the third day, but red wines were used for the first two tasks and whites for the third.

On the second day subjects worked in pairs for a matching experiment. Each subject was given the same three wines, and the first subject had to describe the wines so that his or her partner could match the same wines with the first person's descriptions. Each pair performed this task with three reds and three whites, and each subject had a chance to be both a sender and receiver.

Although it would have been highly desirable to serve wines identical to those used in previous experiments for comparison, this was in fact impossible. The main concern was to select three wines at each experimental session that were from the same general class, such as red table wines or white table wines, but that differed substantially among themselves, such as a German Riesling, a White Burgundy, and a California Chenin Blanc. In no instances did subjects say that two of the three wines tasted identical.

The general hypothesis for these tasks was that there would be greater consensus among the wine scientists than among ordinary wine drinkers as to the properties of each wine.

WINE VOCABULARY

The first question to be answered was whether the inventory of wine descriptors is different for wine scientists than for ordinary wine drinkers. Before the actual testing with wines began, the Davis subjects were presented with the revised list of wine descriptors (Fig. 18) and asked to circle the words that they would use and that they would consider good descriptors, and to cross out those words that they did not consider to be good descriptors, would not use, and perhaps would not understand. The same task had been given to thirteen Tucson subjects.

Listed below are the words that were circled by 75 percent of both the Tucson and the Davis groups (that is, those they considered good wine descriptors) and the words that were crossed out by 75 percent of both groups (that is, those neither group considered good descriptors).

Wine Descriptors Chosen by 75% of Both Groups

acidic	dry	nutty
aged	earthy	perfumed
alcoholic	flat	smooth
aromatic	fragrant	spicy
astringent	fruity	sweet
bitter	full-bodied	tart
bouquet		watery

Wine Descriptors Rejected by 75% of Both Groups

fat	honest	manly
feminine		small

More interesting is the inventory of items on which the scientists and nonscientists differed. Table 29 presents the words that were considered good descriptors by the Tucson subjects but not necessarily by the Davis ones. The first two columns give the number of Tucson and Davis subjects, respectively, who circled the word. The third column shows how many Davis subjects crossed out the word. It is somewhat surprising how few of the Davis subjects circled words like *weak* and *strong*. Wines with such properties were described instead as *low body* for *weak,* and *high body* or *alcoholic* for *strong.*

TABLE 29: Words Considered Good Descriptors by Tucson Group

	No. of Tucson subjects circling (N = 13)	No. of Davis subjects circling (N = 10)	No. of Davis subjects rejecting (N = 10)
bland	13	5	2
insipid	11	4	2
light	7	3	3
lively	8	2	7
mellow	11	4	1
powerful	8	2	4
puckery	12	5	2
refreshing	9	3	4
robust	10	4	2
scented	8	1	7
semisweet	13	5	3
simple	8	3	4
strong	9	1	7
subtle	11	6	2
sugary	12	5	4
syrupy	10	3	3
tangy	11	2	5
velvety	6	2	6
weak	12	2	6

Table 30 contains the words considered good descriptors by Davis subjects. The first column lists the number of Davis subjects who circled a descriptor; column 2 shows the number of Tucson subjects who circled it; and column 3 gives the number of Tucson subjects who rejected the word.

In addition, both groups of subjects were invited to add words to the list. Only one Tucson subject added a word—*raw.* However, Davis subjects added the following: *oxidized* (listed twice), *acetic, estery* (twice,), *sophisticated* (probably with the meaning "adulterated"), *over-ripe, malo-lactic, spoiled, sulfur dioxide, vegy* ("vegetably"), *muscaty, vinous* (nonvarietal).

DESCRIBING WINES

In the word-circling task, subjects were presented with three white wines and one copy of the wine descriptors for each wine. Subjects were asked to taste all three wines and then circle all the words on

TABLE 30: Words Considered Good Descriptors by Davis Group

	No. of Davis subjects circling (N= 10)	No. of Tucson subjects circling (N = 13)	No. of Tucson subjects rejecting (N = 13)
buttery	9	1	10
clean	10	5	4
complex	9	6	5
foxy	8	2	9
gassy	10	2	8
maderized	7	2	8
oaky	10	4	6
peppery	9	6	4
sound	7	1	10
tannic	10	4	5
young	10	5	5

the list that they thought appropriately described each wine. The list contained blank lines where subjects could add additional descriptors, and on some wines many subjects did add to the list. The same task was repeated at the third session, but with red wines. The hypothesis was that, compared to ordinary wine drinkers, more of the Davis subjects would circle the same words for a given wine than the ordinary wine drinkers—that is, there would be greater consensus on what descriptors were appropriate for each wine. Tables 31 and 32 confirm this hypothesis. Table 31 lists the words circled by over 40 percent of the Davis subjects for each wine. Table 32 lists the words circled by over 40 percent of the Tucson subjects. For the Tucson subjects, the tasks were performed near the end of the eight-month-long series of sessions, that is, after the group had been discussing wine for several months. Table 33 presents the number of words circled by 40 percent of the Stanford subjects. (The Stanford subjects had 24 additional words on their list.) The Stanford subjects did better than the Tucson group, though not as well as the Davis one.

The average number of tokens used by the Davis subjects was 10.8 compared to 7.88 for the Tucson group, but this is not statistically significant since there was so much variability in the number of tokens used among the subjects in each group. The range for the Tucson subjects was 1–29 words per wine while that for the Davis group was 5–28.

TABLE 31: Performance of Davis Subjects on Word-Circling Task

White Wines

F   Circled by 50% or more: fruity, unbalanced, flat
                    40%   flowery

W   50% +   acidic, bitter, dry, off, tart,
                                              unbalanced
                    40%   harsh, unripe

In addition, 50% of the subjects added descriptors that indicated defects.

B   50% +   aromatic, balanced, fruity
                    40%   acidic, clean, delicate, flowery,
                                              fragrant, semisweet

Red Wines

S   50% +   dry, astringent, oaky, unbalanced
                    40%   harsh, off, tannic, young

60% of the subjects added descriptors that indicated defects.

H   50% +   balanced, dry, grapy
                    40%   clean, astringent, tannic, thin,
                                              woody

40% made additional comments on the grapiness.

D   50% +   aged, astringent, complex, dry,
                                              full-bodied, oaky, tannic, woody
                    40%   bouquet, balanced

40% mentioned defects.

The Davis subjects used an average of 48 different words per wine, and the average number of words per subject was 8.3. For the Tucson subjects, 49.8 different words were used for each wine, with an individual average of 9. The Stanford subjects, who had 24 words more on their lists, showed a range of 5 to 28 different words per wine with an individual average of 10.6.

A possible objection to basing a conclusion solely on selecting particular words is that, although subjects might agree on the characteristics of a wine, they would select different, but synonymous, words: for example, one subject might circle *thin*, another *weak*, and a third *watery* for the same wine. In scanning the questionnaires to check for this possibility, it did not seem that subjects were doing so.

Table 32: Performance of Tucson Subjects on Word-Circling Task

White Wines

L	Circled by 50% + or more:	fruity
	40%	semisweet
Q	50% +	none
	40%	none
V	50% +	none
	40%	green

Red Wines

E	50% +	astringent, acidic, dry
	40%	puckery, tart
J	50% +	none
	40%	tart, dry
N	50% +	none
	40%	none

Table 33: Performance of Stanford Subjects on Word-Circling Task

White Wines

B	Circled by 50% or more:	none
	40% +	acidic, bland
N	50% +	none
	40% +	light, fruity, semisweet, smooth
W	50% +	none
	40% +	fruity, light, tangy, dry

Red Wines

F	50% +	none
	40% +	fragrant, fruity, semisweet, grapy, perfumed
R	50% +	none
	40% +	dry, smooth
T	50% +	dry
	40% +	acidic, full-bodied, hearty, puckery, astringent

Rather, a subject who circled *weak* for a wine also tended to circle *watery* and *thin*, whereas other subjects would not comment on body at all or would circle a different set of words, such as *robust* and *hearty* for that wine. Thus the difference between the wine scientists and the ordinary wine drinkers in selecting descriptors is that there is greater agreement among the scientists as to how to appropriately describe a wine.

CONSENSUS ON SCALES

The second task which was carried out at the first and third sessions used the same wines as the first task. Subjects were asked to rate each wine on eight seven-point scales (Fig. 17). Subjects were told to judge each wine, using either still white wines or still red wines as the norm. That is, the subject was to decide whether a wine was *sweet, acidic, light,* etc., with respect to white table wines or red table wines. It was hypothesized that there would be more consensus among the Davis subjects than among the Tucson ones, as measured by a smaller variance for the Davis group. Because there was no principled way to match up judgments for wine-by-wine comparison, since the samples were not identical, the average variance was calculated for the three white wines and the three red wines of the Davis subjects. For the Tucson group the mean of the variance was calculated for six whites and six reds. On the red wines, the variance was lower on six of the eight scales for the Davis subjects, but when F-ratios were calculated, none reached significance at the .05 level. On the white wines, the variance was lower on four of the eight scales, but again none of the F-ratios reached a .05 level of significance.

The interesting thing about scalar adjectives is that speakers use them all the time without much concern for the reference point or implicit norm. Among the Tucson subjects, wine descriptors such as *dry, light,* and *tart* were often used for months without anyone asking what the standard of comparison was, and then only when there was an obvious breakdown of communication or considerable disagreement as to the properties of a wine.

In chapter 3 I discussed the many ways of making scalar judgments. When tasting three wines (as in the above task) judgments could be made with a very general reference class, such as white table wines or red table wines, or with respect to a narrower class. For example, a subject may taste a wine, identify it as a Pinot Chardonnay or a White Burgundy from Beaune, and then judge it with respect to Chardonnays or Burgundies.

It is possible that some Davis subjects may have used the last strategy. On the matching task, described below, a subject might describe a wine as having "medium body for its type" or being "typically fruity of its kind," even though the type was not mentioned or explicitly identified. And of course if different subjects were using different implicit norms, there would be greater variation in scaling wines.

Experiments with the Stanford and Tucson subjects showed that a subject's preference often affected his or her judgments when describing a wine and scaling it. There is some evidence that the same mechanism affected some scalar judgments of the Davis subjects. For example, among the white wines, wine B was rated as *too acid* by three subjects who disliked it or were neutral to the wine but rated as *balanced* by the seven who liked it. Wine F was rated as *astringent* by two subjects who disliked it but as *soft* and *smooth* by the rest. The rating on the quality scale of course reflects preference even more directly.

WINES WITH THE MOST AND LEAST OF A PROPERTY

In experiments with the Tucson subjects, it was hypothesized that there would be greater consensus when using common words than when using rare or unusual ones. The eight common words selected were *earthy, flat, grapy, light, perfumed, pungent, smooth, tart;* the eight unusual words were *big, buttery, feminine, honest, manly, positive, round,* and *small.* The subjects had been given three wines and were asked to select the one with the most and the least of each of the sixteen properties.

The same task was performed with the Davis subjects, using the same questionnaire (Fig. 20). However, there were important differences in the vocabularies of the two groups. They differed in their selections of good descriptors, and the Davis group did not discuss the meanings of the sixteen words. The results of the task are given in Table 34 and show that there was greater than chance agreement at the .05 or better level of significance by the Davis subjects on twenty-one measures compared to sixteen for the Tucson group.

The Davis group did better in all categories except that of selecting the white wine with the least of the sixteen properties. It will be recalled that this task was performed by the Tucson subjects after discussing the meaning of the terms while the Davis group did not have this opportunity.

Among the Tucson group there was significant agreement on twelve 'good' descriptors and four 'poor' ones. (For this group, *big, buttery,* and *round* were considered 'poor'.) For the Davis group, how-

TABLE 34: Results of Most and Least *X* Experiments, Davis and Tucson

		Davis Subjects				Tucson Subjects			
		Red Wines N=10		*White Wines* N=10		*Red Wines* N=11		*White Wines* N=10	
		Most	Least	Most	Least	Most	Least	Most	Least
Good Descriptors	Earthy			*				*	
	Flat			**	*	***	*		**
	Grapy	***			**			*	*
	Light				***				
	Perfumed						***		
	Pungent			*		*	**	**	
	Smooth			**					*
	Tart			*					*
	Big	**	*						
	Buttery				*				
	Round								*
Poor Descriptors	Feminine			***	**				**
	Honest			***	***				**
	Manly	***							
	Positive	*	*						
	Small	*	**		**	*			
Total		5	5	5	6	3	3	3	7
Overall		21				16			

Significant Agreement: *p. ≤ 0.05 ; **p. ≤ 0.01 ; ***p. ≤ 0.001

ever, *big*, *buttery*, and *round* were placed with the 'good' descriptors, and among this group there was significant agreement on twelve 'good' descriptors and nine 'poor' ones. As mentioned previously, since *buttery* and *earthy* denote rather specific properties which appear in only a few wines, this choice of descriptors was unfortunate. Several of the Davis subjects reported that none of the wines served was buttery or earthy. However, the hypothesis that there would be greater consensus with common words than unusual ones was confirmed for both groups of subjects. While the wine scientists performed better overall than the ordinary wine drinkers, their superior performance was on the unusual terms. However, as *speakers* of English, they have available to them all of the semantic information and pragmatic strategies to make reasonable inferences; e.g., *feminine*, though considered a poor descriptor, has associations with other words which were considered good descriptors, for example, *light, smooth, round*, and *perfumed*.

MATCHING

The matching task was carried out as with the Stanford and Davis subjects; with those groups, the results showed that one person's matching of wines with a second person's descriptions was not generally better than chance. Where the communication was successfully better than chance, most of the success could be accounted for by different amounts of sugar in the three wines presented, and this fact served as a reliable indicator.

A matching task was presented to the Davis subjects, who were divided into five pairs. Each pair matched three red wines and three whites. The person designated as the sender for the white wines was instructed to add a fake description (as with previous groups). The fake was not supposed to fit any of the three actual white wines, but it was not to be a dead giveaway either. The other member of the pair was designated as the sender of descriptions for red wines, and only three descriptions were given. Subjects could describe the wines in any order. A two-stage procedure was used. At first the sender could use only descriptive, comparative, and evaluative terms (exclusive of color and appearance), but could not identify the wine as to varietal or place of origin. After the receiver made tentative matches, the sender could add information as to the varietal used and the area from which the wine probably came. The receiver could then revise his matches, but in fact none did so. Both senders and receivers made notes on all six wines, and the sessions were tape-recorded.

The white wines presented were a German Mosel, a French White Burgundy, and a California Green Hungarian. Since there was a fourth description, the probability for correct matches by chance would be 1/4 for any given wine. There were eight correct matches, (p = .017). The main problem with matching the whites seemed to be that the fake descriptions were too close to the actual wines. For example, three pairs correctly matched two of the three white wines, but the fake description was selected for the third wine. The other two pairs made one correct match, and the fake was selected for another wine.

The red wines presented were a California Cabernet Sauvignon, a Valpolicella (from Italy), and a Rhône wine. The probability for a correct match was 1/3. There were seven correct matches, (p = .08). Two pairs matched all three wines, one pair matched one, and the other two matches missed all.

Overall, one pair made five correct matches, one four, and the other three pairs made two correct matches. It is interesting that the pair with the most correct matches (5) had belonged to the same tasting group for several months and the subjects were used to talking about wine together.

The actual scores, however, do not tell the whole story, since descriptive notes made by the sender and receiver were often very similar, and so it is instructive to examine the descriptions closely to see what the scource of error was. For example, consider the mismatch of whites shown in Figure 21: the receiver matched the sender's description of E with his 20 (wine N). Apparently the difference in judgment about balance, which is ultimately a quality judgment, caused the mismatch, even though the two most salient descriptive qualities, sweetness and acid, were agreed upon. Since the receiver rated two wines as low in acid, there was another candidate for the description of E.

Consider the descriptions of reds in Figure 22. This receiver matched the descriptions of A with 45, being influenced apparently

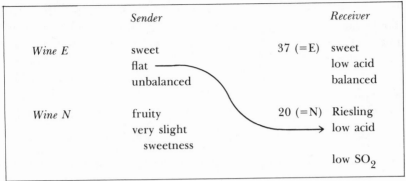

FIGURE 21

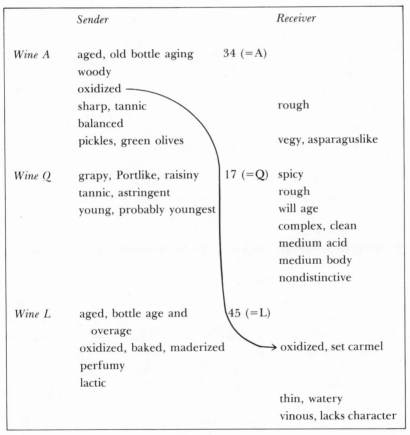

FIGURE 22

by the term *oxidized*. He mentioned that 45 could match either A or L and guessed on A. Q was matched with 34 and L with 17. In this instance, it seems that the individuals were attending to somewhat different aspects of the wines, but where they commented on the same properties, e.g., age, tannin, or oxidation, they seemed to agree. The difficulty of encoding into language unusual smells and aromas can be seen in wines A and Q. On A both individuals described this aroma with reference to green vegetables. In fact, on this wine every pair commented on the nose. The descriptions from the tapes and the receivers' notes included: "bell pepper, berryish"; "bell pepper, green"; "olives, green"; "vegetative, green pepper"; "vegy, green pepper, asparagus"; "green olives, pickle"; "vegy, asparagus"; "green olive nose, green peppery."

John Reid's Later Matching Experiment

Experiments with wine scientists were continued several months later by John Reid, one of the Davis subjects who became interested in the experiments and continued the research. Eight subjects participated in a matching experiment at two sessions. At the first session, five white wines were served; at the second, five red wines. (Six of the subjects had participated in the earlier experiments.) All subjects had been seriously tasting wine for at least one year.

Each pair of tasters was first presented with the five wines in a randomized order (established by the experimenter). And each taster wrote his or her descriptions on a form which elicited information on appearance, aroma and bouquet, taste, and overall impression. Then the pairs were given a fresh set of wines (from the same bottles) and had to match wines by talking about them as in previous experiments. There was one important difference in this experiment, however. Subjects were allowed to refer to color and appearance, and consistently did so. Since there were some mismatches, color was probably not completely defining, but since there were five wines at each session, mention of color was used to narrow the range to two or three wines. For example, a subject might say, "Wine X is one of the two darkest wines." One of the red wines was markedly lighter in color than the rest and this provided the main clue for all subjects.

The white wines presented in John Reid's experiments were premium California wines. They were 1) David Bruce Chardonnay,

1975;   2) Stonegate Chenin Blanc, 1976;   3) Joseph Phelps Johannisberg Riesling, 1976;   4) San Martin Sauvignon Blanc, 1976; and   5) Villa Mt. Eden Gerwurztraminer, 1976. Three of the four pairs matched three correctly and confused two (not the same two), and the fourth pair matched all five correctly. The chance of fourteen correct matches out of twenty is .0000224, a very low probability.

The red wines presented were also California premium wines: 1) Beaulieu Cabernet Sauvignon, 1974;   2) Ridge Lytton Springs Zinfandel, 1975;   3) Beringer Gamay Beaujolais, 1975;   4) Souverain Petite Sirah, 1974; and   5) Johnson's Pinot Noir, 1974. Subjects were not paired with the same partner as for the whites. One of the subjects was not able to attend this session, and the experimenter took her place. Since the experimenter knew the wines ahead of time, he naturally had a decided advantage, but there was some compensation since he described most of the wines which his partner then matched. One pair made only one correct match, but the other three pairs correctly matched all five wines. The probability of sixteen correct matches out of twenty is .0000015, again, very small. Even if the correct matches of the experimenter and his partner are not counted, the probability of eleven correct matches out of fifteen is .0001308.[1]

The descriptions, both written and oral, showed much greater consistency than that found among nonexperts. The Zinfandel, for instance, was described by four of the eight subjects as having a *buttery* nose, and no other wine was described as *buttery*. Chemicals were often referred to: on the reds, two of four of the pairs mentioned *mercaptan*, three *diacetyl*, and two *ethyl acetate*. Rather than describing wines as *acidic* or *flat* or *astringent*, subjects tended to talk about *high acidity*, *low acidity*, or *high* or *low astringency*. In addition to the standard vocabulary and chemical terms, comparisons to other smells and tastes were frequently used to characterize wines: *olivelike, grassy, green pepper, oily, soapy, pickles, vegetative, apples, honeylike, honeysuckle, garlic, minty, eucalyptus, berryish* (this term was frequently used), *Koolade, tutti-frutti, anise, licorice, cardboardy, rubbery, onions, carved oak church pews, skunky, Valley smell* (i.e., a smell characteristic of wines from grapes grown in the San Joaquin Valley), *filter pads, smell of a dentist's office.*

Two wine descriptors appeared in the corpus which I had not found in previous wine literature or conversation, but which would be predicted by my theory of semantic extension presented in chapter 2: one wine was described as *shallow*, "not deep," "lacking depth," and another was described as having a *loud oak character*, "not soft," possibly astringent due to heavy wood flavor. One wine was described as *forward* and *outgoing*. These may be extensions from the personality domain, but they are also words used and defined by Vandyke Price, and so they may not have been original with the speaker.

To show the similarities and differences in description and evaluation among the Davis subjects, Tables 35 and 36 present the description of all subjects for the red wine that was most often matched correctly. Table 35 shows the results of the matching task that I carried out. The descriptions of the senders are based on the tapes made, and those of the receivers are based on their tasting notes, made before hearing the sender's descriptions. Table 36 shows the results of the matching task carried out by John Reid. Descriptions are based on the tasting notes made by all subjects prior to the matching task and those in the discussion during the matching task.

For comparison, descriptions by the Stanford and Tucson subjects are given in Tables 37 and 38. The descriptions are for the red wine on which the largest number of correct matches were made in that session. For the Stanford subjects (Table 37), descriptions are based on senders' notes; in this experiment messages were sent in writing and sender and receiver did not speak to each other. For the Tucson subjects, the discourse was taken from the tape and/or notes made by senders and receivers (Table 38).

On the Valpolicella, the Davis subjects agreed to a large extent on the most salient characteristics of the wine—its age, woodiness, and oxidation. There was some consensus on its tannin and body (by the two subjects who commented on body), but there was disagreement on acid and quality. On the Gamay Beaujolais, Davis subjects agreed on the body, fruitiness, quality, age, and off odor. (Five of the eight tasters remarked that the wine was stinky, skunky, or had a mercaptan smell.) There was no agreement on acid or astringency. Stanford subjects agreed to some extent on taste and body, but disagreed on aroma. Tucson subjects agreed on acid but disagreed on most other features. In general, the Davis subjects described more features of the wine than the other groups.

SUMMARY AND CONCLUSIONS

The Davis subjects did best on the task of describing wines, and in this task they definitely outperformed previous subjects. The result is not surprising since these subjects frequently engaged in this activity. They did not perform better than previous subjects in scalar judgments, and this outcome reflects, I believe, the general problem of implicit norms involved in making such judgments. Though conversations are full of judgments and evaluations like *John is tall, X's ice cream is rich, Lynn is stupid,* reference norms are rarely provided by the speaker or asked for by the hearer. In most everyday conversations, this lack of specificity is not important, but in scientific discourse it is a problem. Davis subjects performed better than the Tucson ones in selecting the wine with the most and least of a property. In this case, the norm was made explicit since the judgments were based on the three wines present rather than an implicit norm.

On the matching task the Davis subjects did not do better than other groups on the experiment that I ran, but they did do extremely well on John Reid's. However, since in the latter the subjects were allowed to refer to color and appearance, the results of the two experiments are not comparable. A second major difference between the two is that in the first instance subjects were presented with several non-California wines, including some that they had had little or no experience with, whereas in the second experiment the wines were limited to premium California varietal wines. The latter experiment shows that when all information can be used, and when the wines are those that subjects are familiar with, wine scientists perform at an extremely high level.

These three sets of experiments with three groups of subjects show that the task of encoding into language the perceptual properties of complex and varied stimuli, such as wines, and subsequently decoding such messages, is an extremely difficult one, even for peope with great knowledge and experience. Contrary to popular opinion, the language provides rich resources for talking about taste and smell. Although few words are used only for these sensory per-

TABLE 35: Results of the Matching Experiment with the Greatest Number of Matches for a Red Wine: Davis Subjects (Lehrer's Experiments)

Pair	1		2		3		4		5	
MATCH WAS	CORRECT		INCORRECT		CORRECT		INCORRECT		CORRECT	
	Sender	Receiver	Sender	Receiver	Sender	Receiver	Sender	Receiver	Sender	Receiver
Aroma and bouquet	Oxidized, light bouquet				Most oxidized, rich aroma		Oxidized, baked or madeira nose	Oxidized, set carmel, more perfumy than A	Oxidized, Sherry-like	
Taste			Dry		Tartest, nice fruit				Slight bitter taste	
Body			Fairly thin					Thin, watery		
Acid			Medium acid			Good acid for red	Distinctly lacked acid			Flat
Tannin	More tannin than Q			Tannin		Moderate tannin	Tannic, more astringent & harsher than A		Small amount of tannin	

TABLE 35 (Continued)

MATCH WAS	1		2		3		4		5	
	CORRECT		INCORRECT			CORRECT	INCORRECT		CORRECT	
Age	Oldest, overaged		Older than the rest, ripe grape	Aged		Aged	Some age			
Woodiness	Oak		Oak	Woody	Woody, burnt wood	Oakiness			Too long in wood	Too much wood
Evaluation		Distinctive					Some complexity	Lacks character		Mediocre
Varietal	Pinot Noir	Pinot Noir	Cabernet		Burgundy or Pinot Noir	Spanish?		Vinous	Partly a Pinot Noir	No varietal character, Pinot Noir that has lost all the [word not legible]

Responses to Valpolicella, 1971 (Gancio)

TABLE 36: Results of the Matching Experiment with the Greatest Number of Matches for a Red Wine: Davis Subjects (Reid's Experiments)

Taster	First Pair		Second Pair		Third Pair		Fourth Pair	
	1	2	3	4	5	6	7	8
Appearance	Deep rosé color	Light cherry red clear	Light red	Light red, slight orange, brilliant *Lightest.*	Very ligth farnet, almost rosé Clear.	Light red to rosé, brilliant. *Lighter than others.*	Light, Lacks deep color, brilliant.	Light red with purple highlights, brilliant.
Aroma and Bouquet	Light aroma, slight artificial sweetness. *Fruity-type aroma*	Light, possible violatile acid or H_2S	Stink, smell of half-rotten onions, H_2S or mercaptan	Sweet-fruity, distinctive. *Stinky.*	Slightly tutti-fruity, low character alcohol pervades.	Fresh, young, no oak, nouveau character, Gamay Beaujclais aroma.	Asparagus odor, seaweed, slight off aroma, shallow, incomplete not pleasing.	Mercaptans, skunky, some fruity character. *Garlicky, sulfides?*
Taste	High flavors	Stinky, undistinguished taste, defective flavor	Onion-like	Dry, distinctive lemonade type	Low intensity of flavors, low alcohol	Some grapy and carbonic marcaration character, clean, not much flavor.	Dry, flavor okay	Some fruity flavors
Body	Somewhat watery	Light		Thin. *Lightest body.*	*Thin*	Watery. *Thin character.*		
Acid		Unbalanced on acid side	Tart	Acid + (high acid')	Low acid	Flat	Acidity okay	Relatively high acid

Table 36 (Continued)

Taster	First Pair		Second Pair		Third Pair		Fourth Pair	
	1	2	3	4	5	6	7	8
Astringency	Low astringency		Astringent		Low tannin		Moderate astringency	
Balance		Unbalanced			Good balance	Unbalanced		
Age							Young, needs time	Young
Evaluation		Mediocre red	Drain it!			Medium-low score	Not too inspiring	An overwhelming fault makes it useless as a drinking wine. Pity.
Varietal/Type				Nouveau-type	Gamay-style	Gamay-Beaujolais		

Responses to Beringer Gamay Beaujolais, 1975. All subjects matched correctly. Descriptions are based on tasting notes and discussion. Items in *italics* were added during the discussion.

TABLE 37: Results of the Matching Experiments with the Greatest Number of Correct Matches for a Red Wine: Stanford Subjects

Sender	1	2	3	4	5	6	7
Match was	Correct	Correct	Correct	Correct	Incorrect	Correct	Incorrect
Aroma and bouquet	Earthy smell, vegetable	Most fragrant	Not a normal red wine aroma, like salad dressing	Less strong aroma	Indefinite, spineless odor		
Taste	Tart		Sour	Less sweet, not a strong taste, little aftertaste	Pleasant taste not definite	Dry, tart	Almost acid, dry dry aftertaste
Body	No legs, weak	Most full-bodied		Less full	Weak, not full or robust	Light	
Acid/Tannin		Smoothest	Harsh, somewhat astringent		Smooth, almost without bite		Smooth at first, somewhat harsh, fairly puckery
Evaluative	Bland			Bland	Agreeable, perhaps intriguing		

TABLE 38: Results of the Matching Experiment with the Greatest
Number of Correct Matches for a Red Wine: Tucson Subjects

Pair	1	2	3	4	5
Match was	Correct	Correct	Correct	Correct	Incorrect
Aroma and bouquet	Burnt rubber, almost perfumy		More pronounced smell, musky	Rose, sulfur, perfume	Fruity
Taste	Medicinal, super dry		Bitter	A little sour aftertaste	2nd driest, salty
Body		Robust			
Acid/Tannin	Tangy, sourish	Harsh, strong acidity, abrasive	Tickly, pungent, biting		
Evaluative		Awful			

ceptions, speakers have at their disposal many general words that
can be applied to various domains, technical words, and productive
means for semantic extension, metaphorical transfer, and comparisons with similar things. But each speaker has a different set of edu-
cational and personal experiences and all this contributes to the variability found in speakers' linguistic behavior.

The experiments show that there is considerable miscommunication, demonstrated by the matching experiments, for example. Yet
in the absence of such tests, speakers seem to think that they are
communicating—that they mean the same thing when they use the
same words. How can this be? Since the speakers generally share the
same intralinguistic connections, and since the differences in denotation are quite subtle, for most purposes the idiolect differences and
the referential discrepencies do not show up. McConnell-Ginet (personal communication) suggests that one reason for the nonexperts'
wanting to learn "proper" wine terminology was that they expected
more wine knowledge, more tasting experience, and a greater familiarity with the vocabulary to enhance their chances of communicative
success. However, simply learning more words and their intralinguistic connections does not guarantee referential consensus.
For a group of people to connect words to wines in the same way
requires a great deal of training. This topic is discussed in chapter
10.

Postscript: Word Clusters

As chapter 3 has shown, when a speaker does not know exactly what a word denotes in a domain but does know how to use it in some other domain, the intralinguistic relationships can be called on to provide an interpretation. I cannot determine what strategies the wine subjects were using in describing wines, but the data on what words were used for the same wine may provide a few suggestions. It may be recalled that the words *feminine, manly, honest,* and *small* were considered by both the Tucson and Davis subjects to be poor descriptors. Yet in one task subjects were forced to use these terms by deciding which wine had the most or least of that property. Figures 23 through 26 show which words were used for the same wine.

Figure 23 shows the word clusters used by the Tucson subjects for the red wines.[2] This task was performed before the word meanings were discussed.

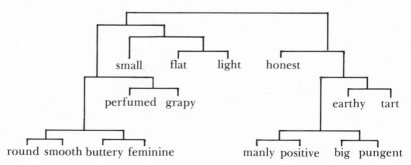

FIGURE 23: Word Clusters Used before Word Meanings Were Discussed: Tucson

One cluster can perhaps be characterized as 'small, smooth, and feminine' and the other as 'strong-tasting and masculine'. *Small* clusters with *flat* and *light,* which can be explained easily since *small* denotes 'less amount, less size' and *light* is used for 'less body' and *flat* for 'too little acid'. *Manly* clusters with *big,* a reasonable association, and *feminine* with *round, smooth,* and, to a lesser extent, *perfumed. Honest* is more or less of an isolate.

Figure 24 shows the results of Tucson subjects' cluster of words for the white wines. The task of selecting the wine with the most X and

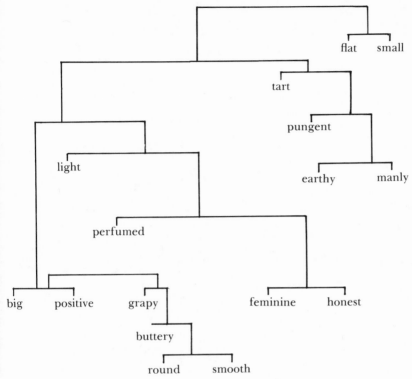

FIGURE 24: Word Clusters Used after Word Meanings Were Discussed: Tucson

least X was done immediately after subjects had discussed the meaning of the words. *Small* is still tied to *flat,* but *honest* has attached to *feminine,* which has in turn become more closely clustered with *perfumed* and *light,* still reasonable associations. However, the clusters themselves are hard to characterize in semantic terms.

One speculation to account for the shift in clusters is that, at the beginning of the year, subjects were relying on intralinguistic networks to attach words to wine. However after discussing the words, new links were made between the words and more specific properties of wines or other tastes or sensations that subjects may have been familiar with. In other words, the experiments provided the subjects with extensions for many words.

Figures 25 and 26 show the word clusters for the Davis subjects.

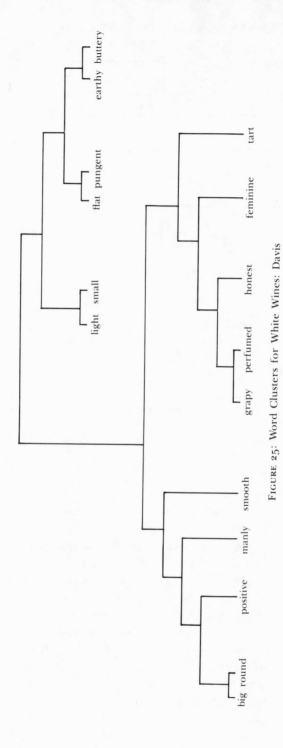

FIGURE 25: Word Clusters for White Wines: Davis

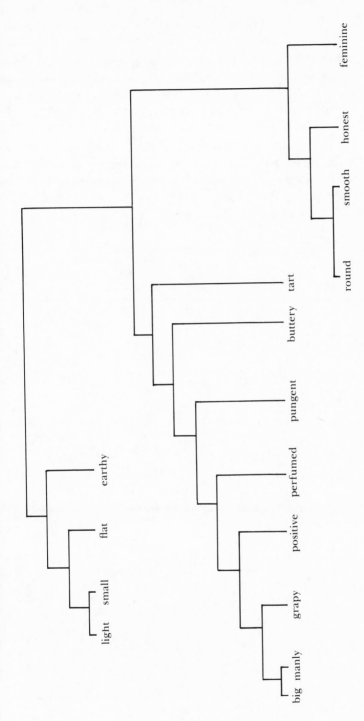

FIGURE 26: Word Clusters for Red Wines: Davis

Small clusters tightly with *light* and then to *flat* and *earthy*. *Honest* clusters with *feminine,* which in turn clusters with *round* and *smooth* for the reds and with *perfumed* for the whites. *Manly* clusters tightly with *big* on the reds and loosely with *big* and other descriptors on the whites. Most of the other words—the ones considered to be good or acceptable descriptors—do not fall into any obvious semantic clusters. This may suggest that the Davis tasters were applying such words directly to the properties of the wine without recourse to intralinguistic relationships—at least for those words they considered to be good descriptors.

Part III

Wine Talk in a Communicative Framework

Chapter 9
Functions of Language

In this and the following chapters that comprise Part III, I speculate about the reasons why people talk about wine. I am not asking a highly abstract question, such as why a particular conversation is about wine instead of about skiing in the Austrian Alps. Such a question may be unanswerable. The narrower question is rather this: in a particular conversation or discourse about wine, what do the participants hope to accomplish? What kind of information do they intend to convey? Is information about wine even relevant?

In chapters 10 and 11 I will also argue that talk about wine, far from being unique or esoteric, has much in common with other topics of conversation, and I have therefore included examples and material from other semantic and conversational domains. In order to prepare for this discussion of the functions of wine conversation, however, I will briefly survey some classifications of the function of speech.

All classification systems reflect the interests and goals of the classifier (cf. Quine 1977), and classifications of the functions of language clearly illustrate the different goals of different systemizers. We are not dealing with natural kinds, like cats or kangeroos, where phenomena neatly divide themselves up into perceptually different categories, and we are a long way from a science of communication. "Ultimately, the functions served in speech must be derived directly from the purposes and needs of human persons engaged in social

143

action. . . . The formal analysis of speaking is a means to the understanding of human purposes and needs, and their satisfaction" (Hymes 1972:70). Although different systems tend to cover the same phenomena, they often give very different weight to the various features. What is a primary division for one taxonomy will be a minor subcategory for another.

Most utterances serve more than one function (Jakobson 1960; Halliday 1975, 1978), so it is difficult if not impossible to say what the function of an utterance is, and of course the decisions made in analyzing a text will depend on the purposes of the analysis—whether one is studying interpersonal relationships during a committee meeting or analyzing a poem.

Since language serves many functions, and since any utterance may serve several purposes, it is unproductive to argue about *the* function of language, or the *primary* function of language. Searle (1972) has argued that communication is the essential function of language. Chomsky (1975) has denied this view, pointing out the importance of language for thought and imagination.

The term *communication* is unfortunately vague, since a speaker communicates not only referential and denotative information about the world but also his or her attitudes, feelings, assessment of the speech situation, and personality. Most of the classification systems on speech functions assume that language serves to communicate these sorts of things, distinguishing, however, between communicating about objective information and using language for various interpersonal functions. Since these classification systems have been devised to analyze actual utterances—texts and conversations—whatever categories are relevant for thinking are little accessible to observation. However, it is possible that some of the categories used for analyzing conversation would also be valid for categories of thinking. Of the systems that I survey, only Soskin & John (1963) allow for a category of thinking to oneself. With respect to using language for thought versus communication, it is enlightening to quote Sapir on this point:

> The primary function of language is generally said to be communicative. There can be no quarrel with this so long as it is distinctly understood that there may be effective communication without overt speech and that language is highly relevant to situations which are not obvi-

ously of a communicative sort. To say that thought, which is hardly possible in any sustained sense without the symbolic organization brought by language, is that form of communication in which the speaker and the person addressed are identified in one person is not far from begging the question. . . . It is best to admit that language is primarily a vocal actualization of the tendency to see reality symbolically, that it is precisely this quality which renders it a fit instrument for communication and that it is in the actual give and take of social intercourse that it has been complicated and refined into the form in which it is known today. (Sapir 1937:159)

The main difference between language function classifications seems to me to be between systems based on speech act theories and those based on theories of social interaction. The first group has been developed by philosophers who have tried to relate utterances to truth on the one hand and action theory on the other. The second group, which includes anthropologists, ethnomethodologists, sociolinguists, and social psychologists, draws a major distinction between referential functions (denotation, descriptions of things and events) and interpersonal, social, and participational functions, and the latter group of investigators has given a great deal of attention to the nonreferential. However, some of the same categories show up in the classes of both groups.

Speech Act Classifications

Classifications of language functions based on speech act theories have grown out of traditional concerns in the philosophy of language (meaning and truth) and action theory. It has been common practice to distinguish between locutionary,[1] illocutionary, and perlocutionary acts. Locutionary acts are concerned with meaning and reference. Illocutionary acts involve the intentions of the speaker and what he wishes to communicate, such as stating a fact, making a request or uttering a greeting. Perlocutionary acts deal with the effects or consequences that result from a utterance, such as persuading or frightening a hearer.

John Austin, whose work *How to Do Things with Words* (1962) was a landmark for speech act theory, took pains to show that earlier theories of meaning were too narrow, since they were concerned solely with truth. Austin introduced the more general notion of felicity conditions, of which truth was only one type. Saying something false is an infelicity connected with statements; promising insincerely would be a infelicitous promise; baptizing a baby with the wrong name would constitute another kind of infelicity. For Austin there was a major difference between utterances that could be true or false and those that could not be. Other philosophers (e.g., Bach 1975; Bach & Harnish 1979) have advocated extending the notion of truth to a wider class of cases than Austin allowed. An utterance like *I order you to close the door* could not be true or false for Austin. Bach, however, argues that it is true if the speaker in fact orders the hearer to close the door, while it could be false if the speaker were joking. Bach admits, however, that the main point of the utterance is to get the hearer to perform the action of closing the door.

The heart of any speech act theory is the illocutionary act, and all major treatments of speech acts give a taxonomy of illocutionary acts. The most complete speech act theory to date is that of Bach & Harnish (1979),[2] and I shall briefly summarize aspects of this work. Following Strawson (1950), Bach & Harnish draw a major distinction between conventional and communicative illocutionary acts. Conventional acts, such as exchanging marriage vows, baptizing a baby, passing sentence on a convicted criminal, and nominating a candidate for an election, are speech acts in which a speaker's utterance changes or maintains an institutional state of affairs. For instance, when a referee in a basketball game calls a personal foul, his doing so brings about a certain state of affairs in the game.

In communicative acts, on the other hand, the speaker wants to communicate something to the hearer, and moreover he wants the hearer to know that what is communicated is intentionally so communicated (cf. Grice 1975). Thus, lying and deceiving cannot be illocutionary acts because the speaker does not want the hearer to know that he (the speaker) is lying.

The Bach & Harnish taxonomy of communicative illocutionary acts contains the following four main categories, with subclasses:

1) Constative: The speaker believes something and wants the hearer to believe it, too. Examples are declaring, reporting, asserting, objecting, hypothesizing, proposing. Bach & Harnish include making appraisals and value judgments, whereas in some

taxonomies, reporting facts and making appraisals are distinguished at the first level.

2) Directives: The speaker wants the hearer to do something. Examples are ordering, requesting, inviting, asking a question, suggesting that the hearer do something.

3) Commissives: The speaker undertakes an obligation to perform some act in the future, e.g., promising, swearing, contracting, guaranteeing.

4) Acknowledgments: The speaker performs some social act. Examples are greeting, congratulating, expressing condolences, apologizing.

In the Bach & Harnish system interpersonal relationships, differences in the status of participants, degrees of formality are of less importance than the above dimensions. Bach & Harnish also acknowledge several classes of auxiliary speech acts, which they claim are not communicative but rather serve to regulate conversation (e.g., changing a topic, breaking off) and small talk (where the participants are talking merely to avoid an uncomfortable silence), joking, and mimicking.

OTHER TAXONOMIES

In contrast to speech act theory taxonomies, the other major classifications of language functions draw a fairly sharp line between informational/referential uses of language and interpersonal functions. However, some of the categories established overlap with some speech act classifications.

One category is a referential-informational one. *Referential* here covers denotation as well as reference proper. Sometimes this category is narrowed to include only public, intersubjectively verifiable reports and may thus contrast with another category in which the speaker reports personal feelings. A category of appraisal and evaluations is distinguished from the informational ones in Soskin & John (1963) (see Table 39).

All taxonomies have a category which is hearer oriented and which includes directives, but other things, such as vocatives, may be included as well.

Beyond these classes, writers establish somewhat different and noncommensurate categories. Jakobson establishes a *phatic* class, which serves to "establish, to prolong, or to discontinue communication, to check on whether the channel works." The term *phatic* is taken from Malinowsky, and although Jakobson includes ritualized formulas in this class, he stresses the aspect of managing the conversation, whereas Malinowsky has stressed the personal and social bonds created by the phatic use of language, defined as "a type of speech in which ties of union are created by a mere exchange of words" (1923:478). Examples of phatic communion would include greetings, formulaic inquiries about the health of the other, "purposeless expressions of preference or aversion, accounts of irrelevant happenings, comments on what is perfectly obvious." For Halliday the personal and social bonding would result from the *interpersonal* function, while the *textual* function would be concerned with the organization of conversation. "The textual function creates text, makes what the speaker says in context operational" (1978:17). For Halliday, the textual function is very general, since it involves the organization of language for all its uses. Three non-speech act classification systems are presented in Table 39. The categories of

TABLE 39: Major Non-Speech Act Classification Systems

	Jakobson (1962)	Halliday[3] (1978)	Soskin & John (1963)
REFERENTIAL			
General Information	Referential	Ideational (includes logical)	Structones
Personal Information	Emotive	Ideational (Experiential)	Signones
Appraisals	Emotive (?)	Interpersonal (?)	Metrones
HEARER ORIENTED			
Directives	Connotive	Interpersonal (Regulative)	Regones
Suggestions	Connotive	Interpersonal (Regulative)	Regones/ Metrones
OTHER CATEGORIES	Poetic Metalinguistic		Expressive Excogitative

most other writers are closely modeled on one of them. In Table 39 the terms for the categories are the writers' own.

Jakobson has two more classes, in addition to those in Table 39: (1) For the *metalinguistic* function, the focus is on the code. Examples would be defining a word or asking for an utterance to be repeated. (2) In the *poetic* function, the focus is on language for its own sake.

Soskin & John also establish two categories in addition to those in Table 39: (1) *Expressive* statements, which "discharge immediately experienced tension," such as interjections (Jakobson includes these under *emotive*), and (2) *excogitative* statements—thinking aloud— which serve to explore a problem, e.g., *I wonder what I should wear today*. These two categories are not intended to be communicative, though they may have an effect on the hearer.

A rather different way of looking at utterances is in terms of the affect and the influence an utterance has on the feelings and attitudes of participants. Such systems are not intended as functional classifications, of course. A very simple system was used by H.E. Miller (1949), in which judges were asked to decide whether a counselor's statement to his or her client was (1) accepting, respecting, or admitting the validity of the client's position, (2) supporting, (3) denying, or (4) neutral.

Bales (1950) uses a classification that makes affect a primary distinctive feature and that combines affect with informational and directive categories:

1) Shows solidarity, raises other's status.
2) Shows tension release, jokes, laughs.
3) Agrees, shows passive acceptance.
4) Gives suggestions, direction, implying autonomy for others.
5) Gives opinions, evaluation, analysis, expresses feeling.
6) Gives orientation, information, reports.
7) Asks for orientation, information, repetition.
8) Asks for opinion, evaluation, analysis.
9) Asks for suggestions, direction.
10) Disagrees, shows passive rejection.
11) Shows tension, asks for help, withdraws.
12) Shows antagonism, deflates other's status.

The first three classes have interpersonal and phatic functions and increase group solidarity. The last three have the same functions but show negative affect. Classes 4 to 6 provide information and direction, while 7 to 9 ask for information and direction.

Hymes (1972:52ff) suggests a number of dimensions and components that might turn out to be relevant for a taxonomy rather than postulating a set of classes. Dimensions would include the speech community, the speech situation, the speech act, and style. Components include the participants, the message form, message content, setting, scene, purpose, key (mock vs. serious, perfunctory vs. painstaking), variety, and genre.

The wine corpus provides a set of data that I wish to explain in functional terms. None of the classification systems is by itself adequate or appropriate for looking at wine conversation in a cultural setting. However, each taxonomy contains some relevant categories or features.

One of the first problems has to do with the nature of denotation. It is generally assumed that speakers agree on the application of words to things, events, properties, and states. But, as we have seen in the last section, this presupposition about conventional meaning is not true. We are of course talking about the more subtle distinctions made by speakers. Presumably all competent speakers of English can distinguish between hammers and horses; we are talking now about the difference between fruitiness and floweriness.

Imagine a conversation about wine in a bar between a wine expert and a casual wine drinker, both of whom are drinking the same house wine. The wine expert is seriously concerned about descriptive accuracy, but the casual wine drinker just wants to converse to pass the time. As the nonexpert talks more and more about the wine, the expert becomes increasingly annoyed at his companion's ignorance. Both are making statements, perhaps asking and answering questions, and performing the same speech acts, in terms of standard speech act theories, but each participant has a different aim in the conversation. The two are at cross-purposes conversationally.

In the following two chapters I will freely and eclectically draw on concepts from the various taxonomies. But I want to focus on an aspect of speech that is a combination of function and genre—one that involves the degree of accuracy and precision required in various types of discourse.

Speakers may discuss wines for scientific purposes, and chapter 10 is concerned with scientific language, the major goal of which is informational: reporting facts, constructing hypotheses, and, at least in the case of wine, making appraisals. The key, to use Hymes's terminology, is serious and painstaking. One salient point about scientific language, however, is that it must serve as an adequate communicative vehicle for a whole scientific community in which personal contact among all the individuals is not possible. Members of this community must agree on the reference and denotation of words as well as on the intralinguistic relationships, since much of the communication will take place through impersonal channels—namely, scientific publications. The reader cannot ask the writer for clarification of what is meant by a particular word.

We have a rather different situation in the case of an informal conversation among participants who are tasting the wine while discussing it. In such a case there is less of a need for the language of the speaker to meet any external public criterion of established use. I call this use of language *critical communication*—a term taken from Eisenberg (1954)—and it is discussed in chapter 11. Also in chapter 11 I will briefly discuss phatic and poetic uses of wine language; and finally, in chapter 12 I will compare talking about wine with parallel phenomena in psychology—namely, talking about feelings and perceptions.

Chapter 10
The Development of Scientific Language

Many philosophers of language have given priority to the scientific use of language. Logical positivists in the earlier part of the century deplored the imprecision of ordinary language, and some (Carnap 1937, for example) set out to construct artificial languages to remedy the defects. Even among those philosophers who made ordinary language a subject of philosophical investigation, there remained an implicit bias in favor of precise use of language, mainly for the purpose of expressing truths, which in turn gave rise to truth conditional theories of meaning. Even Grice (1975) in his seminal paper "Logic and conversation" takes information sharing as the goal of conversation and so proposes such maxims as "Make your contribution as informative as is required" (45) and "Do not say that for which you lack adequate evidence" (46). Austin (1962), in extending a philosophical interest to illocutionary acts other than constatives, still focused on "serious" uses of language and treated remarks like jokes as parasitic.[1]

In the modern technological world it is easy to understand why scientific language has come to be seen as important: since science has been so successful in solving problems, discovering truths about the universe, and creating things for better living, shouldn't we all try to do everything scientifically, even talk scientifically?

Bloomfield (1939) presents an idealization of scientific language that perhaps is commonly accepted as a goal, if not a reality: "The use of language in science is specialized and peculiar. In a brief speech the scientist manages to say things which in ordinary language would require a vast amount of talk. His hearers respond with great accuracy and uniformity" (219). Bloomfield throughout emphasizes the standardization of scientific language. The meaning of a technical term, he writes, "is fixed by an agreement of definition, which receives explicit formulation and strict adherence" (256).

In this chapter I will argue that Bloomfield is indeed correct in suggesting that scientific language is special. In fact, I want to suggest that *precise* language is something special—a marked form of the language. But the need for precision arises only under certain circumstances, for example, when drafting legislation or doing science. I will survey three disciplines in which practitioners are aware of the linguistic problems and have suggested remedies. I am particularly concerned with the problem of observational statements. Do different observers apply the same language in the same ways?

Many difficulties exist even after brushing aside a number of interesting deep philosophical problems. Hanson (1958) and Kuhn (1962) point out that observations may be theory-laden;[2] that is, what one observes is influenced by one's beliefs, expectations, and previous experiences. A behaviorist, for example, would never observe a client manifesting an Oedipus complex. The problem of theory-laden perception is important, but observers can disagree on descriptions even when they share a perspective. I will only discuss cases where people in a field share a theoretical position.

In certain physical sciences, e.g., physics and chemistry, descriptive statements involving perceptual terms like *blue* or *hot* have been replaced by a different set of concepts—color by wave length, temperature by molecular motion, substances like water by molecular formulae. This provides the scientist with a much greater degree of precision than can be found in the vocabulary of any natural language—though many of the scientific terms (names of elements, for instance) are recycled back into the nontechnical vocabulary. An advantage, in addition to the precision gained, is that the terms can acquire universal use, and translation problems of finding an equivalent for *blue* in a language that does not distinguish *blue* from *green*, or which distinguishes *light blue* from *dark blue,* can be avoided. A substance can be described as having a wave length between 450 and 460 nanometers or with a peak of 460 nanometers.[3]

The social sciences present another picture, however. One major concern of the social sciences is the way people perceive, think, and categorize; therefore, scientists cannot *in principle* replace statements of perception and judgment with mechanical or instrumental measurements unless it can be proved that there is a one-to-one correlation between the judgments and the measurement. But this kind of correlation is often not found. One of the major results of acoustic studies of speech has been that perceived sounds cannot be placed in a one-to-one correspondence with the physical signal. In taste, the traditional four basic tastes—sweet, sour, bitter, and salty—have behavioral validity but do not correspond to electrophysiological measurements (Amerine, Panghorn, & Roessler 1965:54; Dethier 1975:225).[4]

An interesting philosophical problem concerns the extent to which different observers share the same perceptual mechanism. This is known as the inverted spectrum problem, but for our purposes we could talk about an inverted palate. Could it be that what tastes salty to me tastes bitter to you and what tastes bitter to me is salty to you? This difference would never show up in our language if we learn to use these words by ostension. A sample of NaCl, for instance, would be labelled *salty,* and everyone would describe this substance as *salty,* but how can we know that everyone has identical (or similar) perceptions?

For scientific purposes (and maybe philosophical ones as well) it is reasonable to assume that the perceptual mechanisms of human beings are quite similar. However, one can legitimately ask whether different individuals are equally sensitive in making discriminations, and here individual differences do show up both in threshold levels and limits of differentiation. There are standard tests for determining whether a person is color-blind, and there are tests that show how well individuals make other sensory discriminations, i.e., how well they perceive pitch, loudness, pressure, heat, cold, tastes, smells. Individuals who are unable to make certain kinds of discriminations are weeded out as potential scientists in some disciplines. Taste-blind individuals would not be promising winemakers, for instance, and people who have trouble distinguishing pitch and tone would be well advised not to become phoneticians. In these cases there are physical or chemical measurements that can be correlated with perception. But in cases where there is no observer-independent method of measuring stimuli, the problems are more difficult, and additional assumptions have to be made; as, for instance, in determining whether two individuals who report sadness or happiness are experiencing the same feeling or whether one can correlate degrees of sadness across individuals.

When we look at technical vocabularies for various disciplines, we need to ask who should fix the denotation of words and arbitrate disagreements. Putnam's theory of the linguistic division of labor (as described in chapter 3) is attractive. An important part of a scientist's education is learning the vocabulary and how to apply it. A scientist writing for the profession assumes that the technical words he uses denote the same things for his readers.[5]

JUDGING FOOD AND WINE

The food and wine industry in investigating the problem of sensory judgment has found that considerable training is required to obtain reliable judges. Judges need to be carefully selected and screened on the basis of their sensitivity, since few people are equally proficient for all products, and each judge varies in his discriminatory abilities from time to time (Amerine, Panghorn, & Roessler, 1965:275ff). Even acute tasters for most stimuli can be insensitive to a particular taste or smell, and occasionally one compound will produce different sensations in different people (Williams 1975:573). Caul reports that it takes six months to a year to train a reliable panel of tasters to use a vocabulary where "all panel members know the exact connotation of each descriptive term applied to the product under study." (1957:28).

The most careful training of panel members for judging flavor that I am aware of is being undertaken by A. Williams and his co-workers at the Long Ashton Research Station in Bristol, England (Williams 1975; Williams & Carter 1977). Williams has investigated sensory judgments of apple cider and perry (a beverage made from pears) and has begun work on wine. In judging the ciders and perries, a panel of twenty-five individuals (sixteen males and nine females) worked to develop a vocabulary and assessment sheet. A final list of 163 words and phrases were collected; 10 for appearance, 125 for aroma, and 28 for taste (Williams 1975). A collection of standard odors was assembled, and samples of each were absorbed into paraffin and stored in small bottles. Panel members could consult the samples at any time to compare the smell in an experimental cider with the standard odor. For example, if a panelist wanted to check and verify whether a particular cider was *earthy*, he could compare the smell of the cider to the standard "earthy" sample.

Williams (personal communication) reported that the first panel required a year of semiweekly sessions to develop a satisfactory vocabulary and learn to use it accurately. However, subsequent panels could be trained in three months. Panelists were continuously tested for reliability, and if a panelist did not receive a minimum score on consistency and discrimination at a particular session, his responses were not tabulated in the judgments and evaluations for that session. (No panelists had to be disqualified from all the testing, however.)

The vocabulary that emerged from the panel is presented in Table 40 (Williams 1975:574–75). Some of the terms are also used in wine tasting. It is interesting to note that the majority of the terms are based on comparisons with other well-known smells: *like onions, like roses, like bananas, like caramel; rubbery, soapy, catty* (the smell of tomcats).

The panelists not only described the samples of cider and perries but also evaluated them using a 0 to 5 scale for intensity of odor (in each of the 11 odor classes) for complexity, and for appropriateness of each adjective listed in Table 40. Williams emphasizes that tasting is a dynamic process and that panelists continue to improve—often noticing new flavors and adding vocabulary or modifying old vocabulary. Most panels change membership over time, and the question of consistency of judgment is a problem. Williams reports (personal communication) that panel satisfaction is higher when members take part in developing the vocabulary to be used than when a ready-made vocabulary is provided. However, if each panel develops its own words and rules for application, there is no guarantee that valid comparisons can be made among panels.

In general, the main interest in assessing food and wine lies in evaluating the products; description is secondary. One may wish to point out the nature of the virtues and defects, but the ultimate goal is an overall value judgment. In judging wines the Davis 20-point scoring method has been widely adopted (Amerine & Roessler

TABLE 40: Categories of Odors for Describing Ciders and Perries

Odour class	Profile sheet adjective number and description	Composition
I. Cough provoking/ irritating	1. Choking, like SO_2	75 µl 5% sulphur dioxide solution
	2. Like high concentration of acetaldehyde	75 µl acetaldehyde
	3. Like high concentration of amyl alcohol	75 µl 3-methylbutanol
	4. Like high concentration of acetic acid	75 µl acetic acid
II. Sharp	6. Like rhubarb	500 µl ethanolic extract natural rhubarb
	7. Like acetic acid	15 µl acetic acid
III. Dry/alcoholic/ fuselly	8. Like ethanol	500–1000 µl ethanol
	9. Like higher alcohols	5–10 µl 3-methylbutanol
	10. Like ethyl acetate	5–10 µl ethyl acetate
	11. Like low concentration of acetaldehyde	5–10 µl acetaldehyde
	12/13. Green	2–5 µl hex-3-enol or 10–20 µl hexanol
IV. Musty	14. Earthy	—
	15. Cardboard	—
	16. Mousey/biscuity	2–5 µl concentrated ether extract of acetamide
V. Sour/stale	17. Like acetic acid (sour character)	10–15 µl acetic acid
	18. Rancid	2–5 µl butyric acid
	19. Old horse	5 mg 2-phenylacetic acid
	20. Fatty	5 µl 2,4-decadienal solution
	21. Soapy	500 mg unperfumed soap
VI. Sulphury	22. Rubbery	2 ml water in which rubber tubing had been boiled
	23. Like bad eggs	Hydrogen sulphide bubbled through molten paraffin wax
	24. Like cooked cabbage	5–10 µl methyl mercaptan
	25. Catty	(i) Catty cider distillate (ii) 10–15 µl p-menthion-8-thiol
	26. Like onions	2–5 µl allyl disulphide
	27. Like shrimps	2–5 ml dimethyl sulphide
VII. Yeasty	28. Like mushrooms	20 µl commerical essence
	29. Like yeast extract	500 mg of "Marmite"
	30. Like dough	500 µl decanted liquor from yeast culture
VIII. Scented	31. Like cucumber (fragrant character)	2–5 µl commercial cucumber essence
	32. Like roses	25–50 µl 2-phenylethanol

continued

Odour class	Profile sheet adjective number and description	Composition
IX. Fruity	34. Like strawberries	2–5 μl commercial essence
	35. Like bananas	2–5 μl commercial essence
	36. Like pineapples	2–5 μl commercial essence
	37. Like pears	2–5 μl commercial essence
	38. Like peardrops	5–10 μl 3-methylbutyl acetate
	39. Like apples	(i) 5–10 μl hexylacetate
		(ii) 2–5 μl ethyl 2-methyl butyrate
		(iii) 5–10 μl natural apple essence
X. Sugary/cooked	41. Like raisins/sweet sherry	10–20 μl commercial red grape essence
	42. Like diacetyl	5–10 μl diacetyl
	43. Like caramel	1 g commercial caramel essence
	44. Like black treacle	1 g commercial back treacle
XI. Phenolic/spicy/ bittersweet	45. Phenolic/carbolic	10–20 μl phenol
	46. Pharmaceutical	2–5 ml methyl salicylate
	47. Like bittersweet cider	(i) 2–5 μl 4-ethylphenol
		(ii) Natural bittersweet cider
	48. Spicy (1) ethyl guaiacol	2–5 μl 4-ethyl guaiacol
	49. Spicy (2) allspice	250 mg allspice
	50. Like celery	2–5 μl commercial celery essence

Reprinted from Williams (1975) by permission.

1976). Wines are evaluated according to the characteristics given in Table 41 with certain weights given for each category. The original score card overemphasized volatile acidity (which was taken to be a vinegary smell) and underemphasized bouquet and aroma. Bitterness and astringency were not distinguished, and the difference between flavor and general quality was not made clear (Amerine & Roessler 1976:123). A modified Davis score card has been proposed which would eliminate the category of volatile acidity and give aroma and bouquet a weight of 6. Since most scientific studies on the evaluation of experimental wines in the United States have taken place at the University of California, Davis, and since the Davis 20-point score card has been used there for many years, it has become a standard measurement tool.[6]

A wine project to determine the feasibility of producing commer-

TABLE 41: Davis 20-Point Score Card

CHARACTERISTIC	WEIGHT		
	Davis Original	Davis Modified	Four Corners Modified
Appearance	2	2	2
Color	2	2	
Aroma & bouquet	4	6	6
Volatile acidity	2	—	—
Total acidity	2	2	2
Sweetness	1	1	1
Body	1	1	1
Flavor	2	2	2
Bitterness (astringency in earlier versions)	2	2	2
General quality	2	2	4

Ratings: superior (17-20); standard (13-16); below standard (9-12); unacceptable or spoiled (1-8)

cial wines in the Four Corners States (Arizona, Utah, New Mexico, Colorado) has been in progress since 1976 (Dutt, Mielke, & Wolfe 1977). The panel, of which I was a member during 1977 and 1978, experimented with several score cards—the Davis card, a Four Corners modified version, and score cards involving only hedonic scales. Hedonic scales measure quality based on the "pleasure that the judge finds in the wine" (Amerine & Roessler 1976:129). The modified Davis score card used in the Four Corners project lumped appearance and color together for a total of 2, gave aroma and bouquet 6, eliminated volatile acidity, and gave 4 points to general quality (see Table 41). Although the panel preferred this score card, the directors of the project decided to have panelists use the unmodified Davis score card on the experimental wines so that the results would be more clearly comparable to published studies which were based on that system.

The criticism I have most often heard about the Davis score card, and the one that most bothered the Four Corners wine tasting panel, is that the rules for assigning numbers to a wine in each category tend to emphasize defects. One takes points off for a wine if it is not clear, not the right color for its type, if there is vinegar in the aroma, and if there is sugar in a wine that is supposed to be dry. As a result, an ordinary, even mediocre, wine can end up with a fairly high score, 15 or 16, simply if it has no defects.

At first some panelists, when they had totaled the points assigned and decided that the overall score was too high for that wine in terms of the ratings (superior, standard, etc.), would go back and subtract a fraction of a point from the various categories. Later the panel developed a different strategy: judges used the categories of flavor and general quality as fudge factors and would assign a 0 to a wine in each of these two classes if it was ordinary and no points could be taken off elsewhere for defects. Amerine & Roessler point out that the definitions of *superior, standard, below standard,* and *unacceptable or spoiled* have varied from judge to judge depending on the experience and severity of judgment of the tasters. However, highly skilled and experienced judges have learned to use the score card with "remarkable precision" (1976:124).

The person who trained the Four Corners project panel received his Ph.D. in Viticulture and Enology from the University of California at Davis and was thoroughly trained in the use of that score card. The panel was trained for four months at weekly sessions, where judges were given eight to ten wines—all of the same varietal—and asked to score them, sometimes using the original Davis card, sometimes the Four Corners modified version, and often both in order to compare the various score cards. Occasionally a score card consisting only of a hedonic scale (1 to 9) was included as well, but the hedonic scale was never used alone. After the panel had tasted and rated the wines, the project director discussed each wine with the panel. He first elicited the panel members' judgments, then gave his own score and explained why he assigned that rating.

The panel tasted experimental wines during 1977, 1978, and 1979. Membership on the panel changed somewhat over the three years, but half of the panel remained during the three years. (There were ten to twelve panelists during any year, but not all attended every session.) The director left after two years, and his place was taken by one of the other researchers, who was not from Davis but who had participated in the training of panels as well as all the other aspects of the tastings.

The directors of the Four Corners wine project let me look at the data collected over the three-year period. I arbitrarily selected the data from three different tastings: March 1977, March 1978, and March 1979. In the 1977 group, the panel was newly assembled. The second (1978) group had been meeting together for three months, and at least half of the panelists had participated the year before. The last group (1979) was composed largely of members from the previous year's panel.

To check for group consistency, F-ratios were calculated on the variance for the three groups. The average variance on the wines at each session was calculated for each group (Table 42). On the basis of the average variance, F-ratios were calculated for groups I and II, II and III, and I and III. As the figures in the fourth column show, the

TABLE 42: Group Consistency: Four Corners Wine Project Panel, 1977–79

	Panel	Number on Panel	Number of Wines	Average s^2	F-ratios
I	1977	10	6	5.98	I – II
II	1978	7	8	2.71	II – III
III	1979	6	8	1.06	I – III

average variance declined. However, the only F-ratio that reached statistical significance ($P > 0.05$) was that which compared panels I and III. That is, the improvement in consensus between I and II or between II and III was not significant at the 0.05 level, but the difference between the inexperienced and the most experienced group was. This small sample at least shows that members of the most experienced panel had learned to use the Davis chart consensually.

ONCOLOGY

In oncology the American Joint Committee for Cancer Staging and End Results Reporting has developed a method of classifying cancers based on the life history or progression of a cancer, rather than on alternative systems such as prognosis or therapeutic criteria. The life history of a cancer (or at least the earliest point at which it can be discovered) begins with a primary tumor.

> As the primary tumor increases in size . . . local invasion occurs, followed by spread to the regional lymph nodes draining the area of the tumor. . . . It is usually later, and often in the middle or oldest period of life span of the cancer, that distant spread or metastasis becomes evident. . . . (1977:1)

Tumors are subclassified T_1, T_2, T_3, etc., on the basis of their size, depth, invasion onto adjacent or surrounding structures, and mobility or fixation of the tumor to another structure. There are a different number of T's for each part of the body, and the definitions differ as well. For example, the size of the tumor assigned a T_2 for the tongue is "between 2 and 4 centimeters," whereas T_2 for the esophagus is "a tumor that involves more than 5 cm of esophageal length without extra-esophageal spread. . . ." Cancer in nodes and metastases are also subclassified in an analogous way: N_1, N_2, . . . ; M_0, . . . M_2. The vocabulary for T, N, and M has a relatively simple intralinguistic structure. All oncologists would agree that a T_3 for a given body site is larger and more serious than a T_1. The parts of the definitions that rely on a precise and universally accepted measuring system, such as 2 cm, are unproblematic.

A problem arises because some of the terms are somewhat vague—in particular terms like *early, localized,* and *resectable.* It is *assumed* that clinicians working independently in different places and trained in different medical schools apply these terms in identical ways, but there is no guarantee that they do so. Since one major purpose of the classification system is to evaluate alternative forms of treatment, if different clinicians apply these terms differently the results will be biased. For example, if one oncologist reports an 80 percent remission rate for T_3, N_1, M_0 in a particular body site, while another reports only a 60 percent rate, we want to know whether the first has a better therapy or whether his patients are better because the categorization is different from that of the second oncologist. Maybe he merely diagnoses patients as having a more serious cancer than the oncologist with the lower remission rate.

There are such discrepancies in the published research results, and several explanations are possible. It could be that some therapies are better or it could be that the theoretical vocabulary is inappropriate. That is, it might be the case that a T_2 for the esophagus should be between 5 and 10 cm rather than between 2 and 5. But it is important not to overlook the hypothesis that different clinicians are diagnosing in subtly different ways—that is, applying the observation terms differently.

PHONETICS

The last field I wish to look at is a part of linguistics—namely phonetics. The question is to what extent linguists and phoneticians apply the phonetic symbols in the same way. On this point, Ladefoged writes:

> It is odd that linguists, who pride themselves on the rigor and scientific nature of many of their concepts, should nevertheless be so tolerant of vague, unverified statements in some parts of the field. . . .
> We need valid phonetic descriptions for two principal reasons. First, a linguist cannot give a comprehensive account of the phonology of a language unless he knows all the phonetic facts; if the original observations made in the field are inadequate, the subsequent analysis is liable to be faulty. Secondly, a linguist usually wants his analysis to be capable of interpretation in phonetic terms. This is obviously the case if the analysis was made for a practical purpose such as teaching the pronunciation of a language. But even if no such purpose is intended, it is still desirable; any account of a language which states simply the phonemic system is obviously not as complete as one which both states that and also gives a phonetic descriptions of the actual sounds in different contexts.
> A phonetic description can be considered to be adequate only if it has the same meaning for all who use it. It is, of course, impossible to find out whether a given description will actually be interpreted in the same way by all the linguists who are likely to read it. But it is quite possible to see whether the members of a particular group of linguists are capable of making descriptions which are meaningful within that group. (Ladefoged 1960:387–88)

After showing that articulatory and acoustic descriptions of sounds are not accurate enough, Ladefoged turns to auditory descriptions, particularly the auditory system devised for vowels by Daniel Jones. This system is based on eight cardinal vowels of more or less acoustic equidistance, which were standardized by Jones, who insisted that "the values of the cardinal vowels cannot be learnt from written descriptions; they should be learnt by oral instruction from a teacher who knows them" (Jones, quoted in Ladefoged 1960:390).

Ladefoged wanted to discover to what extent phoneticians described sounds in the same way. He used fifteen subjects trained in the British tradition of linguistic phonetics. This group included professors and graduate students, both native Britons and foreigners. There were three additional subjects: a Swede, an American, and an Englishman, all noted phoneticians who were acquainted with the Jones system but not trained in it. The eighteen subjects were asked to judge the quality of ten Gaelic vowels and describe them in terms of the cardinal vowels. (None of the subjects knew this variety of Gaelic.)

Results showed that the judgments of the fifteen subjects trained in the British system were more in agreement than those of the three other subjects. Moreover, the three not trained in the British system did not agree very closely with each other.

> All the last three subjects were well-known linguists, accepted scholars in their fields, with a knowledge of many different languages and considerable experience of dialectology. Each of them had spent many years doing fieldwork and research and had published articles involving descriptions of the sounds of speech. They thus had a higher professional standing and a great deal more experience than (the four) subjects . . . who were post-graduate students of the University of Edinburgh. But they are relatively unable to communicate in writing with one another in an unambiguous way about the quality of a vowel sound. (391)

In judging a few words there was a systematic difference between subjects trained in phonetics at the University of London and those trained at the University of Edinburgh. Finally, the differences among the subjects were greater when the Gaelic vowel did not coincide with a cardinal vowel than when it did. Lagefoged concluded that different phoneticians with different training, relying solely on written descriptions, do not provide sufficiently precise and meaningful statements.

Phonological theory and concerns have changed somewhat since Ladefoged's paper appeared. In particular, not all linguists take it as obvious, as the Bloomfieldians and Firthians did, that an accurate, detailed phonetic description necessarily serves as the foundation of phonological description. And in recent years there has been relatively greater concern with morphophonemic alteration and less with what used to be called allophonic variation. On the other hand, there has been a growing concern with phonological universals, and presumably in order to make valid cross-language comparisons, one would need accurate phonetic descriptions. Ladefoged's conclusion is just as important today as it was two decades ago. There is no reason to think that this problem has been remedied.

It is no longer necessary to rely solely on written descriptions, since high-quality recordings are routinely made in doing fieldwork. At the same time, the possibility exists of making available to all linguists everywhere a standard set of sounds. These would then be used to train future phoneticians. If such a standard existed and were adopted, there would be a good reason to think that all phoneticians, wherever they were trained, would be making precise, meaningful, phonetic descriptions.

SUMMARY

Each scientific discipline has its vocabulary, along with definitions of the items in it. Ideally all scientists in that field would know the vocabulary and agree on the intralinguistic relationships. However, even if this were the case, it would not follow that they applied the words in the same way. This problem may be minimal in many of the natural sciences in which an important part of the vocabulary is defined in part operationally and in which measurements are made on instruments calibrated according to international standard. However, scientists in the social sciences are not so well off. It should be possible to find out how much agreement there is among scientists in different places, but one may ask whether it is worth the effort. The margin of error may be acceptable. At any rate, awareness of the possibility of different groups of social scientists applying expressions in ways that differ systematically should be kept in mind as a source of miscommunication.

POSTSCRIPT: VARIATION IN NAMING

The kinds of observations and distinctions discussed in this chapter involve fairly subtle properties and qualities. When mature speakers are asked to name and distinguish between rather different objects or properties, such as a cup and a bowl (Labov 1978) or a chair and a sofa (Faust 1978), they have no trouble. If pictures of objects are used that are borderline, variation of response can be observed. Just how much variation is tolerated may vary from community to community, and of course the semantic domain would also be a relevant factor. Two interesting examples reported in the anthropological literature by Heider (1975) and Rosoldo (1972) show two communities where extreme imprecision is found in naming objects.

Heider, in his studies of the Dani of New Guinea, gave a naming task to Dani men from two different groups who were asked to name twenty-five stone adze blades at two different times. Heider selected twenty-five tools, taped a number on each one, and put them in a bag so that they could be drawn out randomly. All the men in Heider's study were over thirty and were functioning adults who had been using stone tools before steel ones were introduced. Previous ethnographic research had convinced Heider that all normal men were equally expert in their knowledge of stone adze blades, since they all traded for them and used them and sharpened them. (The division of expertise was true of some realms of Dani culture, but not of this one.) There were seven men from one region and five from another. Each man individually was asked to name each of the twenty-five adze blades; and the task was repeated at a later time (nine days to three months later). Each man gave all answers without hesitation. During the session five men changed their minds on a name a total of six times (out of 300 responses). Both groups used a large number of names. "The most remarkable result was not the disagreement between the men, . . . but rather the inconsistency between the first and the second namings of each man" (1975:11). Heider discusses various possible explanations and rules out possibilities such as a large number of synonyms or the use of descriptions. No informant responded with two names. "In the six cases where a second word was given, the first word was withdrawn. . . . In summary, the evidence on naming stone adze blades shows that the Dani have a large vocabulary which they use with considerable inconsistency" (17). Heider goes on to compare this behavior to other Dani behavioral patterns and concludes that "although the Dani do have many names in their vocabulary, they do not invest the psychic or intellectual energy necessary to keep the words ordered in a systematic fashion" (19).

Rosaldo (1972) studied the Ilongots (in the Philippines) with respect to the names they gave to plants used for particular kinds of spells. The spells could be performed by anyone at any moment of misfortune. The practitioner would collect appropriate plants, including various types of orchids. "The practitioner uses whatever words, whatever metaphors, seem appropriate" (1972:85). Rosaldo found no regularity in the magical usage. Inconsistencies appeared at all levels, and the "Ilongots themselves did not seem troubled by the irregularities; when two men called one plant by different names and I asked for an explanation, they answered that each had learned the words from his own father—of course they didn't agree" (86). Plants used only for spells could be identified by thirteen different labels. Informants not only disagreed among themselves but were inconsistent in their own use. Body part terms were used to name orchids, but any body part term could be used for any kind of orchid. "If an informant is asked to label any one kind of orchid, he may call it at one time 'their fingers,' at another 'their thighs,' and so on . . . In any one context, Ilongots insist that the name they are giving is the name for the orchid in question" (90). On the other hand, names for peas were more stable, and the names for poisonous peas were consistently distinguished from names for edible kinds. Rosoldo explains that the magical practitioner has no need to discriminate kinds of orchids used for spells. "He uses orchid names largely to signify the name of plants in his set." She concludes that the importance and stability of lexical variation depends on the importance of the discrimination (87).

Chapter 11
Nonscientific Uses of Language

CRITICAL COMMUNICATION

Wine talk, as we have seen, shares some properties with other kinds of aesthetic discourse. It is in fact interesting to note that many of the wine descriptors listed in chapter 1 are also found in descriptions of music and art: *austere, balanced, charming, complex, empty, flamboyant, forceful, graceful, insipid, majestic, rough, soft, sweet,* and *warm,* to mention a few.[1] Some aestheticians have been concerned with the language used to describe works of art and more specifically with the function of criticism. Of the aesthetics literature I have read, the best piece I have found in helping to understand wine conversation outside of a scientific setting is Isenberg's article "Critical Communication" (1954).

The function of criticism, writes Isenberg, is "to bring about communication at the level of the senses, that is to induce a sameness of vision, of experienced content" (1954:138). The critic tries to point out something—to get the hearer to see or perceive some nonobvious thing, property, or quality in a work of art or a piece of music. "Criticism does not actually designate the qualities to which it somehow directs our attention" (140), and so to read criticism "otherwise than in the presence, or with direct recollect, of the objects discussed is a blank and senseless employment" (139).

Wine talk among people who are drinking and discussing the

same wine seems primarily to serve this function. Suppose two individuals are drinking a wine together and A says to B, "Do you notice the *earthy* quality, especially strong in the aftertaste?" If B then notices that property, A's communication has succeeded, even if wine experts would deny that the property in question was earthiness. And if two different individuals, C and D, are drinking the same wine, but C calls this property *chalky,* and D thereby notice the same property, then his communication would succeed as well. Suppose further that E describes the very same property as *metallic* and successfully gets F to pick it out. In all cases, if the speaker gets the hearer to notice something, then the communication is successful. Semantically, *earthy, chalky,* and *metallic* contrast, so from a standard, normative scientific point of view, they cannot all be right. But with respect to critical communication, the point is that the question of correctness is irrelevant. The only thing necessary is accord.

This view is in some ways analogous to Donnellan's position on definite descriptions (1966). Donnellan argues that some (but not all) definite descriptions function to pick out a referent. Even if a description is inaccurate, if it succeeds in getting the hearer to pick out the referent correctly, then the sentence might be true. For example, if someone says "The man with the martini is a philosopher," and the man in question is actually holding a glass of Perrier water with an olive in it, if the hearer picks out the referent correctly, and if that man is in fact a philosopher, then the utterance, according to Donnellan, is true.

Most of the examples that Donnellan and other philosophers use contain descriptions whose truth is rather easy to assess: *the man with the martini, the woman in the red dress, the boy in the corner.* When we look at wine descriptions, the truth of such statements is much harder to determine, and for scientific purposes we call on experts: is the salient property in the wine *earthiness* or *chalkiness* or *metal?* In critical communication truth plays a secondary role. The function of an utterance like *a bit of earthiness on the back of the palate in the aftertaste* is not to state a truth but to point out a quality. Isenberg's main point about critical communication is that since these kinds of utterances look like other kinds of statements, philosophers have been misled into trying to analyze them like other kinds of statements. Isenberg, following other widely held theories of criticism, distinguishes between a judgment or verdict (V), e.g., *this is good,* and a reason (R), e.g., *because it has such-and-such a quality* (131). But "the truth of R never adds the slightest weight to V, because R does not designate any quality the perception of which might induce us to assert to V" (139).

Yet there are limits to attaching words to properties. *Sweet* and *burnt rubber* cannot be used interchangeably for the identical property. "The links between aesthetic qualities and non-aesthetic ones are both obvious and vital. Aesthetic concepts, all of them, carry with them attachments and in one way or another are tethered to or parasitic upon non-aesthetics features" (Sibley 1959:442). The more definite the denotation of a word, the less likely it is to be extended in the wine realm. Conversely, the easier it is to identify a property of a wine, the easier it is to label it with a common and widely used descriptor. The difficult and interesting cases are those where the speaker gropes for an appropriate term—groping because the property is subtle and the perfect word does not leap to mind. It is in these cases that words are selected creatively and imaginatively.

Transcriptions of the experimental wine sessions reveal the process of critical communication. At these sessions people were required to talk about the wine, but the kinds of things said were very much like the spontaneous comments and natural wine conversations I have observed. The first illustration is with four Tucson subjects at a pre-session, where the four are trying to describe a wine for the rest of the group to match later.

E: Oh, there's something in Z. When you smell it, before you drink it.

W: Yes, I smelled it when I first sat down. You just take a sniff . . . .

E: I think burnt rubber.

D: Burnt rubber! . . . I think it smells woody or something.

W: I think it smells perfumy.

E: Woody. I said straw—old . . .

W: Aftersmell of some woodhue.

E: Woody is not bad, it seems.

A: Reminiscent of a woody perfume.

E: But only at the first smell.

D: Vegetable or something organic.

W: It's organic to me. It smells like 401 labs.

E: Maybe it's slightly rotten . . . I feel there's a chemical. Chemical seems to be right . . . medicinal. I feel that about this. It's not a natural grape.

W: Almost plastic.

E: Straw.

Another example can be seen where speakers are trying to describe astringency. Compare the way two different groups of speakers characterize this word and property. In the first example, three wine tasters are describing a wine at a pre-session.

F: I'm talking about what it does to my tongue—not about how it actually tastes. Something physical that it does to my tongue.

L: Do you find a sort of—what's the word—cotton candy? But not candy—cotton mouth?

A: Puckery.

L: Yeah, and dry.

F: Yeah. I think I would go with that.

The second excerpt is from a session in which the speakers try to characterize the difference between tannin and acid.

E: It seems to me that acidity and tannin are hard to distinguish.

O: Yeah, how *do* you distinguish those?

E: Acidic strikes me as the contrast between grapefruit and milk. Roughly, with grapefruity being acidic and milk being flat . . .

O: What is tannin?

E: It's an acid, and it's a puckery quality.

O: Aha!

E: So astringency or tannin tends to be an unpleasant sharpness. Right? Puckery. . . .

R: Persimmons.

E: Acidic isn't necessarily unpleasant. Grapefruit, for instance. But astringency is a sort of unpleasant harshness. I would say, as contrasted with—just goes down awfully smooth. Velvety, or soft.

O: If you were thinking about, say you were eating pork or something, wouldn't astringency be a kind of nice thing? Wipe out the grease?

E: Yeah. You'd want something with tannin or acidity. One or the other would do.

N: Have you ever had a cup of tea that was too strong? Took a mouthful, and it made the inside or your mouth feel dry?

In both cases the speakers draw on comparisons, calling up other similar experiences, but rather different comparisons are used— cotton in one case, tea in the other.

Two of the Davis subjects were discussing a wine in the matching experiment (unfortunately their conversation did not result in a match):

C: Now, my remaining number is 52. Just mediocre red wine, probably jug wine, and it has a kind of strange smell.

L: Sort of has a Valley smell to it? . . . Valley—overripe grape almost?

C: No, it smells like . . .

L: Filter pads.

C: Something like that, you know, that smell [when] you walk into a dentist's office.

L: Yeah.

C: That kind of smell.

L: I would call that filter pad.

If scientific language is judged by criteria of correctness, critical communication is judged by a criterion of success. The following excerpts from the communication experiment illustrate a case where matching did not succeed. The first excerpt is from the pre-session, where four subjects selected descriptions for the others to match.[2] Since the small group agreed, *their* critical communication was successful.

E: I think this wine is spicy with dill or something.

W: [Expresses disagreement.]

D: Smell is sort of dill.

W: I agree on the spicy, but—

E: Not dill. Hm.

D: This one (O) is just sort of spicy and tangy, and this one (F) is really pungent.

E: Not dill. Huh. Some vegetable though.

The final description eventually agreed on was *spicy bouquet, spicy on the palate, tangy, intermediate in flavor* and *body, good character.* However, this description was inadequate for some speakers. Below are comments made by subjects after they had matched their wines with the comments of the small group and learned the results:

H: I had trouble with the word *spicy.* How do people usually use that? I don't think of oregano.

E: How would *dill* have been? Would that have been helpful?

O: That would have been much better. *Spicy* I think of maybe cinnamon.

H: When I think of *spicy,* I think of the sweet side—I think of spice cake rather than garlic pizza.

E: What do you think about *spicy?*

N: Think same things, spice cake.

E: Yeah, I thought *dill* or *oregano*—in that direction.

A: Would *herbal* have been better?

E: *Herbal.* That would have been better.

H: Yeah.

Although I have stressed the distinction between scientific and critical communication, where in the first case it is important that speakers use language conventionally and agree on the meaning and denotation of words and in the second case it is not important, I now want to blur that distinction somewhat. In our society there is a strong belief in linguistic correctness. Many of my nonexpert subjects were apologetic about not knowing how to use the wine descriptors correctly. When people drink a wine together and try to describe and characterize it, this activity provides a way for speakers to check on the accuracy of their words and at the same time for individuals to check on their perception of reality—to find out if a wine is *salty* or *herbaceous.*

If speakers can agree on a characterization, they assume that their perceptions and their word use are conventional. If they disagree, they can try to determine whether the discrepancy is linguistic or perceptual. We have seen examples where the disagreement seemed linguistic; for example, the case above where *herbal* would have been a better descriptor than *spicy,* or a case described in chapter 5.

A: I tend to think it smells *perfumy*.
B: I don't think the smell is sweet enough to be called *perfumy*.
A: So *perfumy* is sweet to you.
B: Yes.

So where does this leave us? In critical communication, as long as the participants are satisfied with a description and as long as there is nothing jarring, then any words that are used to call attention to some property will do. The fact that experts might use different and inconsistent words is irrelevant. However, when there is a disagreement about descriptions, then the specter of correctness arises to challenge the linguistic (or possibly perceptual) competence of the speakers. If one conversational participant is clearly more knowledgeable about wine, the others will probably concede and accept the expert's judgment. If there are no experts, various outcomes are possible. But since there is a general belief that there are correct and mistaken descriptions (a belief which is perhaps controversial in aesthetic domains), then in case of disagreement, the conversationalists may be left wondering who is right and who is wrong. If experts disagree, then what do we do?

PHATIC COMMUNION

The use of language to check on one's perception of reality and to share an experience blends into another function of language — phatic communion. The concept of phatic communion is usually characterized as language used to establish and maintain social bonds. The term is taken from Malinowski (1953), and has been widely referred to, but in fact it has not been well explicated. Examples of phatic communion offered by Malinowski are "inquiries about health, comments on weather, affirmations of some supremely obvious state of things—all such are exchanged, not in order to inform, not in this case to connect people in action, certainly not in order to express any thought" (476). Malinowski relates the requirement to converse with "the well-known tendency (in all human beings) to congregate, to be together, to enjoy each other's company" (477).

The most extreme form of phatic communion involves talking to animals and babies. It may even be pushing the concept of phatic

communion to apply it to such creatures. There is a growing literature describing the ways adults speak to children and infants (e.g.,
Snow & Ferguson 1977). Ferguson (1964) mentions that speakers
use baby talk (forms used when talking to babies) for pets as well. It
is reasonable to assume that talking to infants and children is necessary to enable them to learn the language besides providing needed
emotional contact. But pets?

A survey I conducted among twenty-six undergraduate students
revealed that all respondents talked to their pets. All used greetings
and commands (which the animals could perhaps understand)[3]. But
twenty-one reported that they say things which their pets probably
could not understand. Explanations offered were "it makes me feel
better," "it comforts and soothes the animal," "it's better than talking
to oneself," or "the animal likes to be talked to." In fact all respondents said they believed their pets liked to be talked to. Twenty reported that they used a special tone of voice, but only fifteen said it
was the same tone they would use with an infant.

When one is talking to an infant or pet and saying something un-
intelligible to the "hearer," it does not really matter *what* is said, so
long as the tone of voice is appropriate. It may be easier for the
speaker to construct appropriate rather than inappropriate utterances—for example, "You're a nice little pussy cat" rather than "E
equals mass times c^2," uttered in the same tone of voice—just as it is
easier to produce grammatical utterances than deliberately ungrammatical ones. Some aspects of speech are so thoroughly learned
that it takes extra effort to violate the pattern. A parallel might be
found in human gatherings such as a crowded cocktail party or re-
ception line, where nobody is paying attention to content, and where
one can make outrageous remarks without being heard.

But in true phatic communion, it *does* matter what is said.
Malinowski has made too sharp a break between discourse used to
communicate thought and phatic communion (cf. Lyons 1968). "It's
a nice day" said non-ironically when the weather is ghastly is not
appropriate, nor is "Merry Christmas" appropriate at Easter time.

Gossip also serves the function of phatic communion:

Such gossip, as found in Primitive Societies, differs only a little from our
own. Always the same emphasis of affirmation and consent, mixed
perhaps with an incidental disagreement which creates the bonds of an-

tipathy. Or personal accounts of the speaker's views and life history, to which the hearer listens under some restraint and with slightly veiled impatience, waiting till his own turn arrives to speak. For in this use of speech the bonds created between hearer and speaker are not quite symmetrical, the man linguistically active receiving the greater share of social pleasure and self-enhancement. But though the hearing given to such utterances is as a rule not as intense as the speaker's own share, it is quite essential for his pleasure, and the reciprocity is established by the change of roles . . .

[Gossip] consists in just this atmosphere of sociability and in the fact of the personal communion of these people. But this is in fact achieved by speech, and the situation in all such cases is created by the exchange of words, by the specific feelings which form convivial gregariousness, by the give and take of utterances which make up ordinary gossip. The whole situation consists in what happens linguistically. Each utterance is an act serving the direct aim of binding hearer to speaker by a tie of some social sentiment or other. (Malinowski 1953:478–79)

To understand fully the function of gossip it is necessary to go beyond linguistics and into psychology and sociology—into theories of group cohesion and individual personality. Gluckman (1963) discusses the social functions of group cohesion served by gossip, stressing the rules and constraints about whom one may gossip with and about. Gossip keeps people in line, since individuals may behave conventionally to avoid being talked about.

There are also constraints on content which—though not as strict as in truth-seeking communicative speech—carry over to gossip. One can exaggerate, make up details, and make assertions without sufficient evidence, but one is not supposed to lie or make up facts and events. (Fiction is in a different category.) And after a topic is selected, the same rules of discourse and the same kinds of illocutionary acts are operative.

The speech corpus from my wine experiments does not contain much gossip because the sessions were task oriented. However, casual wine talk is commonly heard at social gatherings, where people express their preferences, relate their experiences, and display their knowledge. Such conversations still follow patterns characteristic of conversations for information-exchange. There are limits on what is acceptable, especially with the more descriptive parts of the vocabulary. A wine with 2 percent sugar could be described as *sweet* or *dry;* a wine with 10 percent sugar cannot be labeled *dry.* But the required precision is much lower than for scientific language. It is really only necessary to be in the right ballpark.

For the evaluative or descriptive-evaluative words, the speaker expresses his or her assessment and preferences, and such comments will be interpreted as such. Even if the hearer disagrees, he may not express his disagreement if the purpose of speaking is to pass time and/or establish a bond. The same is true of novel and imaginative descriptions, such as describing a wine as *roguish* or *disciplined* or *pretentious.* A puzzled hearer might ask for clarification if he is sufficiently interested in the topic to continue, but asking for justification would push the conversation out of phatic communion and into an information-exchanging conversation.

Phatic communion can probably not be sharply divided from critical communication. In the latter case, the speaker really wants to communicate something about the piece of art or wine or music. But the motivation for doing so may well stem from a wish to share an experience, and thus create a sense of communion. Although the clearest examples of phatic communion might be ritualistic and mechanical remarks (*it's a nice day; that's a good wine*), a conversation confined to such remarks does not create meaningful bonds between people because such remarks are too superficial, possibly insincere, and emotionally and intellectually insignificant.[4]

THE USE OF HUMOR

My wine studies have provided me with a corpus of discourse, and I have tried to look at different aspects of the semantics and pragmatics. Most of the utterances could be classified according to a speech act taxonomy and categorized as making a request, asking a question, answering a question, making a statement, or making an appraisal. The application of functional categories such as Jakobson's could be applied, but it is difficult to decide how to pigeonhole each utterance. Is a remark such as *This is a delicious wine* an instance of referential or phatic communication, or both? I have argued that the distinction is not always clear cut and that many utterances are multifunctional. In the wine corpus it is also hard to distinguish between metalinguistic and referential functions. A discussion about whether a particular wine is fruity or flowery can be looked at as one involving the properties of the wine itself *or* as the appropriateness of one word rather than another to a given property.

The wine corpus contains many humorous remarks that do not fit easily into the categories provided by functional classifications. Nor would it do simply to establish a new category for humorous remarks, since such comments serve a variety of purposes and overlap with established categories as well. Perhaps the closest category so far proposed is Jakobson's *aesthetic* function, where the form of the language gives pleasure. But this category is not quite right either. Hymes has proposed a category of jokes (1974), but this is a genre which contrasts with conversation. Hymes (1972) also distinguishes between mock and serious key, although a humorous remark can at some deeper level be serious.

Humor—jokes, puns, and other witticisms—is virtually ignored in speech act theories. Austin describes jokes and other nonserious uses of language as parasitic on other language function (1962:22). No taxonomy of speech acts or illocutionary acts lists humor. In many speech act theories joking and punning would not be illocutional acts, though it is possible to give such an account in which meaning, including the illocutionary act, is defined in terms of the speaker's intention and his attempt to bring about a recognition of that intention in the hearer. Thus joking would be characterized as an act whereby a speaker by saying X intends to amuse the hearer and to bring about an understanding in the hearer of the speaker's intention. In any case, whether joking can be considered as an illocutionary act, it certainly has an intended perlocutionary effect: to amuse the hearer, and/or get the hearer to think that the speaker is witty and clever (depending on whether joking is perceived altruistically or egotistically).

One problem in analyzing humor is that it must be examined at many levels. One level is conscious and intentional. Another level goes beyond linguistics and into psychology, where theories of humor intersect with theories of personality, interpersonal relationships, the unconscious, and more. Such theories propose that humor functions as tension release (Freud 1916; Bales 1950), veiled aggression or apprehension (Koestler 1964), expression of superiority (Hobbes 1651), or as a liberation from all of our social constraints

(Mindess 1971). Mindess's theory is the most general because it incorporates the functions of the other theories. Most of life, write Mindess, consists of conventions and organization. "Humor frees us from the chains of our perceptual, conventional, logical, and moral systems" (28).

Mindess also points out that having fun is central to any theory of humor:

> Let us not overlook the obvious: we all *like* to laugh. From infancy to old age, regardless of intellectual or social status, people in all groups and cultures enjoy a smile or a chuckle. Laughter, in short, is fun. It is gratifying in itself, no matter under what conditions it has been elicited. As such, it is part and parcel for relaxation, ease, delight, for happiness in all its many hues. Any explanation of humor that professes to dig its roots must keep this point in hand.

> The liberation theory does precisely that. It elucidates the entire, varied range of things that make us laugh, omits neither intellectual, perceptual, nor emotional components, and—most important—makes convincing sense of the fact that wit and comedy are above all, delightful. (Mindess 1971:241)

Kris (1940) also points out the bonding function of laughter in a group. When people laugh together about something, there is a stimulus, and a stranger who has not heard or seen it cannot join in and be a part of this alliance. But laughing together creates an alliance among the group, and after this alliance is formed, one can laugh along with others without knowing what the laughter is about. "The laughter of the group no longer requires a 'butt' to laugh at, it can itself represent both content and sealing of the pact" (Socarides 1977:92).

The wine corpus of the Tucson subjects provides many instances of humor. What appears funny depends on the total social context, of course, so although the remarks presented below as illustrations may not be amusing when read out of this context, they produced laughter when originally uttered. (Drinking wine also contributed to this total context.) The subjects at the wine sessions worked hard at their tasks—describing wines, making subtle judgments, and evaluating the judgments of others, and laughter provided a release from the tensions and hard concentration.

ADRIENNE: What about wine L?
HENRY: Sexy?
ADRIENNE: What's a sexy wine?
HENRY: I don't know. It's a wine I had on a good night.

Henry's remark serves as a way of getting out of having to defend a characterization.

DONNA: Does it smell like soy sauce?
HENRY: No. I eat in better restaurants.

Henry's remark is a complete non sequitur, but it provides a way of forcefully rejecting the characterization. This example might count as veiled aggression, although there seemed to be little aggression or hostility displayed during the wine sessions that I could perceive.

LINDA: I thought that the smell was soapy.
EDWARD: Soapy, not bad. . . . If I were to take a bath in one of them, I'd prefer that one.

Although Edward initially seemed to accept the characterization, his final remark could be interpreted as a way of rejecting it and implicating that *soapy* was a silly wine word.

The following example is from a session when subjects were defining words on the work sheet with the eight scales.

ADRIENNE: Age.
WILMA: How do you judge that?
TOM: Look at the label.

Tom's remark can be interpreted as denying that people can tell age by taste and thus attacking people who claim to be able to do so.

Some remarks do not seem to reveal even the faintest aggression; they seem to be spontaneous expressions of perceived incongruity or instances of pure silliness, liberation from logic and reason, to use Mindess's categories.

SAM: Wine K tastes mossy.
CAROL: Have a little taste of mold!

WILMA: I have a question. I was curious about the word someone used. They said some wine had *legs*, and I say "Oh, this had legs." But what are legs?

HENRY: Small bacteria.
WILMA: Anti-arms?

A reason I have dwelled on humor is that some of the remarks in a conversation may actually interrupt the exchange of information. But such remarks contribute to the satisfaction and pleasure of the participants and contribute to the social, noninformational functions of talk-exchanges. Conversation satisfies social and emotional purposes as well as communicative functions. Much conversation is concerned with phatic communion, that is, with establishing and maintaining social bonds and with passing time in an enjoyable way. Humor—jokes, puns, and other sorts of witticisms—contributes to the enjoyment and fun of such conversations and therefore enhances them, even though it may interrupt whatever information-communication goals the conversation also may have.

DISCOURSE FEATURES

Although there is a wealth of data on discourse features in the wine corpus, there is one feature that I want to mention: first, because it involves humor, and second, because it is not given sufficient attention in the literature on conversational analysis. This is the topic of discourse cohesion—the succession of utterances and how the contribution of one speaker is related to and/or influenced by what the last speaker has said. "Conversational analysts take most seriously the claim that the context for any strip of behavior is the behavior which precedes it, follows it, and co-occurs with it across persons in an interaction" (McDermott & Roth 1978:340). The phrase "behavior which precedes" is sufficiently vague to be interpreted as anything earlier in the conversation, but, in general, conversational analysis focuses on the immediately preceding utterances.

Conversations, at least some good ones, have structures like those found in consciously created literary texts. We may normally think of a conversation as consisting of blocks of topics, lined up like cars of a train, and after one topic is exhausted, speakers go on to the next.[5] However, conversationalists, like poets or novelists, make remarks that allude to previous topics or expressions in the conversation, and so a conversational structure is built up which is more than just a string of relevant remarks in a strict order. The structure has an aesthetic dimension.

One simple example is taken from a wine session in which subjects were to agree on the descriptions of three wines. Notice the way in which the prefix *semi-* is developed during the conversation. Wine F was being discussed.

WILMA: Sweet—
TOM: Semisweet.
WILMA: Semisweet?
            ●●●
EDWARD: Semisweet.
IDA: Sticky.
BETTY: By that you mean cloying?
IDA: Yeah, it sticks around.
HENRY: I don't think so.
ADRIENNE: What about sticky?
EDWARD: It's like that if there were a little more of it.
HENRY: Yeah, but there's not enough of it.
EDWARD: It would be cloying and syrupy if there were a little more of that quality.
DONNA: Semisyrupy!
EDWARD: Semisyrupy!
BETTY: Why not!

Later in the sessions wine H was being discussed.

BETTY: How about a bitter aftertaste.
WILMA: I think *bitter* is pretty good.
TOM: Bitter.
ADRIENNE: Bitter.
RICHARD: Bitter.
HENRY: I think *bitter* is too strong. I would call *bitter* excessive.
RICHARD: *Bitter* is too hard a word for it.
TOM: Semibitter?
RICHARD: Semibitter!

Although *semi-* is a semiproductive prefix, the previous use of *semisweet* and *semisyrupy* makes the use of *semibitter* special in this context. The fact that the wine tasters laughed is evidence that they appreciated its "aesthetic" function in this context.

A second example is taken from the session in which sixteen words were to be defined by the group. The battle between the sexes serves as a unifying theme in this conversation.

ADRIENNE: What about *feminine*?

LINDA: You should be careful.

BETTY: We might say *delicate*. . . . If you're going to use *feminine*, I think of *delicate*, rather than *robust*.

NED: It's opposite of a *big* wine.

EDWARD: But delicate is more positive than just *light*, right?
            ••

JOHN: Without bite, too.

EDWARD: Right, it shouldn't have any bite.

LINDA: Lots of claw, but no bite.

EDWARD: *Delicate*, but not very substantial.

CAROL: Keep going!

EDWARD: I think we've about done that one pretty well.

ADRIENNE: What about *flat*?

EDWARD: No bite?

CAROL: Claw?

HENRY: Claw.

Three words later, *light* was discussed.

EDWARD: How can we distinguish *light* from *feminine*? . . . *Delicate* seems to have something a little more positive. Doesn't it seem to suggest [something] more positive?

CAROL: I'm still offended by *insubstantial*.
            ••

ADRIENNE: What about *manly*?

CAROL: What about *heavy, rough,* and *gross*?

HENRY: Not close. Dishonest, destructive.

EDWARD: Takes a chunk out of the tip of your tongue.

HENRY: Okay, we got it; let's move along.

EDWARD: Are we going to stick with that? Does it have to be bad in order to be manly?

[Two words later]

ADRIENNE: The next one should be tough—*positive*.

EDWARD: Well, that's the opposite of *feminine*.
LINDA: It's also the opposite of *manly*.

In these excerpts, since the remarks were intended to be humorous and were perceived as humorous, as evidenced by the laughter of the group, the structure of the conversation and the allusions to previous remarks considerably earlier in the discussion were apparent to and appreciated by the participants. This phenomenon occurs in nonhumorous discourse as well, as when a speaker connects his or her contribution with that of another remark much earlier in the conversation.

Although most work on discourse analysis has focused on local control or cohension—that is, on the relevance of an utterance to the utterance immediately preceding it—conversational structure also shows evidence of nonlocal control. A speaker's contribution may be related to something much earlier in the conversation. Many utterances play a dual role, of course; they are related to the immediately preceding utterances, but to fully appreciate their significance, they must be connected with earlier utterances as well.

SUMMARY

In this chapter I have used examples from the wine corpus to illustrate some of the nonscientific uses of language. There are perhaps a variety of dimensions which separate the various forms of discourse. One is an objective-subjective dimension. Science tends to be about the objective world while phatic communion often deals with attitudes and opinions. Another is descriptive accuracy and precision. For scientific purposes, it is necessary to use words carefully and precisely. Phatic communion can succeed with vague expressions. It is, however, possible to be precise about subjective matters,[6] and we shall see in the next chapter attempts by psychologists and psychiatrists to deal scientifically with feelings and with personality types. Social bonding has high value in phatic communion, but little in scientific discourse. For critical communication, which is somewhere between the scientific and the phatic, the speaker wishes to communicate information but cannot use a standard vocabulary, either because none exists or the speaker does not know it. Critical communication also involves the sharing of experience, and when language is used for this function, it blends into phatic communion. I have stressed that there are some constraints on the language used. Descriptions must loosely correspond to—or at least not conflict with—what they denote. If one is seriously describing a dessert wine such as Port, one cannot describe it as a *dry white wine*. The difference between scientific and nonscientific language is a matter of degree, not kind, when description is at stake.

When speakers joke, their remarks are intended to be understood as nonserious, and are perhaps to be understood at several levels. Humorous remarks in a conversation often interrupt the exchange of information, but they serve other functions in conversation, one important one being to enchance the enjoyment of the participants in the talk exchange.

PART IV

The Semantics of Personality

Chapter 12
Describing People

Or, Where Angels Fear to Tread

> Everybody knows that language is a very poor medium for expressing our emotional nature. It merely names certain vaguely and crudely conceived states, but fails miserably in any attempt to convey the ever moving patterns, the ambivalence and intricacies of inner experience, the interplay of feelings with thoughts and impressions, memories and echoes of memories, transient fantasy, or its mere runic traces, all turned into nameless, emotional stuff. (Langer 1957:100–101)

Up to now we have been concerned in one way or another with wine—with a structural analysis of the vocabulary, with descriptions of how people apply this vocabulary to real wines, with the problems of making the vocabulary more precise for scientific purposes, and with the functions of talking about wine with one's friends and colleagues. However, wine talk is not an unusual or esoteric semantic domain. The problems of meaning and reference which have been discussed exist in other—perhaps all—semantic domains. In this chapter, I will sketch out parallels between the semantic problems in wine and those in personality.

It would obviously require many volumes to adequately cover the topic of how speakers of English describe people—their personality, behavior, moods, and attitudes—since these domains are far more complex than that of wine and since the vocabulary is enormous. I can only refer to a few articles that are concerned with topics in psychology and psychotherapy which are parallel to some of the problems that have been raised in the chapters on wine.

189

In the section on scientific language in personality theory and psychotherapy, scientists and clinicians are still in the process of selecting and defining the vocabulary. In applying some of these words to individuals, for example, in diagnosing mental illness and labeling patients with these terms, such as schizophrenic, physicians and clinicians have acknowledged the problems of unreliability and have begun to work toward solutions.

I also see close parallels between talk when used in critical communication and the psychotherapeutic interview. The patient must figure out some way of encoding into language his or her feelings. Each patient and clinician must work out some sort of vocabulary for themselves, though it may be highly personal, unconventional, and idiosyncratic. This vocabulary will almost certainly be different from that of the technical vocabulary used in journals for reporting research results or discussing psychoanalytic theory. Transcripts of therapy interviews illustrate beautifully the creative use of language which patients exhibit—their ability to convey their feelings using metaphors, imagery, comparisons, and associations.

Finally the topic of gossip is mentioned, since people frequently gossip about each other, using this large vocabulary of personality descriptors. What words do people actually use when they talk about their friends (and enemies) and how much consistency and reliability is there in their application of words to people? I have not developed this subject at all, however; I have only brought it up as a fascinating topic for future research.

Langer (1957) laments the inadequacy of language for describing emotions, as the quotation at the head of this chapter shows. She distinguishes between discursive language—the language for science and other 'referential' functions—and nondiscursive symbolic processes. She argues that what cannot be adequately described in discursive language, however, can often be expressed in other symbolic systems—music, ritual, poetry, dreams, metaphor, myth, and art. "The limits of language are not the last limits of experiences, and things inaccessible to language may have their own symbolic devices" (ibid.: 265).

Yet it is possible to create a science of human emotion and construct an adequate language. Langer would probably admit this. A psychologist or therapist engaged in research about feelings and personality who wishes to report his or her findings must rely on language to communicate with others. Individuals may be described as *aggressive, introverted, sociable, lonely, angry, unhappy, horrified, pampered, neurotic,* or *schizophrenic.* What is the status of these words? Are they descriptors with a clear denotation in the world, like *blue,* or are they vague, like *tall?* Are they theoretical terms, whose meaning can only be understood in relationship to a particular theory of personality or affect? To what extent are evaluative components a part of their meaning?

I will discuss in this chapter problems involved in the development of an adequate scientific language for personality types, mood, affect, and personality disorders; linguistic and other symbolic systems which clients use to communicate their feelings to a therapist; and phatic uses of this vocabulary.

Scientific Language

For the purposes of describing personality it is not yet clear what descriptors or words will turn out to be useful. Ordinary language is as good a place as any to begin, however, and most psychologists and therapists will have to use some terms from ordinary language, although additional theoretical terms may be used as well. Goldberg (1981) describes a long-term research project the ultimate aim of which is to provide an observational language for general personality description.

> In our most grandiose moments, my colleagues and I see our scientific task as one of discovering the basic elements that underlie the personality compounds found in the various natural languages. Specifically, we want to provide a compelling structure for all personality-descriptive terms in English and then compare this with its equivalents in other languages. Our ultimate goal is to discover as much as possible about the processes involved in describing oneself and others and about the role of language and culture in these processes. (1981:44)

The number of words in English for describing personality traits is very large. Allport & Odbert (1936) assembled a list of 17,953 such descriptors. A list, however, fails to show the intralinguistic structure of this vocabulary. Goldberg asked 100 subjects to rate these and other terms in this taxonomy of personality terms. The Allport &

Odbert list has been reduced to 7,294 by eliminating terms that are purely evaluative *(nice)*, anatomical or physical *(hairy)*, vague or metaphorical *(oceanic)*, and obscure or little known *(bevering)*. A few new terms were added. These terms have been divided into three major categories: (1) stable traits *(meek)*, (2) temporary states or activities *(lonesome)*, and (3) social roles, relationships, or effects *(dangerous)*. Using a variety of semantic techniques—scaling, card sorting, similarity judgments—a taxonomy was constructed. (Subjects were college students, many of them graduate students in English.)

The semantic structures found in the personality domain are similar to those found in wine description. For one thing, there is a strong evaluative dimension built into many descriptors. Contrast *thrifty* with *stingy*, for example. If one looks at the abstract semantic structure for wine in chapter 1, Figure 1, the dominant pattern is

Too little X   Right Amount   Too much X

An identical structure exists with words that refer to 'a tendency to share one's possessions'.

Pole A ← keeps | gives → Pole B
Gives too little   Acceptable   Gives too much
stingy miserly frugal thrifty | *generous philan-   over-   wasteful*
                                       | *thropic charitable*
(Adapted from Goldberg 1981:55)

FIGURE 27

A group of 100 subjects rated these and other terms in this semantic domain on a desirability scale from 1 (least desirable) to 9. *Generous* received the highest desirability rating of 7.8, *thrifty* received 5.7, *wasteful* was rated as 2.9, and *stingy* as 2.2.

One reason for constructing a taxonomy is to try to determine to what extent the correlation between personality traits is a factor of the semantic structures themselves. One controversy in personality theory revolves around this problem. If a psychologist reports that people who are generous also tend to be warm, is he judging these attributes independently or is he responding to a possible semantic overlap of *generous* and *warm*? As we saw in the case of the wine vocabulary, although subjects rejected *feminine* as a good descriptor and claimed not to know its meaning, they could use it reasonably well (i.e., consensually) because of its intralinguistic relationships to other words with a clearer denotation. Goldberg says that one aim of the project is to separate the similarity of meaning from "true relationships among personality traits" (1975:13). It is possible to argue that the semantic similarity reflects the correlation of personality traits—that *generous* and *warm* overlap because people who have one property also have the other.

Goldberg and his associates are only concerned with intralinguistic relationships and with providing a set of words for psychologists to choose from. The problem of denotation is a different one. How does one "properly" apply *generous* to some people and *stingy* to others? We find here the same kind of vagueness that occurs among wine descriptors like *light* and *robust*. Some reference groups or criteria are implied, but they need to be made explicit. Even so there are likely to be disagreements that reflect different value judgments. If A gives away 15 percent of his property, B gives away 10 percent, and C gives away 5 percent, B may be considered *wasteful* by C but *stingy* by A. All three may agree on the intralinguistic relationship (e.g., that *generous→good, stingy→bad*) but disagree on application and denotation. Getting the whole community of psychologists who use English to apply these descriptors consistently and consensually would be a mammoth task, but it is not impossible in principle.

For some purposes denotation may not be so important. For example, if a psychologist or clinician is interested in a person's self-image, then he will want to know whether the patient describes himself as *generous* and *kind* or as *selfish* and *mean*. On the other hand, if the therapist wishes to determine whether the patient's self-image is realistic, then additional sources of information will be required—either other people's descriptions, or his own knowledge of the individual's behavior. But then, the problem of variation of individual norms arises. If the patient gives away 2 percent of his property and believes that such behavior constitutes generosity, while the therapist and the patient's associates believe that one must give away 15 percent to be generous, then there will be mismatch between a self-report and objective (i.e., intrasubjective) accounts of others.

In fact, one could not define *generosity* as 'giving away X percent of one's property', since factors of motivation for sharing, the attitude displayed, etc., will also be important. Someone who grudgingly gives away 15 percent of his income solely to avoid paying a greater amount of income taxes could hardly qualify as generous. And giving of one's time, effort, and affection may be as important or more important than giving away property or money.

The language of emotions is interesting in many respects. We assume that there is an underlying biological foundation for the species, with an overlay of cultural and subcultural patterns and values, and with some range of individual variation. Individuals who lack certain emotions or are removed from their emotions may be analogous to color-blind or tone-deaf individuals in that they are incapable of perceiving, responding, or sensing what most people can. However, society's value judgments toward such people[1] are quite different than toward color-blind individuals.

With emotion words it is much harder to show that speakers apply words in the same way—or in different ways—than with certain other semantic domains. When dealing with words for color, sound, or taste, the same stimulus can be presented to hundreds of subjects, but such stimuli may be harder to find for emotion. It could be that we all experience the same feeling of sadness, and all of us who speak English would describe the feeling as sadness, but that different sorts of events make different individuals feel sad. I do not think that sadness would be confused with happiness or anger, but where the differences are subtle there could well be differences in application, e.g., jealousy vs. envy, fear vs. anxiety, sadness vs. depression, arrogance vs. smugness, or sourness vs. bitterness. Perhaps films or works of literature could serve as adequate stimuli for investigating consensus on these matters.

For scientific purposes words for emotions have been defined not only to describe feelings in terms of ordinary languages but partly in terms of casual events producing that emotion and partly as theoretical entities, relative to a particular theory. For example, Owens & Maxmen argue that there has been a semantic confusion between *mood* and *affect*. Inferences about mood stem from present observations and past events, whereas those about affect "pertain only to current observations" (1979:99).

An interesting collection of easays, *The World of Emotions*, edited by

Charles Socarides, deals with a variety of emotions, largely in terms of psychoanalytic theory. Socarides writes, "Over the years of teaching and clinical practice, I have been struck by the extent to which such words as *arrogance, envy, boredom, smugness, gloating,* and *enthusiasm* are regarded as self-explanatory or in a sense taken for granted" (1977:3). Socarides goes on to advocate connecting these descriptive words with the "rich unconscious psycho-dynamic material underlying every affective state," and many of the essays are concerned with this, but they also include attempts to distinguish between closely related emotions.

Zilboorg distinguishes between fear and anxiety. Anxiety is intimately connected with or accompanied by a feeling related to fear. Anxiety is not related to any specific object, while fear is. "Clinically, however, i.e., as far as the subjective perception of the affective tone is concerned, it is well-nigh impossible to distinguish anxiety from fear" (in Socarides 1977:46).[2]

In distinguishing boredom from depression and apathy, Greenson writes that boredom can be described as dissatisfaction and a disinclination to act, as a state of longing without being able to say what is longed for, and an empty, passive feeling, but with the hope that the world will provide satisfaction (in Socarides 1977:221). Depressed persons have lost something but have fantasies about regaining an unloving object. Apathetic persons have given up longing, while bored individuals long for the lost satisfactions as do the depressed, but they experience the empty feelings of the apathetic (237).

The conceited person, unlike the smug one, appears foolish, because he constantly tries to call attention to himself. "He needs witnesses to overcome his own doubts concerning his worthwhileness." But the smug person needs no external confirmation of his feelings of self-satisfaction (Arlow, in Socarides 1977:262).

Alexander tries to distinguish between sourness and bitterness. The embittered person feels deeply that he has been treated unjustly. He feels "reproachful, resentful over pain whose reason he cannot understand, which appears to him unnecessary" and he feels victimized (in Socarides 1977:296). The sour person feels more completely rejected than the bitter person. He is cross, ill-tempered, and less likely than the bitter person to be verbal, to defend his right to anger and to demand redress for injustices.

The distinction between faith, trust, and gullibility is discussed by Isaacs, Alexander, & Haggard. The trustful person has little anxiety about dangers—inner or outer—and he is free to have new experiences. He sees others as friendly and cooperative and treats others with sympathy and compassion. The nontrusting person is wary of others, if not frightened, expecting harm and perceiving the world as a dangerous place. The gullible person has unrealistic hopes of a sane and comfortable world. The realistically trusting person knows when to be wary and when he can relax and be trusting (in Socarides 1977:366–70). Then the authors go on to distinguish between mistrust and distrust. In transitory mistrust, the "patient diminishes his credulity and thus his capacity to take seriously what the analyst says," but the analysis may remain on sound grounding. But if the patient feels *distrust* the analysis may falter or end. "The distrusting patient carefully fends off the analyst" (371).

Whitman & Alexander draw a subtle distinction in terms of the situation and casual events between jealousy and envy. "Envy is the hostile feeling that another is enjoying superiority, advantages, or success, that one would like to have oneself. The envious impulse is to take it away or spoil it. . . . Jealousy is based on envy, but implies a relation to at least two other people; love has been taken away from the subject by another person, love which was his due" (in Socarides 1977:433).

Is there really a problem about the uniformity of application of such terms? Davitz (1964) says that researchers are aware of possible differences of meaning and extension but apparently believe that there is sufficient uniformity among speakers for research purposes (10). Ordinary speakers make the same assumption. Davitz and others conducted a series of experiments to test the ways in which emotional meaning are communicated:

> It is somewhat surprising that among the hundreds of subjects we studied, none asked us what sadness or anger or joy meant. The only category of emotional meaning that anyone ever asked about was love, but even questions about the meaning of love were fairly rare. (194)

In these experiments, subjects we've asked to identify emotions conveyed by means of paralinguistic cues—repetitions of the same sentence, uttered differently to convey different emotions; line drawings, music, vocal and facial expressions, Rorschach inkblots, and brief descriptions of situations. Subjects chose from five different emotions in some tests (anger, anxiety, joy, love, sadness), from ten in other tests (anger, admiration, amusement, boredom, despair, disgust, fear, impatience, joy, and love). In most cases subjects matched the intended meaning with better than chance accuracy. The percentage correct for each of the experiments tended to vary from 50 to 85.[3] However, the emotions selected were in general maximally different from each other, especially when there were only five choices. Would the subjects have judged as accurately if the choice had been among more closely related feelings, anger, hostility, and jealousy, for instance? Each experiment, on the other hand, looked at a single variable, so it is possible that when a hearer has access to all information (content, facial expression, vocal cues, plus background information), he can identify the speaker's emotion with great accuracy.

PSYCHIATRIC DIAGNOSIS AND INTERPRETATION

There is a large literature on the problems of reliability in psychiatric diagnosis. First of all there are disagreements involving vocabulary and intralinguistic relationships. At the highest level there is a disagreement over whether abnormal behavior is an illness and therefore to be conceived of as a medical or health problem or not. Szasz (1969) has been a leading opponent of the medical model and has argued that psychological problems are to be looked at as "problems in living." Others view the problem as one of "interpersonal behavior" (Adam 1969, McLemore & Benjamin 1979). Yet the medical model remains a predominant one and has been adopted by the World Health Organization and the American Psychiatric Association.

The classification of mental and emotional disorders and the diagnosis of patients has been acknowledged as unreliable (a list of articles showing such unreliability can be found in Ziegler & Phillips 1969, McLemore & Benjamin 1979, and Cooper et al. 1973). Scheflen (1973), in discussing the interpretation of psychotherapeutic events, describes attempts to find a system of interpretation that all observers or participants could use to come up with reliably similar descriptions.

The first method we tried was very popular at the time. We conducted structured interviews with therapists and patients, or else we had them fill out rating scales and questionnaires. Then we tried to determine statistically whether the various raters had achieved consensual validation.

This procedure caused us endless difficulties. We were never certain that various subjects and raters attributed similar meaning to the items. We could obtain a statistically significant consensus only among raters who had been trained in psychoanalysis by the same training analyst. (1973:3)

A particularly interesting study was carried out by Cooper et al. (1973). It had been noticed that in comparative studies of mental illness in the United States and Great Britain, there was a much higher proportion of schizophrenia in the United States and a much higher proportion of mania-depression in Britain, although the proportion of the population admitted to mental hospitals was similar in the two countries.

TABLE 43: Comparison of American and British Mental Disorders (per 100,000 population)

	U.S.A.	England & Wales
All disorders	102.1	115.7
Schizophrenia	24.7	17.4
Major Affective Disorder	11.0	38.5

(from Cooper et al. 1973:20)

The doctors involved in this project intended to spend most of their time studying the different causative factors in American and British society that would account for this difference, but they needed first to determine the accuracy of the diagnoses. A team of six British psychiatrists, four of whom were trained at the same British hospital, spent several weeks learning to administer and score psychological interviews. At the end of this period the six psychiatrists achieved a fairly high degree of reliability (33–34).

Netherne Hospital in London and Brooklyn State Hospital in New York were selected for this project because the patients admitted were typical of London and New York respectively but would reveal differences in populations in the two cities. At each hospital, 250 patients between the ages of 20 and 59 were interviewed. The project psychiatrists' diagnoses were completely independent of the diagnoses given by the hospital staff, so that independent correlations could be made. Table 44 shows a few of the discrepancies in the diagnostic categories between the project psychiatrists and those done by the hospital staff. Further investigations showed that the hospital diagnoses at other New York hospitals were similar to those at Brooklyn, just as those at other London hospitals were similar to those at Netherne. The discrepancies in diagnoses between the project psychiatrists and the hospital staff at other hospitals were as great as between those in Table 44. With respect to the project diagnosis, there was no significance between the proportion of patients diagnosed as schizophrenic in the two populations. Although there still remains a significant difference between the New York and London patients diagnosed with depressive neurosis, the difference is much smaller in the project diagnoses (18% in Brooklyn to 26% in London) compared to the hospital diagnoses (7.2% to 32.8%).

TABLE 44: Comparison of Diagnoses by Different Clinicians

	BROOKLYN		NETHERNE	
	Hospital Diagnosis	*Project Diagnosis*	*Hospital Diagnosis*	*Project Diagnosis*
	%	%	%	%
Schizophrenia	65.2	32.4	34.0	26.0
Depressive Psychoses	7.2	18.0	32.8	26.0
Mania	0.8	8.8	1.6	5.6

(from Cooper et al.1973:98–99)

In addition, eight videotapes of psychiatric interviews were made and shown to a total of over 700 psychiatrists in America and Britain, who were then asked to make a diagnosis for each interview they watched (no psychiatrist viewed all eight tapes).

For the three patients whose symptoms were fairly typical of classical sterotypes there was substantial agreement between American and British raters, at least for the major category of illness involved. For three other patients with a mixture of schizophrenic and affective symptoms the majority of both American and British raters diagnosed schizophrenia, but for all three a substantial minority of British raters (20% to 34%) diagnosed an affective psychosis instead. For the two remaining patients there was really serious disagreement, with most British raters diagnosing either a personality disorder or a neurotic illness but the majority of the Americans again diagnosing schizophrenia. (Cooper et al. 1973:124)

The accuracy of diagnosis is important for several reasons. First of all, it has been found that lithium salts provide an effective treatment specifically for manic illnesses (Cooper et al.1977:81). Secondly, the fact that the same proportion of schizophrenia is found in various populations around the world has been used as evidence for considering it to have a genetic basis (see Goldstein & Goldstein 1978 for a discussion of this point).

Aware of the problems of reliability found in previous studies, the World Health Organization, conducting an international study of schizophrenia, carefully set up a procedure to improve reliability. In addition, procedures were established so that reliability could be measured. First, the group in charge of the study developed standardized techniques for collecting data. They developed interviewing instruments for a Present State Examination (PSE) of the patient, for a clinical history, and for other historical and pathological information (WHO 1973:36). The psychiatrists who would be interviewing patients were trained in using these examination instruments, especially the PSE. Each clinician was apprenticed to someone who was already proficient in applying the PSE and in scoring it (ibid.: 81). Videotapes were made and shown to all the clinicians at various states of their training in order to clarify the meaning of the questions, to increase similarity of ratings, and to check on reliability among the participating psychiatrists (ibid.: 82).

The study was carried out at nine medical centers throughout the world. In order to check on reliability within each center, some patients were rated simultaneously by two psychiatrists, one acting as the interviewer and the other acting as observer. Additional patients were interviewed twice by different psychiatrists. Videotapes and films were made to be rated by all participating investigators during their annual meeting (ibid.: 11). To improve reliability among the different centers, investigators visited other clinics (ibid.: 44). Intercenter reliability was measured by showing videotapes to the participating investigators, who then had to diagnose on the basis of these videotapes.

Although the measure of reliability was to some extent dependent on the statistical method used, the investigators felt that the overall reliability was high. The intracenter reliability, with an average R of .83, was higher than the intercenter reliability.

> The results of the PSE reliability evaluations showed generally high re-
> liability by items . . . when the PSE was used by investigators from the
> same centre. When investigators from different centres were compared,
> however, there was less reliability. . . . In all situations, ratings made on
> the basis of observed behavior had considerably lower reliability than
> ratings based on patients' responses to specific questions. (ibid.: 135)

Overall the group felt that the interviewers within a center obtained high reliability but that further work was necessary to achieve greater intercenter reliability (ibid.: 145).

In the United States the major classification system for mental disorders is the *Diagnostic and Statistical Manual,* the third edition of which was published in 1980 (DSM-III). In the earlier version, DSM-II (1968), the disorders are based on etiology, where known, rather than on treatment or prognosis, whereas etiology is used less as a criterion in DSM-III (Gelman 1979).

DSM-II draws a broad distinction between the psychoses (subclassified into those associated with organic brain syndromes and those not so associated) and the neuroses. There are several other broad classes as well, one of which is "personality disorders and certain other non-psychotic mental disorders," including sexual deviation and drug addiction. Ziegler & Philips report that reliability in diagnosis is reasonably reliable for these broad classes, but as the classes are subdivided and categories become narrower and more specific, reliability decreases (1969:30–31).

DSM-III provides much more detailed and elaborate descriptions than DSM-II. Consider the following descriptions for Schizophrenia. From DSM-II:

> Schizophrenia. This large category includes a group of disorders man-
> ifested by characteristic disturbances of thinking, mood and behavior.
> Disturbances in thinking are marked by alterations of concept forma-
> tion which may lead to misinterpretation of reality and sometimes to
> delusions and hallucinations, which frequently appear psychologically
> self-protective. Corollary mood changes include ambivalent, constricted
> and inappropriate emotional responsiveness and loss of empathy with

others. Behavior may be withdrawn, regressive and bizarre. The schizo-phrenias, in which the mental status is attributable primarily to a thought disorder, are to be distinguished from the Major affective illnesses (q.v.) which are dominated by a mood disorder. The Paranoid states (q.v.) are distinguished from schizophrenia by the narrowness of their distortions of reality and by the absence of other psychotic symptoms.

Schizophrenia is further divided into various subtypes: simple, hebephrenic, catatonic, paranoid, latent, residual, schizo-affective, childhood, chronic undifferentiation, and other (unspecified). For example, simple type schizophrenia is characterized as follows:

Schizophrenia, simple type. This psychosis is characterized chiefly by a slow and insidious reduction of external attachments and interests and by apathy and indifference leading to impoverishment of interpersonal relations, mental deterioration, and adjustment on a lower level of functioning. In general, the condition is less dramatically psychotic than are the hebephrenic, catatonic, and paranoid types of schizophrenia. Also, it contrasts with schizoid personality, in which there is little or no progression of the disorder.

Compare the characterization for schizophrenia in DSM-III:

Diagnostic criteria for a Schizophrenic Disorder
A.   At least one of the following during a phase of the illness:

(1) bizarre delusions (content is patently absurd and has no possible basis in fact, such as delusions of being controlled, thought broadcast-ing, though insertion, or thought withdrawal)

(2) somatic, grandiose, religious, nihilistic, or other delusions without persecutory or jealous content

(3) delusions with persecutory or jealous content if accompanied by hal-lucinations of any type

(4) auditory hallucinations in which either a voice keeps up a running commentary on the indiviudal's behavior or thoughts, or two or more voices converse with each other

(5) auditory hallucinations on several occasions with content of more than one or two words, having no apparent relation to depression or elation

(6) incoherence, marked loosening of associations, markedly illogical

thinking, or marked poverty of content of speech if associated with at least one of the following:

(a) blunted, flat, or inappropriate affect

(b) delusions or hallucinations

(c) catatonic or other grossly disorganized behavior

B. Deterioration from a previous level of functioning in such areas as work, social relations, and self-care.

C. Duration: Continuous signs of the illness for at least six months at some time during the person's life, with some signs of the illness at present. The six-month period must include an active phase during which there were symptoms from A, with or without a prodromal or residual phase, as defined below.

Prodromal phase: A clear deterioration in functioning before the active phase of the illness not due to a disturbance in mood or to a Substance Use Disorder and involving at least two of the symptoms noted below.

Residual phase: Persistence, following the active phase of the illness, of at least two of the symptoms noted below, not due to a disturbance in mood or to a Substance Use Disorder.

Prodromal or Residual Symptoms

(1) social isolation or withdrawal

(2) marked impairment in role functioning as wage-earner, student, or homemaker

(3) markedly peculiar behavior (e.g., collecting garbage, talking to self in public, or hoarding food)

(4) marked impairment in personal hygiene and grooming

(5) blunted, flat, or inappropriate affect

(6) digressive, vague, overelaborate, circumstantial, or metaphorical speech

(7) odd or bizarre ideation, or magical thinking, e.g., superstitiousness, clairvoyance, telepathy, "sixth sense," "others can feel my feelings," overvalued ideas, ideas of reference

(8) unusual perceptual experiences, e.g., recurrent illusions, sensing the presence of a force or person not actually present.

Before the final version of DSM-III was released, field trials were conducted with a preliminary version and diagnostic reliability was tested. Clinicians were invited to participate in these field trials.

Each clinician in this study was expected to participate with another clinician in at least two reliability evaluations. These two evaluations were to be done after each clinician had already used the DSM-III draft in evaluating at least 15 patients selected from his or her patient population as either consecutive admissions or "catch-as-catch can" (an approximation of the ideal of random sampling). The reliability interviews, with only a few exceptions, were given to the clinicians to avoid possible biases. (Spitzer et al. 1979:815)

The two evaluations could either be done jointly or separately. 274 clinicians participated in this study, and 281 adult patients were involved. Reliability on schizophrenic disorders was .82 for both the joint interviews and the separate interviews. (Reliability is expressed with a kappa index, and .7 is considered high.) With affective disorders, the index was .77 for joint interviews with the patient and .59 for separate ones. Spitzer et al. conclude:

> For most of the classes, the reliability for both interview situations is quite good and, in general, is higher than that previously achieved using DSM-I and DSM-II. . . . It is particularly encouraging that the reliability for such categories as schizophrenia and major affective disorder is so high. . . . As expected, the reliabilities are high when the interviews are done jointly. (1979:817)

In another study the preliminary DSM-III was used to evaluate individuals charged for crimes in order to decide if they were competent to be tried. Ciconne & Barry report,

> At first, the new classification was deceptively simple to implement. . . . On second look, however, we found the operational criteria to be disappointingly subjective in many instances, e.g., the adjective "excessive" is often used to describe the degree to which a particular trait must be present in order to make a diagnosis. . . . Our fascination with the operational criteria was further dimmed by a blinding glimpse of the obvious fact that they were simply aids in ordering one's thinking about the data gathered in the clinical interviews; in no way did they confer on the diagnostician the vital ingredient of clinical judgment, nor did they substitute for the seasoned clinician's ability to elicit the signs and symptoms of mental disorder. Despite these shortcomings, the operational criteria are more explicit and denotative than the descriptive statements in [DSM] II. . . . (1978:27)

The preliminary work suggests that DSM-III provides better guidance in diagnosing and classifying mental disorders than previous systems. However, it should be pointed out that the field studies reported by Spitzer et al. (1979) involved two clinicians working at the same institute or hospital. What still remains to be determined is the reliability among clinicians working at different places, trained by different teachers. Although DSM-III provides more explicit descriptions of behavior than its predecessors, I doubt that one can learn to use it accurately just by reading the definitions. New practitioners must learn to use it as part of their training under the guidance of experienced clinicians who have already learned to use it correctly.[4]

The present situation is encouraging. It is in principle possible to develop standard teaching or testing materials using videotapes, for example. (Sheflin 1973 and Erikson 1964:79-80 advocate this method.) These materials might serve as standard stimuli, analogous to a standard set of tapes for phonetics or a standard set of odors like those used by Williams in his research on ciders and perries.

I do not wish to underrate the importance of social, political, and personal difficulties involved. Clinicians in one place whose diagnosis or coding procedures systematically differ from the "standard" might be unable or unwilling to change. There are delicate matters involved, such as who should establish the standard criteria, make decisions on what constitutes "correct" application, and evaluate the performance of practitioners in a field. There may also be a problem of giving a group in charge too much power in a field where there are basic theoretical disagreements.

Another approach would not involve imposing a standard on everyone, but would attempt to determine whether there were systematic differences that could be calibrated. Just as it is possible to convert liters to gallons or centigrade to Fahrenheit, so it might be possible to work out correspondences between research institutes.

At any rate, the practitioners in psychiatry have recognized that there is a problem, and they have begun to try to remedy it.

THERAPY INTERVIEWS

When a psychologist or psychiatrist writes an article for a journal in order to share his or her discoveries, for successful communication to take place the audience must understand the words used in the same way that the writer does. However, when a patient and a psychotherapist discuss the patient's problems, it is only necessary that each understand the other—it does not matter whether the words they use or the extension of those words is similar to or different from that of other patients and therapists.

The use of language in a therapeutic situation shares some of the properties of critical communication (chapter 11). The essence of critical communication is that the speaker tries to get the hearer to perceive or notice something, "to induce a sameness of vision, of experienced content" (Isenberg 1954:138). Isenberg was discussing art, where a specific stimulus exists and where the speaker wants the hearer to notice something about it. The situation in the psychotherapeutic session is different; in it there is usually no such common stimulus.

According to Freudian theory there may be differences between one's conscious and unconscious states, feelings, or motives. In such cases what a patient says he feels may differ considerably from his "actual" feelings.[5] The therapist has a special problem in presenting an interpretation which is both "accurate" and acceptable to the patient. In cases where the patient is trying to describe his feelings, rather than trying to conceal them, therapy talk is similar to critical communication in that the patient must convey to the therapist how he feels, using whatever linguistic and nonlinguistic means he has available. The therapist must convey his interpretation to the patient in a way that is appropriate to the patient. Communication is successful if the speaker's feelings, beliefs, and interpretations of those feelings and beliefs are communicated to the hearer. It does not matter whether the participants are using language in accord with the norms of correctness established by scientists. Nor does it matter if distinctions such as those discussed earlier as between envy and jealousy or smugness and conceit are recognized.

There are many ways of communicating information about feelings, language being only one. Balint (1963) and Rogers (1965) describe patients who used drawings to convey their feelings. Langer (1957) and Davitz (1964) discuss music and art as means of communicating emotions. And of course paralinguistic and prosodic features together with facial expressions carry a great deal of the message. However, language remains the primary means of communication in the therapeutic situation, and I want to briefly look at the way in which patients, drawing on the resources of their language, describe their feelings.

Labov & Fanshel (1977) point out that the therapeutic literature takes texts of what patients say for granted. This literature consists largely of the interpretation of patients' utterances, with little concern for precisely *what* they say and *how* they say it (14–15). Since therapy is a communicative process between two individuals, we can look at problems from the point of view of both participants—the ability of the patient to convey his feelings and experiences to the therapist and the ability of the therapist to convey his interpretation to the patient. The literature contains even less on the latter point than on the former. However, Greenson, Sullivan, and Rogers mention this problem and give examples.

> Skill in imparting insight to a patient depends upon one's ability to put into words the thoughts, fantasies, and feelings which the patient is not fully aware of and to present them in such a way that the patient can accept them as his own. One must translate from one's own vocabulary into the living language of the patient at the moment. (Greenson 1967:385)

Greenson gives an example of a patient who suffered from shame and embarrassment in a variety of social situations. The patient's mother had used the Yiddish word *pischer* to express her contempt after he wet his pants as a child. By using the same word, Greenson provided an insight for the patient by recreating his feeling of shame and by eliciting recollections of several incidents when he had had this feeling.

> Facility in selecting the right word or language is similar to what one observes in storytellers, humorists, and satirists. . . . My own personal observations seem to indicate that among psychoanalysts, the best therapists do seem to possess a good sense of humor, do have ready wit, and do enjoy the art of storytelling. (Ibid.: 386)

In discussing the kinds of things an interviewer should or should not say, Sullivan discusses psychiatric banalities.

> Still another thing that the interviewer should eschew is all meaningless comment and clouding of issues. We often fail to realize just how meaningless many comments are. A lot of bromides from the culture and

psychiatric banalities are handed out with the utmost facility, but I defy anyone to determine what most of them mean. For example, people refer to a 'mother-fixation'—and when this is done by a psychiatrist in the course of a psychiatric interview, I think it deserves nothing short of a spanking . . . 'Mother-fixation' may be a beautiful abstract idea, useful for the psychiatrist's private ruminations, but to the person who suffers the 'mother-fixation', the term is as nearly devoid of meaning, as near to being claptrap, as anything I can think of. (Sullivan 1954:35–36)

The point is that although theoretical terms or even precise descriptive terms may be necessary or at least useful for scientific purposes, they may be ineffective or detrimental in a therapeutic interaction.

Finally, Rogers (1951) quotes a testimonial from a patient whose therapist, Mr. L, was able to find the right words.

Many of the thoughts and fears in my mind were vague—I couldn't put them into exact, clear words. The fear was the thing that overwhelmed my thoughts. . . . Mr. L. took these vague thoughts and fears and put them into words that I could understand and see clearly. . . . During the second meeting I received my first jolt. Taking my vague thoughts he told me in a few words what they really meant. I broke out into a sweat, I was trembling, somewhat panicky. Those few words opened the door for me. When I walked out into the street after that meeting it was as though I were in a new world. (Rogers 1951:78)

The therapeutic literature contains a few references to the problems of patients trying to explain their feelings. Two points emerge. First of all, there are great differences among individuals, and some patients apparently have just not learned how to talk about their feelings. Secondly, there are no convenient labels in the language. "The fact that the client's concepts do not readily lend themselves to organization within the verbally labeled parts of the system makes it difficult for a person to be very articulate about how he feels, or for him to predict what he will do in a future situation . . ." (Kelly 1955, Vol. 1:110). Thirdly, what the patient says may be limited by what he can accept at the time.

The interviewer develops an impression of the *intelligence* of the interviewee. First impresssions of the intelligence of another can be quite misleading. . . . Thus one must always realize that intelligence, in the sense of something which is useful as an aid in living, is by no means necessarily measurable by verbal dexterity. Verbal dexterity is closely related to intelligence only if there has been an opportunity for the development of verbal skills. (Sullivan 1954:115).

As I have tried to suggest before, it is easy to believe that you understand everything said to you, and vice versa, but if you did not overlook negative instances, you would be greatly impressed with what queer things people mean by words that you use to mean something else. Sometimes the patient's use of words is extraordinary. He is apparently depending on a word to communicate something to you which it doesn't communicate at all, and you realize that he is still quite autistic in his verbal thinking and that there has been a very serious impairment of this extremely important aspect of his socialization. (Ibid.: 152)

Rogers (1951) quotes a patient who describes the difficulties she had in expressing herself.

I found that I ran into the most extraordinary grammatical difficulties in expressing myself. I was dissatisfied with the expression. I knew I hadn't expressed what I meant, but it was the best I could do at the time. That it was the best I could do at the time probably indicates that it was all I could face at the time. (From Miss Cam's notes, Rogers 1951:92)

Rogers also generalizes about other aspects of the process of encoding. A patient will suddenly be "hit" by a feeling. "He is hit by a feeling—not something named or labelled but an experiencing of an unknown something that has to be cautiously explored before it can be named at all" (Rogers 1961:129). With respect to finding a name or label, he writes,

Still another of these naturalistic observations has to do with the importance which the client comes to attach to *exactness* of symbolization. He wants just the precise word which for him describes the feeling he has experienced. An approximation will not do. And this is certainly for clearer communication within himself, since any one of several words would convey the meaning equally well to another. (Rogers 1961:130)

These quotations testify to the difficulty of finding the right words for the therapeutic interaction, but they still do not show very much about what patients and therapists say. Below are a few examples taken from transcripts of therapeutic sessions. In some instances, the patient and therapist are trying to identify a feeling. Two examples occur in the case of Mrs. Oak (Rogers 1961):

In earlier interviews [the patient] had talked of the fact that she did not love humanity, and that in some vague and stubborn way she felt she was right, even though others would regard her as wrong. She mentions this again as she discusses the way this experience has clarified her attitudes toward others.

C[lient]:   The next thing that occurred to me that I found myself thinking and still thinking, is somehow—and I'm not clear why—the same kind of a caring that I get when I say "I don't love humanity." Which has always sort of—I mean I was always convinced of it. So I mean, it doesn't—I knew it was a good thing, see. And I think I clarified it within myself—what it has to do with this situation. I don't know. But I found out, no, I don't love, but I do care terribly.

T[herapist]:   M-hm. M-hm. I see. . . .

C: . . . It might be expressed better in saying I care terribly what happens. But the caring is a— takes form— its structure is in understanding and not wanting to be taken in, or to contribute to those things which I feel are false and— It seems to me that in—in loving, there's a kind of final factor. If you do that, you've sort of done enough. It's a—

T: That's it, sort of.

C: Yeah. It seems to me this other thing, this caring, which isn't a good term—I mean, probably we need something else to describe this kind of thing. To say it's an impersonal thing doesn't mean anything because it isn't impersonal. I mean I feel it's very much a part of a whole. But it's something that somehow doesn't stop. . . . It seems to me you could have this feeling of loving humanity, loving people, and at the same time—go on contributing to the factors that make people neurotic, make them ill—where, what I feel is a resistance to those things.

T: You care enough to want to understand, and to want to avoid contributing to anything that would make for more neuroticism, or more of that aspect in human life.

C: Yes. And it's—(pause). Yes, it's something along those lines. (Rogers 1961:82–83)

Caring is not a precise enough word, so the patient must go on to elaborate in order to clarify this feeling. Consider an analogous excerpt from the wine discussions:

L: Wine K seems very acidic to me.

F: Does it? Maybe I don't have quite the word. It just seems less bitey. K seems least bitey of all.

B: Do you think K is thinner than M?

F: No, I'm talking about what it does to my tongue—not about how it actually tastes. Something physical that it does to my tongue.

L: Do you find a sort of—what's the word—like cotton candy? But not candy—cotton mouth?

In the next example, the same patient is searching to identify the feeling of bitterness. She also describes the specific experiences which evoke that feeling.

C: I have the feeling it isn't guilt. (Pause. She weeps) Of course I mean, I can't verbalize it yet. (Then with a rush of emotion) It's just being terribly hurt!

T: M-hm. It isn't guilt except in the sense of being very much wounded somehow.

C: (Weeping) It's—you know, often I'ven been guilty of it myself but in later years when I've heard parents say to their children "stop crying," I've had a feeling, a hurt as though, well, why should they tell them to stop crying? They feel sorry for themselves, and who can feel more adequately sorry for himself than the child. Well, that is sort of what—I mean, as though I mean I thought that they should let him cry. And—feel sorry for him too, maybe. In a rather objective kind of way. Well, that's—that's something of the kind of thing I've been experiencing. I mean, now— just right—now. And in—in—

T: That catches a little more the flavor of the feeling that it's almost as if you're really weeping for yourself.

C: Yeah. And again you see there's conflict. Our culture is such that—I mean, one doesn't indulge in self-pity. But this isn't—I mean, I feel it doesn't quite have that connotation. It may have.

T: Sort of think that there is a cultural objection to feeling sorry about yourself. And yet you feel the feeling you're experiencing isn't quite what the culture objected to either.

C: And then, of course, I've come to—to see and to feel that over this—see, I've covered it up. (Weeps) But I've covered it up with so much bitterness, which in turn I had to cover up. (Weeping) That's what I want to get rid of! I almost don't care if I hurt.

T: (Softly, and with an empathic tenderness toward the hurt she is experiencing) You feel that here at the basis of it as you experience it is a feeling of real tears for yourself. But that you can't show, musn't show, so that's been covered by bitterness that you don't like, that you'd like to be rid of. You almost feel you'd rather absorb the hurt than to—than to feel the bitterness. (Pause) And what you seem to be saying quite strongly is, I do hurt, and I've tried to cover it up.

C: I didn't know it.

T: M-hm. Like a new discovery really. (Rogers 1961:93–94)

A very interesting case involving a specific word is discussed by Labov & Fanshel (1977); in this instance the patient resists using the "correct" word and will only accept a mitigated expression. The patient, Rhoda, cannot admit that she feels anger toward her mother and aunt but will only admit to feeling *bothered* or *annoyed*. The following excerpts are taken from a fifteen-minute segment.

> Rhoda: If I see the house getting dirty, it sort of *bothers* me . . . (193)
> •
> Rhoda: I don't know why, but it *bothers* me when they say that, because they look at me as if—(307)

In both of these instances, Labov and Fanshel interpret *bother* as "angry."

> Therapist: So—then—and for some reason you feel they're *angry* because you're so underweight, or because they—think you're underweight.
>
> Rhoda: I don't— I dunno, I don't— I don't— I never felt like that— it's just that . . . no I never thought if I like that and I don't— I don't think I feel anger because I mean I just get annoyed, like I'm not— I don't say I get—angry, but it just gets annoying, to hear the same thing.
> •
> Therapist: So there's a lot of anger passing back and forth.
> (This remark is followed by a long silence)
>
> Rhoda: Yeh. (Labov & Fanshel 1977:318–20)

Frequently patients will use metaphors, analogies, or comparisons to communicate their feelings. Motion metaphors are relatively common. Three examples are taken from the notes of Miss Cam, who kept a diary of her feelings (Rogers 1951):

> I'm just so miserable and discouraged. . . . A sea, a rising tide of chaotic emotions rises up from deep, deep within me. (94)

It took four hours to write that page and a half—four hours of sinking down—no, it's not sinking down, it's more like expanding, as if bonds were loosened, and a homogeneous design got larger and larger, until you could see that what looked like continuous lines were really composed of rows of separate points, and as the design spreads out, the points get farther and farther apart, until finally the connections become so tenuous that it [sic] snaps, and the pattern collapses into a wild jumble of unrelated bits and pieces. (95)

There's a deep joy and happiness here . . . a real belongingness, a flawless functioning, in which I am a steady glow, active but unchanging though bathed in an active changing medium—a medium composed of an infinite variety of things, yet all harmoniously blended. They have individuality and form yet are not rigid: they are full of light and color but not transparent: substantial, yet not solid. The pattern moves and changes as if full of life. It's not like a kaleidoscope, not full of bits and pieces held together in harsh geometric patterns, nor changing what that abrupt collapse and re-formation. There's none of that lifeless rigidity—rather, all the parts are alive, smoothly flowing into new, dynamic, harmonious relationships. (96)

Rogers himself generalizes about the changing feelings of patients, using a movement metaphor.

The second observation is difficult to make, because we do not have good words for it. Clients seem to move toward more openly being a process, a fluidity, a changing. They are not disturbed to find that they are not the same from day to day. . . . They are in flux, and seem more content to continue in this flowing current (1961:171).

Other kinds of comparisons include feeling like a dam or an animal or working out a jigsaw puzzle.

It suddenly became clear that loving and hating, for example, are neither right nor wrong, they just are. After this, the wall seemed to disappear but beyond it, I discovered a dam holding back violent, churning waters. I felt as if I were holding back the force of these waters and if I opened even a tiny hole, I and all about me would be destroyed in the ensuing torrent of feelings represented by the water (Rogers 1951:169).

I have felt it . . . inside as though it were a little animal coming out of a cave—just a defenseless animal, who has been unmercifully defeated, horribly lacerated and bleeding. . . . Now I don't feel any longer as though I see him. I feel as though I *am* that little animal, whipped and helpless and terribly wounded. (From Miss Cam's notes, Rogers 1951:124)

This last description is interesting in several respects. First the patient has to imagine and project what a beaten and wounded animal must feel like. Then in comparing herself to this animal, she must assume that the therapist would also be able to imagine and project the same thing.

The final example is taken from Mrs. Oak, who describes the experience of the therapeutic process and of becoming aware of herself.

> Client: It all comes pretty vague. But you know I keep, keep having the thought occur to me that this whole process for me is kind of like examining pieces of a jigsaw puzzle. It seems to me I, I'm in the process now of examining the individual pieces which really don't have too much meaning. Probably handling them, not even beginning to think of a pattern. That keeps coming to me. And it's interesting to me because I, I really don't like jigsaw puzzles. They've always irritated me. But that's my feeling. And I mean I pick up little pieces (she gestures throughout this conversation to illustrate her statements) with absolutely no meaning except I mean the, feeling that you get from simply handling them without seeing them as a pattern, but just from the touch, I probably feel, well it is going to fit someplace here. (Rogers 1961:77)

These excerpts illustrate some of the conceptual and linguistic devices available for encoding and describing feelings. Since they are taken out of context, they may not successfully convey to the reader the patient's feeling. Moreover, a conversation between speakers with a long history of interaction has deep meaning and interpretations that outsiders would not notice (Labov & Fanshel 1977:271–72). In therapy "both patient and therapist are presumably working towards making certain propositions explicit" (Labov & Fanshel 53); that is, the patient tries to explain his feelings and experiences to the therapist, and the therapist helps the patient to do so, in part by getting the patient to recognize feelings that the patient is not aware of.

The important way in which the therapeutic session resembles critical communication is that each pair works out its own vocabulary of words, phrases, and other kinds of expressions. If one pair uses *anger* to talk about a feeling and another pair uses *hostility* to talk about the same feeling, it would not matter, so long as each understood the other. The case of Rhoda is interesting because she could admit to feeling only *bothered* at one stage of her treatment. Communicative success is determined by the satisfaction of the participants, and the language must be meaningful to each patient and therapist. Scientific accuracy, as determined by an authoritative body of psychological experts, is irrelevant.

This phenomenon parallels the discussions of wine and art. Each conversational participant wants the other(s) to recognize or perceive or experience something, and each uses whatever linguistic or other means achieves this purpose. In the case of wine or art there is an independent object that all participants can experience. In the therapeutic situation there is not; the therapist and patient must assume that both share a sufficiently similar range of feelings, background, language, and experience.

In scientific discourse it is necessary for all the speakers and hearers to share the same vocabulary and agree on the extensions and intensions of this vocabulary. For critical communication, this situation is not necessary, and it may even be detrimental. A patient could become very annoyed by a therapist who constantly "corrected" his descriptions.

The problem is this: psychiatrists and psychologists who write articles for the scientific community on therapy draw on their experience with patients. To what extent is the scientific language of the therapists *qua* scientists influenced by the language of their patients—language which is appropriate to the therapeutic sessions? Do the therapists translate what the patients say into the scientific language (of the theory they are working in), or is their use of even scientific language influenced by the ways in which their patients use these expressions? The psychiatrist or psychologist *qua* scientist must learn and use a standardized language—to the extent that such a language exists or could be developed; *qua* therapist he must relate his language to the needs, abilities, and knowledge of the patient. Yet it is not unreasonable to suppose that the types of language used in the two roles influence each other.

PHATIC COMMUNION AND DESCRIBING PEOPLE

Gossip was briefly discussed in chapter 10, and certainly one favorite topic of gossip is other people: the kind of people they are, how they behave, and why they do what they do. How accurate are such remarks? They need not be very accurate at all. If the purpose of gossip is to pass time, create social bonds, and maintain social control, the degree of accuracy may be similar to that of nonexpert wine drinkers describing wine.

In fact, I propose the following experiment for anyone to conduct who cares to: select three people—three men or three women—and describe their personality, character, and moods, but do not mention age or appearance. Give these three descriptions and the three names to someone else who knows them and see if that person matches correctly. Of course, to be comparable to the wine experiments, the persons cannot be maximally different. In my wine tests, the three wines were never Sherry, Port, and Champagne. Or have several pairs of people independently agree on a characterization of someone known by all. Would the various descriptions show any resemblances?

I would expect to find many similarities between performance on such a test and on the wine tests. Descriptions would reveal the subjective attitude or bias of the describer. The choice of a descriptor such as *generous* vs. *overextravagant* or *thrifty* instead of *stingy* would reveal this. If people were to discuss the meaning of the words as well as describing other individuals who had these properties, I would expect to find fair agreement on the intralinguistic relationship of the words (*generous* → *not stingy; generous* → *good*) but considerable variation in applying the words to people. And for nonscientific conversational purposes, that is good enough.

Conclusion

We have surveyed many aspects of talking about wine. As we have seen, there is a large vocabulary, which is by no means a closed set. The language has productive means of expanding the vocabulary—one of which is to add suffixes to stems and to make use of the processes of derivational morphology, but a second and more important way is to extend the meaning of existing words—via semantic widening, metaphorical transfer, and exploitation of the various lexical relationships which are proposed by semantic field theories. These intralinguistic relationships provide a lexical structure which not only plays a crucial role in extending word meaning to new semantic domains but also explains why communicative success is possible in the absence of definite reference or denotation.

In addition to intralinguistic relationships, words (at least many words) are connected to the world; that is, they denote some object, property, event, process, or situation. Many of these words, wine descriptors for example, are learned in rather casual ways. In addition, many terms are vague, for example the gradable adjectives, which presuppose a norm or reference class. As a result, there is considerable variation among speakers in the way they apply words to the world.

It is a mistake to think of each word as having a fixed, specific meaning, where meaning includes both intra- and extralinguistic relationships. Language is dynamic and fluid, and the semantic part of

217

our language is highly flexible, enabling speakers to talk about new things, events, and situations, and to encode into language things which no one has talked about before.

Sometimes there arise circumstances when speaker variability and indefinite denotation cannot be tolerated. This occurs when doing science and reporting the results to an audience of strangers via technical journals. In such situations the participants must trouble themselves to find out whether they mean the same things by the words they use, and if they do not, then for successful communication, they must do something to achieve consensus, or at least to make the others aware that there are dialect and idiolect differences.

However, there are other situations, such as engaging in critical communication or just gossiping, when an insistance on accuracy might be out of place and destroy the purpose of the conversation. Many discourse purposes require little, if any, attention to precise reference. And some, such as telling jokes, require none.

I have used wine talk as a example of the various intra- and extra-linguistic aspects of meaning. But I do not believe that wine conversation is unique. I have tried to draw parallels in the area of person and personality description. And probably similarities can be found in the problems of encoding into language other perception (how things sound, look, and feel) and other aesthetic domains. Investigating how people talk about music would be an interesting topic. Much of the vocabulary would be similar to that of talking about wine.

I have not provided a conceptual framework for the place of semantics in a grammar, nor have I provided an account of what meaning is. However, the wine vocabulary shows that an account of meaning must take into account both intralinguistic relationships and denotation. It is not possible to reduce one to the other. In addition, the wine vocabulary shows great differences among the words as to their connnections with the world. Some terms like *grape* have a fairly tight connection, while others, like *grapy,* have a much weaker connection, and still others, like *elegant,* have still less connection, or at least their connection is mediated by the preferences of the speakers. Any complete semantic theory must take into account this variety in the lexicon.

POSTSCRIPT

One aspect of the wine literature that I have not mentioned is the satirical material which puts down wine experts and implies that the whole business of making subtle judgments and discriminations and of identifying wines is fraudulent—that describing wines in a manner more sophisticated than "good" or "bad" is an attempt to show off, and that people who claim to be able to distinguish between Moselle and Rhine wines are putting on airs.

I have no doubt that some people can make very fine discriminations and can identify wines which they have had considerable experience with. But to do so requires an excellent memory for taste and smell as well as a sensitive palate. It may be that relatively few people have this ability, so that the majority, who lack this capacity, are suspicious of the abilities of those few.

Most people have good musical memories and can easily identify composers and pieces of music. But suppose things were otherwise and that although everyone liked music, only five percent of the population could distinguish Beethoven from Bach or could recognize specific works, such as the Jupiter Symphony. Would many of the nonmusical individuals have a suspicious attitude toward the musical experts?

From my own experience in wine tasting over these past years as researcher, subject, and just plain wine drinker, I have concluded that my palate is reasonably good—I can distinguish tastes well and make reasonable evaluations, but my wine memory of specific wines is not so good. I could select a good wine cellar but never become a wine writer.

Before I worked on this project I used to enjoy describing wines and finding the "right" word. But after carrying out these experiments and learning how difficult it is, by expert standards, to describe wines I would now rather drink and enjoy wines nonverbally. Perhaps this is a disadvantage of taking a hobby and turning it into one's work.

Notes

1. WINE WORDS

1. Frank Lewis points out that some of the descriptors in Table 1 are closely associated with specific wines, e.g., *chalky* with Chablis, *grassy* with Sauvignon Blanc, and *mint* or *eucalyptus* for certain Cabernet Sauvignon wines.

2. Some tannin may get into wine that is aged in wood.

3. French has a more elaborate and precise classification for sparkling wines. First of all there is a distinction between *mousseux*, "full sparkling," and *petillant*, "light natural sparkle." A more precise classification is based on "atmosphere"—pressure behind the cork. *Mousseux* has at least 5.5 atmosphere; *cremant* has 2.5 to 4 atm., and *perlant* has 1.5 to 2.5 atm. (Vandyke Price 1975:101.)

4. Other wine words on Table 2 in chapter 2 will be discussed after describing the resources available to speakers for extending word meanings and using words in novel ways.

5. Whether or not the definition can help one use and understand the meaning of *round* in a wine context, it is certainly a marvelous use of language.

2. EXTENDING THE VOCABULARY

1. I am no longer as willing as previously to mark forms as impossible, since with a suitable context and a good story a plausible context can be found.

2. Arnoff makes a similar point with respect to partially productive affixes. If an affix is partially productive but would create a new word that already has a rival, the new word is *blocked* (1976:45). However, a completely productive affix, such as *-like*, would not be blocked. Marchand (1960) classifies *-like* as a semisuffix, halfway between a suffix and *a full word*.

3. *Flat* and *sharp* are used in the domain of spatial dimension. *Flat* was used as a dimensional term by 1400. However, the first citation for it as a taste word is listed as 1607 in the OED. If we examine the meanings of *sharp*, we can see that *sharp* was used for touch by 825, for taste by 1000, and for dimension by 1537. I claim that it was only at this later period, when *sharp* and *flat* developed their antonymous relationship, that *flat* became available (via its antonymy with *sharp*) to be used for taste and feel in the mouth.

4. Perhaps one could make out a case that *silky* and *velvety* are derived morphologically from *like silk, like velvet*. But it is the properties of softness and smoothness that are relevant. One cannot experience the qualities of a velvety wine by sticking a piece of velvet in one's mouth.

5. Frank Lewis (personal communication) has suggested this interpretation.

3. THERE ARE INTENSIONS AND INTENTIONS

1.   It is an irony of modern linguistics that although linguists have emphasized the need to develop grammars and semantics that go beyond describing corpora, they have not yet even developed descriptive devices capable of dealing with substantial corpora.

2.   This part of Kripke's view is implausible for most of our nontechnical natural kind vocabulary. It may do for scientific names like *Cabernet Sauvignon*, but hardly for *grape*. At any rate, that part of linguistic history is not likely to be discovered.

3   I believe that Putnam's prediction about what scientists would do is correct. But suppose that they were to do otherwise. Would Putnam say that the scientists had made a wrong choice or would he go along with their judgments? In other words, to what extent is Putnam's position a normative one about how scientists ought to behave? This topic is taken up in chapter 9.

4.   Notice the semantic drift of *type*. A Cabernet-type wine is not necessarily a type of Cabernet wine.

5.   Tom Larson and Frank Lewis have questioned my use of *real*. Might not a native of Los Angeles, having drunk only California Sauterne, on drinking Sauternes in Paris, ask for a real Sauterne, meaning a California one? I suppose that, as with brand names, the first one to establish a name has the priority and the right to call it *real*.

6.   I am aware of problems with the definition of synonymy as bilateral entailment. For example, there must be some way to rule out pathological entailments such as

Red Bordeaux   ⟷   Claret v. round square.

However, for descriptive purposes concerning the semantic relationships in a natural language, the use of statements such as

Red Bordeaux   ⟷   Claret

remain empirically important.

7.   Although Rosch and Mervis (1975) and Labov (1978) have explored the notion of applying scalar judgments to nouns and the problem of class membership, the words they deal with are clearly different from the gradable predicates dealt with here. Boertien (1975) and Faust (1978) also investigate speakers' responses in classifying objects.

8.   My discussion is an informal account of McConnell-Ginet (1973). See also Kamp (1975) and Fine (1975) and formal semantic treatments of vague predicates.

9.   Occasionally wines with 0% sugar are judged sweet because of a fruity aroma, a lack of sour-bitter-harsh elements, or from other ingredients in the wine.

10.   Not all antonyms are gradable ones. Examples of nongradables are *male-female, married-single, dead-alive*. Nongradable antonyms can be handled successful by meaning postulates such as the following for *dead* and *alive:*

dead → not alive
not dead → alive
alive → dead
not dead → alive

11. Additional conditions are necessary to show the relationship of *excellent* to *good* and *warm* to *hot* and to rule out treating *warm* and *hot* as antonyms. See A. Lehrer & K. Lehrer (1982).

12. Katz (1972) is an exception, since he has analyzed *good*, but he deals with only some of its uses. See also McConnell-Ginet (1979).

13. Gale (1975) argues that wine judgments are true or false because there are significant inferential steps from the judgments that a wine has certain descriptive properties (which Gale assumes are true or false) to evaluative ones.

14. Many papers in Ortony (1979) discuss the problems of whether metaphorical statements can be true. The papers by Searle and Black in particular address this issue.

15. See K. Lehrer (1977, 1978) for a method of evaluating conflicting judgments among experts.

4. REMARKS ON METHODOLOGY

1. A general problem in all the sciences has to do with the relationship between theory and data, where *interpretive* statements relate the two (see Hempel 1958). For example, a scientist may argue that a particular experimental outcome will confirm theory A but disconfirm theory B. However, these interpretive statements may themselves be controversial, and, in the social sciences at least, different investigators may argue about which of several incompatible theories is supported by a piece or set of data.

5. EXPERIMENTS AND SUBJECTS

1. At some sessions three white wines *and* three red wines were served.

2. Some subjects must have had terrible memories, because they seemed to need an enormous amount of wine to complete the experiments.

6. THE STANFORD SUBJECTS

1. I was intrigued by the fact that a few subjects, on seeing the list, commented that they had not known before that certain descriptors could be applied to wine, and they promptly used these words.

2. I am grateful to Marge Cruse for help with the statistical analysis.

3. At later sessions Stanford subjects were served whites at room temperature because of the problem of trying to keep the temperature constant for all tasters. Temperature affects discrimination of certain tastes (Geldard, 1953).

4. The subjects actually preferred wines with some sugar (1%–2%).

5. A white wine aged in wood might pick up some tannin, but it is unlikely that wine B had any wood aging.

6. The percentage of sugar for Z, 1.5% was supplied by the winery. My own measurement was close to 1.3%. Either my measurement was too low,

or, in the particular bottle served, some of the sugar had converted to alcohol. The latter hypothesis is plausible, because the wine showed some signs of secondary fermentation.

7. The probability of a correct match was ¼ since there was one fake description as well as the three real ones.

7. THE TUCSON SUBJECTS

1. Subjects were free to perform this task by ordering wines or words as they pleased. Some started with the *most* X on some wines and the *least* X on others. Probabilities were figures as $1/3$ even though some would be conditional. That is, after a subject selected one wine as the *biggest*, he would have a choice of two for the *least big*.

2. A buttery nose is produced by any of a number of aliphatic alcohols (butanol, pentanol, propyl, butyl, amyl) which have the fusel oil odor (Amerine & Roessler 1976:75).

3. I have treated the trio as two pairs: the two who matched all wines correctly were one pair and the third subject and the previously defined pair comprised the second pair.

4. This definition is different from Casagrande & Hale's (1976) definition and use of the term *exemplification*.

5. See K. Lehrer (1977, 1978) for a method of rating judges.

8. WINE SCIENTISTS—THE DAVIS SUBJECTS

1. I wish to thank Steve Rust for working out the statistical results.

2. David Sankoff designed the cluster program used for Tucson subjects; the one used for the Davis subjects was taken from Anderberg (1973). The clusters were determined by the words applied to the same wine, regardless of which wine. For example, if subject A said that wine 1 was *soft* and *round* and subject B said that wine 2 was *soft* and *round,* there were two instances of *soft* clustering with *round.*

9. FUNCTIONS OF LANGUAGE

1. Searle (1969) uses *proposition,* a somewhat different concept, in place of locutionary act.

2. Other illocutionary taxonomies can be found in Austin (1962), Searle (1969), Fraser (1974), Sadock (1974), McCawley (1979), and Vendler (1972) to name a few.

3. More specific categories of language function can be found in Halliday (1975), but those categories have been devised to account for child language acquisition.

10. The Development of Scientific Language

1. Friedrich (1979:493–95) traces the scientific models in anthropology and anthropological linguistics.

2. This view is also implicit in Quine (1953).

3. The existence of "independent" measures assumes that the scientific community subscribes to the same theory of measurement for what is being measured.

4. Schiffman & Erickson (1971) reject the notion of primary tastes, replacing them with a model of parameters or dimensions, to which they add alkaline as a fifth parameter.

5. Eugene Mielke points out that when writers suspect a word is confusing, they must be careful to define the usage. For example, among grape growers in the English-speaking world there is much confusion about the meaning of *frost* and *freeze* and *rest* and *dormancy*.

6. Current American systems tend to be based on a 20-point scale. See Amerine & Roessler (1976:124ff) for a discussion of various scoring systems; also Machamer (1977).

11. Nonscientific Uses of Language

1. These descriptors are used for many beverages—tea, coffee, beer. The following descriptions of coffee were taken from a coffee shop menu: *fragrant, sweet, rich, full-bodied; aromatic, rich* and *sweet, lively; rich* and *sharp, lively, heavy body.*

2. The matching experience does not exactly involve critical communication. Critical communication would more appropriately be applied to a situation where all the individuals had the same wine and were trying to characterize the flavor.

3. Hymes (1974:109) reports that different groups have different beliefs about what an infant can understand, and individuals in a group may also vary considerably. The same may be true of pets, and it is hard to tell how much people believe their pets can understand. I once brought my kitten to the vet, and the kitten constantly meowed in the waiting room. A man and woman, owners of a large grey cat, told their cat to talk to my kitten. The man said to his cat, "Talk to the cat" (my kitten). The woman added, "Tell him in your language it's all right. He's nervous. Talk to the pretty cat." This conversation could have been intended for their cat, my kitten, me, the other spouse, or some combination. Or this couple may have believed that: (1) animals understand human language and (2) can convey human messages via some communication system of their own.

Speaking to animals or infants (or for that matter inanimate objects) in the presence of other speakers creates another dimension for the ethnography of communication, since the intended receiver is not formally the addressee.

4. Language can also be used to prevent or destroy bonds. A speaker can be quarrelsome or critical. Malinowski (1953:478) uses the expression *bonds of antipathy* but does not elaborate.

5. Sacks points out also that talking does not consist simply of blocks of

talk about a topic. He also suggests that "conversation has much of the additional phonological, grammatical, and thematic patterning which is usually thought to typify works of literature." Reported in Coulthard (1977:71). See also Philips (1976).

6. I am indebted to Dick Oerhle for pointing out the need for this distinction.

12. DESCRIBING PEOPLE

1. Thakurdas & Thakurdas (1978) in their list of 16 characteristics of psychopaths include: (1) lack of remorse or shame, (2) incapacity for love, (3) general poverty in major affective reactions, and (4) unresponsiveness in general interpersonal relations.

2. An interesting discussion of threat, fear, anxiety, and guilt can be found in Kelly (1955: vol. I, ch. 11) in which these concepts are handled as theoretical and defined within the psychological theory of personal constructs.

3. For an individual item accuracy was sometimes as high as 100% or as low as 25%.

4. Bloomfield's discussion of scientific language (1939) shows an awareness of the problem of variations in the meaning of terms, but he overrates the ability of making the meanings precise through definition. Wilson, in his review of Bloomfield's 'Linguistic Aspects of Science', points out that scientists in taxonomic biology tried to rely on careful definitions, but they finally had to turn to type specimens, which were deposited in museums (1940:259–60).

5. There are serious epistemological problems concerning the truth or falsity and the verification of statements like "Jones believes that he loves his mother but he really hates her." (Of course, the status of such statements must be considered relative to a psychological theory.) We can imagine a situation involving a beginning therapist and a patient who excels in deceiving himself and the therapist. Both individuals might agree on the description of the patient's feelings, but a more experienced therapist might recognize this situation. 'Correctness' here would be determined by the judgment of the more experienced therapist, and verification might consist of his persuading the beginning therapist and ultimately the patient to reject the original characterization and accept a different one. (I am indebted to Keith Lehrer for insightful discussions on this point.) Erikson (1964:53) admits that therapy is subjective at the center, but talks about a "disciplined subjectivity." He goes on to advocate that the therapist include his own feelings and responses to the patient in his interpretation (ibid.: 72–73). When a therapist suggests an interpretation to a patient, assent by the patient is evidence for the correctness, but that alone is not sufficient. Such an interpretation must also lead to new insights and progress (ibid.: 74–75).

Bibliography

Adam, Henry B. 1969. 'Mental illness or interpersonal behavior?' in *The Study of Abnormal Psychology*, M. Zax and G. Stricker, eds. New York: Macmillan.

Alexander, James. 1960. 'The psychology of bitterness', in Socarides 1977:295–310.

Allport, G.W., and H.S. Odbert. 1936. 'Trait-names: A psycholexical study', *Psychological Monographs*, 47.

American Joint Committee. 1977. *Manual for Staging of Cancer*. Chicago.

American Psychiatric Association. 1968. *Diagnostic and Statistical Manual of Mental Disorders*. 2nd ed. Washington, D.C.

American Psychiatric Association. 1980. *Diagnostic and Statistical Manual of Mental Disorders*. 3rd ed. Washington, D.C.

Amerine, Maynard, Rose Marie Panghorn, and Edward Roessler. 1965. *Principles of Sensory Evaluation of Food*. New York: Academic Press.

Amerine, Maynard, and Edward Roessler. 1977. *Wines: Their Sensory Evaluation*. San Francisco: Freeman.

Amerine, M.A., E.B. Roessler, and F. Filipello. 1959. 'Modern sensory methods of evaluating wine', *Hilgardia* 28:477–567.

Amerine, M.A. and V.L. Singleton, 1965. *Wine: An Introduction for Americans*. Berkeley and Los Angeles: University of California Press.

Anderberg, Michael. 1973. *Cluster Analysis for Applications*. New York: Academic Press.

Arlow, Jacob A. 1957. 'On smugness', in Socarides 1977:259–82.

Arnoff, Mark. 1976. *Word Formation in Generative Grammar*. Cambridge, Massachusetts: MIT Press.

Asher, Gerald. 1974. 'Wine journal', *Gourmet* 34.5:12–14, 52.

Austin, John. 1962. *How to Do Things with Words*. Oxford: Oxford University Press.

Bach, Kent. 1975. 'Performatives are statements, too', *Philosophical Studies* 28:229–36.

Bach, Kent, and Robert M. Harnish. 1979. *Linguistic Communication and Speech Acts*. Cambridge, Massachusetts: MIT Press.

Bales, Robert. 1950. *Interaction Process Analysis*. Cambridge, Massachusetts: Addison-Wesley.

Balint, Enid. 1963. 'On being empty of oneself', in Socarides, 1977:335–54.

Berlin, Brent, and Paul Kay. 1970. *Basic Color Terms*. Berkeley: University of California Press.

Bespaloff, Alex, ed. 1977. *The Fireside Book of Wine*. New York: Simon & Schuster.

Bion, W.R. 1958. 'On arrogance', in Socarides 1977:283–94.

Black, Max. 1979. 'More about metaphor', in Ortony 1979:19–43.

Bloomfield, L. 1939. *Linguistic Aspects of Science*, in *International Encyclopedia of Unified Science*, Vol. 1.4. O. Neurath, R. Carnap, and C. Morris, eds. Chicago: University of Chicago Press.

227

Boertien, Harmann. 1975. Vagueness of container nouns and cognate verbs. Ph.D. dissertation. Austin: University of Texas.

Botha, Rudolph P. 1973. *The Justification of Linguistic Hypotheses: A Study of Non-Demonstrative Inference in Transformational Grammar.* The Hague: Mouton.

Botha, Rudolph P. 1979. 'External evidence in the validation of mentalistic theories: A Chomskyan paradox', *Lingua* 48:299–328.

Broadbent, J. 1977. *Wine Tasting.* London: Christie's Wine Productions.

Carnap, Rudolf. 1937. *Logical Syntax of English.* Repr. ed., London.

Casagrande, Joseph, and Kenneth Hale. 1967. 'Semantic relationships in Papago folk definitions', in *Studies in Southwestern Ethnolinguistics,* Dell Hymes and William Bittle, eds. pp. 165–96. The Hague: Mouton.

Caul, Jean. 1957. 'The profile method of flavor analysis', *Advances in Food Research* 7.1:1–40.

Chomsky, Noam. 1975. *Reflections on Language.* New York: Pantheon.

Ciccone, J. Richard and David J. Barry. 1978. 'The experience of using DSM III in a court clinic setting', *Bulletin of the American Academy of Psychiatry and Law.*

Clark, Eve V., and Herbert H. Clark. 1980. 'When nouns surface as verbs', *Language* 55:767–811.

Cooper, J.E., R.E. Kendell, B.J. Garland, L. Sharpe, and J.R.M. Copeland. 1972. *Psychiatric Diagnosis in New York and London.* London: Oxford University Press.

Coseriu, E. 1966. 'Structure lexicale et enseignement du vocabulaire', *Actes du premier colloque international de linguistique appliquée.* Nancy, France.

Coseriu, E. 1968. 'Les structures lexématiques', *Zeitschrift für französische Sprache und Literatur* Beiheft 1:3–16.

Coulthard, Malcolm. 1977. *An Introduction to Discourse Analysis.* London: Longmans.

Davitz, Joel R. 1964. *The Communication of Emotional Meaning.* New York: McGraw-Hill.

Dermer, O.C., G. Gorin, and K.L. Loening. 1977. 'The standardization of chemical language', *International Journal of the Sociology of Language* 11:61–83.

Dethier, V.G. 1978. 'Other tastes, other worlds', *Science* 201:224–228.

Dickie, George, 1971. *Aesthetics.* Indianapolis: Bobbs-Merrill Co.

Donnellan, Keith. 1966. 'Reference and definite descriptions', *Philosophical Review* 75:281–304.

Dutt, Gordon, Eugene A. Mielke, and Wade H. Wolfe. 1977. Final Report Regional Grape Development Project—Phase I—Four Corners Regional Commission Demonstration Project. Tucson, Arizona.

Erikson, Erik. 1964. 'The nature of clinical evidence', in *Insight and Responsibility.* London: Faber & Faber.

Esau, Helmut. 1973. *Nominalization and Complementation in Modern German.* Amsterdam: North Holland.

Faust, Manfred. 1978. 'Wortfeldstruktur und Wortverwendung.' *Wirkendes Wort* 6:365–401.

Ferguson, Charles. 1964. 'Baby talk in six languages', *American Anthropologist* 66.II:103–14.

Fine, Kit. 1975. 'Vagueness, truth, and logic', *Synthese* 30:265–300.

Fraser, Bruce. 1974. 'A partial analysis of vernacular performative verbs', in *Toward Tomorrow's Linguistics*, R. Shuy and C.J. Baily, eds. Washington, D.C.: Georgetown University Press.

Freud, Sigmund. 1916. *Wit and Its Relation to the Unconscious*. London: K. Paul, Trench, Trubner & Co.

Friedrich, Paul. 1979. *Language, Context, and the Imagination*. Stanford: Stanford University Press.

Gale, George. 1975. 'Are some aesthetic judgments empirically true?' *American Philosophical Quarterly* 12:341–48.

Geldard, Frank. 1953. *The Human Senses*. New York: Wiley.

Gelman, David. 1979. 'Beyond neurosis', *Newsweek*, Jan. 8.

Gluckman, Max. 1963. 'Gossip & scandal', *Current Anthropology* 4:307–15.

Goldberg, Lewis R. 1975. 'Toward a taxonomy of personality descriptive terms', *Oregon Research Institute Technical Report* 15.2. Eugene, Oregon.

Goldberg, Lewis R. 1981. 'Developing a Taxonomy of trait-descriptive terms', in *New Directions for Methodology of Social and Behavioral Science: Problems with Language Imprecision*. D. Fiskke, ed., pp. 43–65. San Francisco: Jossey-Bass.

Goldstein, Martin, and Inge F. Goldstein. 1978. *How We Know*. New York: Plenum Press.

Goodman, Nelson. 1968. *Languages of Art*. Indianapolis: Bobbs-Merrill Co.

Greenson, Ralph. 1967. *The Technique and Practice of Psychoanalysis, I*. New York: International Universities Press.

Greenson, Ralph. 1953. 'On boredom', in Socarides 1977:219–38.

Grice, H.P. 1957. 'Meaning', *Philosophical Review* 66:377–88.

Grice, H.P. 1975. 'Logic and conversation', in *Syntax and Speech Semantics*, Vol. 3 *Speech Acts*. P. Cole and J. Morgan, eds. pp. 44–58.

Halliday, M.A.K. 1975. *Learning How to Mean*. London: Arnold.

Halliday, M.A.K. 1978. *Language as Social Semiotic*. Baltimore: University Park Press.

Hanson, Norwood Russell. 1958. *Patterns of Discovery*. Cambridge: Cambridge University Press.

Heider, Karl G. 1975. 'Inconsistencies and elaborations: Two lexical studies of Dani cognition', MS.

Hempel, Carl G. 1958. 'The theoretician's dilemma', in *Minnesota Studies of the Philosophy of Science Vol. II*, H. Feigl, M. Scrivan, and G. Maxwell, eds., pp. 37–99. Minneapolis: University of Minnesota Press.

Hobbes, Thomas. 1651. *Leviathan*.

Hymes, Dell. 1972. 'Models in the interaction of language and social life', in *Direction in Sociolinguistics*, J. Gumpers and D. Hymes, eds., pp. 35–71. New York: Holt, Rinehart, & Winston.

Hymes, Dell. 1974. *Foundations in Sociolinguistics*. Philadelphia: University of Pennsylvania Press.

Isaacs, Kenneth S., James Alexander, and Ernest A. Haggard. 1963. 'Faith, trust, and gullibility', in Socarides 1977:355–76.

Isenberg, Arnold. 1954. 'Critical communication', in *Aesthetics and Language*, William Elton, ed., pp. 114–30. New York: Philosophical Library.

Jakobson, Roman. 1960. 'Linguistics and poetics', in *Style in Language*, Thomas Sebeok, ed., pp. 350–77. Cambridge: MIT Press.

Kamp, J.A.W. 1975. 'Two theories about adjectives', in *Formal Semantics of*

Natural Languages, E. Keenan, ed. Cambridge: Cambridge University Press.

Katz, Jerrold S. 1972. *Semantic Theory.* New York: Harper & Row.

Katz, Jerrold S. 1977. *Propositional Structure and Illocutionary Force.* New York: Crowell.

Kelly, G.A. 1955. *The Psychology of Personal Constructs.* New York: Norton & Co.

Kempson, Ruth M. 1977. *Semantic Theory.* Cambridge: Cambridge University Press.

Kittay, Eva, and Adrienne Lehrer. 1981. 'Semantic fields and the structure of metaphor', *Studies in Language* 5:31–63.

Klapp, Orrin E. 1962. *Heroes, Villains, and Fools.* Englewood Cliffs: Prentice-Hall.

Koestler, Arthur. 1964. *The Act of Creation.* New York: Macmillan.

Korzybrski, Alfred. 1933. *Science and Sanity: An Introduction to Non-Aristotelian Systems and General Semantics.* Lancaster, Pa.: Science Press Printing Co.

Kripke, Sol. 1972. 'Naming and necessity', in *Semantics for Natural Language,* D. Davidson and G. Harmon, eds., pp. 253–355. Dordrecht: Reidel.

Kris, Ernst. 1940. 'Laughter as an expressive process', in Socarides 1977:87–108.

Kuhn, Thomas. 1962. *The Structure of Scientific Revolutions.* Chicago: University of Chicago Press.

Labov, William. 1972. 'Some principles of linguistic methodology', *Language in Society* 1:97–120.

Labov, William. 1975. *What Is a Linguistic Fact?* Lisse: Peter de Ridder Press.

Labov, William. 1978. 'Denotational Structure'. *Papers from the Parasession on the Lexicon,* D. Farkes, W. Jakobson, and K. Todrys, eds., pp. 220–60. Chicago: Chicago Linguistic Society.

Labov, William, and David Fanshel. 1977. *Therapeutic Discourse.* New York: Academic Press.

Ladefoged, Peter. 1960. 'The value of phonetic statements', *Language* 36:387–96.

Lakoff, George, and Mark Johnson. 1980. *Metaphors We Live By.* Chicago: University of Chicago Press.

Langer, Susanne K. 1975. *Philosophy in a New Key.* Cambridge, Massachusetts: Harvard University Press.

Lehrer, Adrienne. 1974. *Semantic Fields and Lexical Structure.* Amsterdam: North Holland.

Lehrer, Adrienne. 1975. 'Talking about wine', *Language* 51:901–23.

Lehrer, Adrienne. 1978a. 'Structure of the lexicon and transfer of meaning', *Lingua* 45:95–123.

Lehrer, Adrienne. 1978b. 'We drank wine, we talked, and a good time was had by all', *Semiotica* 23:243–78.

Lehrer, Adrienne, 1982a. 'Critical communication: Wine and therapy.' In *Exceptional Language and Linguistics,* L. Obler and L. Menn, eds., pp. 67–79. New York: Academic Press.

Lehrer, Adrienne. 1982b. 'Die Sprache der Weinprobe—Zur Entwicklung und Verwendung wissenschaftlicher Terminologien'. Christoph Küper, trans. *Zeitschrift für Semiotik* 4.4.

Lehrer, Adrienne, and Keith Lehrer. 1982. 'Antonymy'. *Linguistics and Philosophy* 5.4:483–502.

Lehrer, Keith. 1977. 'Social information', *The Monist* 60:473–87.

Lehrer, Keith. 1978. 'Consensus and comparison: A theory of social rationality', in *Foundations and Applications of Decision Theory* Vol. 1, C.A. Hooker, J.J. Leach, E.F. McClennen, eds., pp. 283–310. Dordrecht: Reidel.

Levin, Samuel P. 1977. *The Semantics of Metaphor*. Baltimore: John Hopkins University Press.

Lexique. 1963. *Lexique de la Vigne et du Vin*. Paris: Office International.

Ljung, Magnus. 1970. *English Denominal Adjectives*. Lund: Acta Universitatis Gothoburgensis.

Loewenberg, Ina. 1975. 'Identifying metaphors', *Foundations of Language* 12:315–38.

Lyons, John. 1977. *Semantics*. Cambridge: Cambridge University Press.

Lyons, John. 1968. *Introduction to Linguistics*. Cambridge: Cambridge University Press.

Machamer, Peter. 1977. *A Wine Evaluation System*. Pittsburgh, Pennsylvania.

Malinowski, Bronislaw. 1953. 'The problem of meaning in primitive language', in supplement to *The Meaning of Meaning*, C.K. Odgen, I.A. Richards, eds., pp. 451–510. New York: Harcourt Brace.

Marchand, Hans. 1960. *The Categories and Types of Present-Day English Word Formation*. Munich: Beck.

McCawley, James. 1978. 'Logic and the lexicon', *Papers from the Parasession on the Lexicon*, D. Farkas, W. Jacobsen, and K. Todrys, eds., pp. 261–77. Chicago: Chicago Linguistic Society.

McCawley, James. 1979a. 'Remarks on the lexicography of performative verbs' in *Adverbs, Vowels, and Other Objects of Wonder*, Chicago: University of Chicago Press.

McCawley, James. 1979b. 'Some ideas not to live by', in *Adverbs, Vowels, and Other Objects of Wonder*. Chicago: University of Chicago Press.

McConnell-Ginet, Sally. 1973. Comparative constructions in English: A syntactic and semantic analysis. Ph.D. dissertation, Rochester, New York: University of Rochester.

McConnell-Ginet, Sally. 1979. 'On the deep (and surface) adjective *good*' in *Contributions to Grammatical Studies*, Linda Waugh, Frans Van Coetsem, eds., pp. 132–50. Leiden: Brill.

McDermott, R.P., and David R. Roth. 1978. 'The social organization of behavior: Interactional approaches', *Annual Review of Anthropology* 7:321–45.

McLemore, Clinton W., and Lorna S. Benjamin. 1979. 'Whatever happened to interpersonal diagnosis?' *American Psychologist* 34:17–34.

Miller, David. 1967. *Scientific Sociology*. Englewood Cliffs: Prentice-Hall.

Miller, H.E. 1945. ' "Acceptance" and related attitudes as demonstrated in psychotherapeutic interviews', *Journal of Clinical Psychiatry* 5:83–87.

Mindess, Harvey. 1971. *Laughter and Liberation*. Los Angeles: Nash.

Moskowitz, Howard R. 1970. 'Ratio scales of sugar sweetness', *Persception & Psychophysics* 7:315–20.

Nida, Eugene. 1975. *Exploring Semantic Structures. Componential Analysis of Meaning*. Munich: Fink.

Nunberg, Geoffrey. 1978. *The Pragmatics of Reference*. Bloomington: Indiana University Linguistics Club.

Ortony, Andrew. 1979. *Metaphor and Thought*. Cambridge: Cambridge University Press.

Owens, Howard, and Jerrold S. Maxmen. 1979. 'Mood and effect: a semantic confusion', *Am. J. Psychiatry* 136.1:97–99.

Philips, Susan. 1976. 'Some sources of cultural variability in the regulation of talk', *Language in Society* 5:81–95.

Porzig, W. 1950. *Das Wunder der Sprache*. Berne.

Putnam, Hilary. 1975. 'The meaning of meaning' in *Language, Mind, and Knowledge, Minnesota Studies in the Philosophy of Science*. VI, K. Gunderson, ed., pp. 131–93. Minneapolis: University of Minnesota Press.

Quine, Willard Van Orman. 1953. 'Two dogmas of empiricism', *From a Logical Point of View*, pp. 20–46. Cambridge: Harvard University Press.

Quine, Willard Van Orman. 1977. 'Natural kinds', *Naming, Necessity, and Natural Kinds*, Stephan Schwartz, ed., pp. 155–75. Ithaca: Cornell University Press.

Robinson, S.O. 1970. 'The misuse of taste names by untrained observers', *British Journal of Psychiatry* 61:375–78.

Rogers, Carl R. 1951. *Client-Centered Therapy*. Boston: Houghton Mifflin.

Rogers, Carl R. 1961. *On Becoming a Person*. Boston: Houghton Mifflin.

Rosaldo, Michelle Z. 1972. 'Metaphors and folk classification', *Southwestern Journal of Anthropology* 28:83–98.

Rosch, Eleanor, and C.B. Mervis. 1975. 'Family resemblances: studies in the internal structure of categories', *Cognitive Psychology* 7:573–605.

Rubin, Philip. 1973. 'A unified classification of cancers: An oncotaxonomy with symbols', *Cancer* 31:963–82.

Sadock, Jerrold M. 1974. *Toward a Linguistic Theory of Speech Acts*. New York: Academic Press.

Sapir, Edward. 1939. 'Language', *Encyclopedia of the Social Sciences*, Vol. 9:155–68. New York: Macmillan.

Sapir, Edward. 1944. 'Grading: A study of semantics', *Philosophy of Sciences* 11:93–116. Repr. in *Selected Writings of Edward Sapir in Language, Culture, and Personality*, D. Mandelbaum, ed., pp. 122–49. Berkeley: University of California Press.

Scheflen, Albert. 1973. *Communicational Structure: Analysis of a Psychotherapy Transaction*. Bloomington: Indiana University Press.

Schiffman, Susan S., and Robert P. Erickson. 1971. 'A psychophysical model for gustatory quality', *Physiology & Behavior* 7:617–33.

Schoonmaker, Frank. 1965. *Frank Schoonmaker's Encyclopedia of Wine*. New York: Hastings House.

Searle, John. 1969. *Speech Acts*. Cambridge: Cambridge University Press.

Searle, John. 1972. 'Chomsky's revolution in linguistics.' *New York Review of Books*, June 29.

Searle, John R. 1979. 'Metaphor', in Ortony, 1979:92–123.

Sibley, Frank. 1957. 'Aesthetic concepts', *Philosophical Review* 63:421–50.

Small, George W. 1924. *The Comparison of Inequality: The Semantics and Syntax of the Comparative Particle in English*. Greifswald: Abel.

Snow, Catherine E., and Charles A. Feguson. 1977. *Talking to Children*. Cambridge: Cambridge University Press.

Socarides, Charles, ed. 1977. *The World of Emotions*. New York: International Universities Press.

Soskin, William, and Vera P. John. 1963. 'The study of spontaneous talk', in *The Stream of Behavior*, R. Barker, ed. New York: Appleton-Century-Crofts.

Spencer, Nancy. 1973. 'Differences between linguists and nonlinguists in intuitions of grammaticality-acceptability'. *Journal of Psycholinguistic Research* 2:83–98.

Spitzer, Robert L., Janet B.W. Forman, and John Nee. 1979. 'DSM-III field trials: I. Initial interrater diagnostic reliability, *American Journal of Psychiatry* 136.6:815–17.

Strawson, Peter. 1950. 'On referring', *Mind* 59:320–44.

Sullivan, Harry S. 1954. *The Psychiatric Interview*. New York: Norton.

Szasz, Thomas. 1964. *The Myth of Mental Illness*. New York, Hoeber-Harper.

Teller, Paul. 1977. 'Indicative introduction', *Philosophical Studies* 31:173–95.

Thakurdas, Harold, and Lyn Thakurdas. 1978. *Dictionary of Psychiatry*. Lancaster, England: M & P Press.

Trier, Jost. 1931. *Der Deutsche Wortschatz im Sinnbezirk des Verstandes*. Heidelberg: Winter.

Urmson, J.O. 'On grading' in *Logic & Language*. 2nd series, A.G.N. Flew, ed., pp. 159–86. Oxford: Alden Press.

Vandyke Price, Pamela. 1975. *The Taste of Wine*. New York: Random House.

Vendler, Zeno. 1972. *Res Cogitans*. Ithaca, New York: Cornell University Press.

Waugh, Alec. 1968. *Wine and Spirits*, New York: Time-Life Books.

Weinreich, Uriel. 1962. 'Lexicographic definition in descriptive semantics' in *Problems in Lexicography*, Fred Householder and Sol Soporta, eds., pp. 25–43. Bloomington: Indiana University Research Center in Anthropology, Folklore and Linguistics.

Weinreich, Uriel. 1966. 'Explorations in Semantic Theory' in *Current Trends in Linguistics III*, T. Sebeok, ed. The Hague: Mouton.

Wheeler, Samuel. 1972. 'Attributives and their modifiers'. *Nous* 6:310–34.

Whitman, Roy, and James Alexander. 1968. 'On gloating', in Socarides 1977:427–44.

Williams, Anthony A. 1975. 'The development of a vocabulary and profile assessment method for evaluating the flavour contribution of cider and perry aroma constituents'. *Journal of the Sciences of Food and Agriculture* 26:567–82.

Williams, Anthony A., and Caroline S. Carter. 1977. 'A language and procedure for the sensory assessment of Cox's Orange Pippin apples', *Journal of the Sciences of Food and Agriculture* 28:1090–1104.

Wilson, J.W. 1940. Review of *Linguistic Aspects of Science* by L. Bloomfield. *Language* 16:347–51.

World Health Organization. 1973. *Report of the International Pilot Study of Schizophrenia*, vol. 1, Geneva.

Zigler, Edward, and Leslie Phillips. 1967. 'Psychiatric diagnosis: A critique' in *The Study of Abnormal Behavior*. M. Zax and G. Stricker, eds. New York: Macmillan.

Index

Acidity: words for, 6, 20; masks sweetness, 52–53
Adam: 197
Adjectives: *See* Descriptors
Aesthetics: applied to wine evaluation, 42–47; theories, 168–170; function of language, 178
Age: and astringency, 9; words for, 26–27
Agreement: on descriptions, 169, 173. *See also* Consensus
Alexander: 195
Allport & Odbert: 191–192
American Joint Committee for Cancer Staging and End Results Reporting: 161
American Psychiatric Association: 197
Amerine, Panghorn, & Roessler: 69, 77, 154, 155
Amerine & Roessler: 156, 159, 160, 224n, 225n
Amerine, Roessler, & Filipello: 13
Amerine & Singleton: 6, 70, 74
Antonymy: 19, 40–41, 42, 51, 221n, 223n
Anxiety: 195
Apathy: 195
Appearance of wine: 12
Appellation Contrôlée: 34
Arlow: 195
Arnoff: 221n
Aroma: 10
Asher: 22
assertive wine: defined, 14
Astringency: 8; defined by subjects, 171
Austin: 145–46, 152, 178, 224n

Baby talk: 174
Bach: 146
Bach & Harnish: 146–147
Balance: 7; words for, 24; as aesthetic quality, 43
Bales: 149–150, 178
Balint: 206
Beardsley: 43
Berlin & Kay: 12
big: 10, 22, 122–123, 136–140

bitter: confused with *sour,* 76–77, 82; personality, 195
Black: 223n
Bloomfield: 152–153, 226n
body: 9–10, 22, 24, 36
Boertien: 222n
Bonds: *See* Social bonds
Boredom: 195
Botha: 58
Bouquet: 10; has positive connotation, 91
Broadbent: 6, 9, 10–11, 12, 13, 26
buttery: 96, 117, 122–123, 127, 224n

California wine laws: 33, 34
Carnap: 152
Casagrande & Hale: 106, 107, 224n
Caul: 155
Chemical terms: for defects, 8; as natural kinds, 33–34
Chomsky: 144
Ciconne & Barry: 204
Ciders and perries: 155–156 *passim*
Clarity, of wine: 12
Clark & Clark: 48
Classification: of language functions, 145–151; of speech acts, 145–147; of cancers, 162; of mental diseases, 197–205
Clustering: task, 74; of words, 136–140
Color, of wine: 12, 13
Communication: experiments, 80–85, 96–102, 123–129. *See also* Matching task; framework for, 143–151; function of language, 144, 181
Comparative constructions: 37–39
Complexity: defined, 12; words for, 26
Concentration: of dissolved solids, 24. *See also* Body
Connoisseurs: of wine, 51, 74
Consensus: 63; experiments, 70–79, 83–85, 89–94, 114, 116–120; importance for scientists, 113; greater among experts, 120; among Four Corners States subjects, 161; among social scientists, 165. *See also* Agreement
Consistency: 92–94. *See also* Retesting
Conversation: spontaneous, 58; experi-

ments, 83–85; functions of, 143 *passim;*
satisfies social needs, 181
Cooper et al: 197–200
Correctness: in wine description, 169,
172; in linguistic usage, 173–174; of
psychiatric diagnosis, 205; in therapy,
212, 215, 226n
Correlation of preference and description. *See* Preference
Coseriu: 18
Critical communication: 151, 168–174,
184; and psychotherapy, 190, 200,
214–215, 218; in matching task 225n
Criticism, literary: 168 *passim*

Dani: 166
Davis: subjects, 66–67, 68, 113–140,
172; compared to Tucson subjects:
115–116, 118–119, 121–122, 128,
131–135; compared to Stanford sub-
jects: 119, 128, 131–134; score card:
156–157, 159–160
Davitz: 196–197, 206
Deese: 106
Defects: in wine, 43; noted by experts,
125–126; emphasized by score cards,
159–160
Definite descriptions: 169
Denominal verbs: 48
Denotation: 30–31 *passim,* 35, 40, 50–51,
150, 151, 155; *See also* Reference; of
personality descriptors, 193.
Dethier: 154
Depression: 195
Descriptive: statements, 153, 154; words
express evaluation, 46–47. *See also*
Preference
Descriptors: for wine, listed, 5, 72, 88;
good and poor, 115–117, 121; most
frequently used, 71–73, 76, 79, 93,
106. *See also* Most and least task;
pragmatically interpreted, 48–50, 51;
for coffee, 225n; for people, *See* Per-
sonality
Diagnostic and Statistical Manual (DMS):
201–205
Dickie: 42, 43
Directives: 147
Discourse: 181–184, 225n–226n
Donnellan: 169
dry: bone dry, 7; has evaluative component, 73–74, 76
Dutt, Mielke, & Wolfe: 157

earthy: 75, 96, 108–109, 115, 123,
136–140, 156, 169
Emotions: describing, 189–191, 194–197
Emotivism: 42
Empirical studies: 61 *passim*
Entailment: 35, 40–41, 222n. *See also*
Meaning postulates
Envy: 196
Erikson: 205, 226n
Esau: 17
Evaluation: affects description, 6, 71
passim, 79, 177; terms of praise and
derogation, 11–12; theories of, 41–47,
51. *See also* Preference
Experimental semantics: 57 *passim*
Experiments: wine, 43, 61, 67–69; in
psychology, 58–59; controlling vari-
ables, 61–62
Experts: determine denotation 32,
39–40, 44, 50–51; use narrower refer-
ence class, 38; disagree, 43; winetast-
ers, 62, 63; connoisseurs vs. scientists,
113
Extending the vocabulary: 48–50
Extension: 35, 41. *See also* Denotation
and reference

Faith: 196
Faust: 165, 222n
Fear: 195
Feel: of wine in mouth, 9; words for, 20,
21. *See also* Body
feminine: 29, 50, 115, 122, 136–140,
183–184, 193
Ferguson: 175
Fillipello, Berg, & Webb, 74
Fine: 222n
flabby: 6
flat: 9, 20, 96; and *sharp,* 221n
Flavor: defined, 6
Finish: lingering vs. short: 11
Four Corners States wine project: 157,
159–161
foxy: defined, 13
Fraser: 224n
Freud: 178, 200
Friedrich: 225n
Functions of language: 143–151

Gale: 223n
Gelman: 201
General semantics: 41–42
generous: 192, 193–194, 216
Generic wines: 34
Gluckman: 176

Goldberg: 191–193
Goldstein & Goldstein: 200
good: 41–47
Goodman: 49
Gossip: 175–176, 216, 218
Gradable expressions: 36–41; 51
Grading: 43
Greenson: 195, 207
Grice: 48, 146, 152
Gullibility: 196

Halliday: 144, 148, 224n
Hanson: 153
Hearer-oriented: 147, 148
Hedonic: *See* Scales
Heider: 166
Hempel: 223n
Hobbs: 178
honest: wine, 28, 50, 115, 136–140
Humor: 177–181, 182–184
Hymes: 144, 150, 178, 225n
Hyponymy: 19, 35, 40, 44–45, 46, 51

Ilongots: 167
Incompatibility: 35, 41, 45, 51
Indices: for interpreting scalar terms, 37–38; *very* indexer, 46–47; *too* indexer, 47
Intension: 30–31 *passim*, 41
Interdisciplinary studies, value of, 57
Interpersonal: relationships, 144, 147 *passim;* functions of language, 147, 149
Intralinguistic relationships: 30, 35, 50–51; explored by subjects, 84; agreement by subjects, 95; used to define, 106–107 *passim*, 151; agreement by scientists, 165; among personality descriptors, 193; disagreement among therapists, 197
Intuitions: 58
Inverted spectrum: 154
Isenberg: 151, 168, 169–170, 206
Issacs, Alexander, & Haggard: 196

Jakobson: 144, 148, 149, 178
Jealousy: 196
Jokes: parasitic on serious language, 153; category of, 178. *See also* Humor
Jones, Daniel: 163
Judging food and wine: 155–161

Kamp: 222n
Katz: 41, 48, 223n
Kelly: 208, 226n
Kempson: 48

Kittay & Lehrer: 19, 49
Klapp: 41
Koestler: 178
Korzybski: 41
Kripke: 31–34, 52, 222n
Kris: 179
Kuhn: 57, 153

Labov: 58, 165, 222n
Labov & Fanshel: 207, 212, 214
Ladefoged: 163–164
Lakoff & Johnson: 49
Langer: 189, 190, 206
Laughter: *See* Humor
Learning new words: *See* Vocabulary
Legs: caused by glycerine, 9
Lehrer, A.: 19
Lehrer, K.: 223n, 224n
Lehrer & Lehrer: 41, 223n
Levin: 49
Lexical structure: of wine descriptors, 4. *See also* Intralinguistic relationships, Meaning postulates
Lexique: 9, 26
Ljung: 17
Loewenberg: 49
Logical positivists: 152
Lyons: 18, 19, 41, 175

Machamer: 12, 225n
Malinowsky: 148, 174, 175–176, 225n
manly: 183–184
masculine: 29
Matching task: 80–83, 96–102, 123–129, 130–131
McCawley: 58, 224n
McConnell-Ginet: 37–39, 222n, 223n
McDermott & Roth: 181
McLemore & Benjamin: 197
Marchand: 221n
Meaning: postulates, 35, 40–41, 47, 222n; explored by subjects, 84; general vs. specific, 44–45. *See also* Denotation, Intralinguistic relationships, Semantic fields
Measurement: of sugar and alcohol, 69; theory, 225n
Mental illness: 197–205
Metaphor: 48, 49–50; for describing feelings, 212–214
Methodology: in the social sciences, 57–60, 61
Metzger & Williams: 106
Miller, D.: 59, 60

Miller, H. E.: 149
Mindess: 179
Miscommunication: 81–82, 84, 86, 135, 165
Miss Cam: 209, 212–214
Morphology: suffixes, 16–17, 221n; of comparative constructions, 38
Moskowitz: 52
Most and least experiment: 94–96, 121–123
Mr. L.: 208
Mrs. Oak: 209–212, 214

Naming: of objects, 165–167
Natural kind terms: 31–35, 39
Nida: 18, 106
Nonexpert winetasters: 62, 150
Nonscientific uses of language: 168–185
Norms: no stable set developed, 111; rarely made explicit, 120, 129. See also Reference class
Nounty: 17
Nose: dimension of smell, 10
Nunberg: 45

Observational studies: 59–60
Odor: vocabulary for ciders and perries: 155–156 passim
Oncology: 161
Owens & Maxmen: 194

Perceptions: impossibility of determining instrumentally, 154. See also Sensory discrimination
Personality: terms for wine, 13–14, 26–28; describing, 189–197
Pets: talking to, 174–175, 225n
Phatic communion: 148, 149, 174–177, 181, 184–185, 216
Philosophy of language: 30, 152 passim
Phonetics: 163–165
Porzig: 18
Pragmatic: theories, 36; functions, 45, 46
Precise language: 153 passim
Preference: questionnaires, 63, 64, 67; affects description, 71 passim, 79, 82, 93–94, 121, 176–177; and trusting others' judgments, 112
Preferred words: 89, 115–117. See also Descriptors
pretentious: 28, 50, 117
Profile of tastes: 14
Psychiatric diagnosis: 197; U.S. vs. Britain, 198–199
Psychopath, defined, 226n

Psychotherapy: 190; interviews, 205–216; skill in communicating, 207 passim; determining correctness, 212, 215, 226n
Putnam: 31–34, 155, 222n

Questionnaire: on preference, 63, 64, 67; on knowledge, 63, 65; on most and least task, 95
Quine: 143, 225n

Reference: 31; See also Denotation; class for gradable predicates, 37–38, 42, 120–121, 193; and definite description, 169
Referential functions of language: 144, 146, 147
Reid, John: 126–129, 132–133
Rejected words: 89, 115–117
Relativism: 43
Reliability: short term, 103–105; See also Retesting in diagnosing schizophrenia, 200–201, 203–204
Retesting: 78–79, 92–94, 103–105, 111
Rhoda: 212, 215
Rigid designators: 32
Robinson: 77
Rogers: 206, 207, 208, 209–212, 213–214
Rosch & Mervis: 222n
Rosoldo: 166, 167
round: 14, 26, 110–111, 122–123, 136–140, 221n

Sacks: 225n–226n
Sadock: 224n
Sapir: 37, 144–145
Satisfaction: expressed by subjects, 84–85, 111–112; on descriptions, 174
Sauterne(s): 34–35, 43, 222n
Scalar terms: 19, 36–41, 44–45, 51. See also Antonymy; judgments, 120–121, 129
Scales: for judging wine, 90; hedonic, 157, 160
Scheflen: 197–198, 205
Schiffman & Erickson: 225n
Schizophrenia: 190; diagnosing, 198–204; definitions of, 201–203
Schoonmaker: 9
Scientific language: 151, 152–167; vs. phatic communion, 184–185; for describing people, 191–194; for emotions, 194–197; in therapy, 207–208, 215

Scientists: of wine, 113 *passim;* determine denotation, 32, 50
Searle: 144, 223n, 224n
Semantic: extension of word meaning 17–20 *passim;* fields, 18–20 *passim,* 48–49; theories, 30–31 *passim,* 41; relationships among words 35, 40–41, 44–47, 51; relationships between nouns and verbs, 48
semi-: 182
Sensory discrimination: 154
Shape: of a wine, 14, 24
sharp: as taste word, 20; and *flat,* 221n
Sibley: 170
Size: words for wine, 22, 24
Smugness: 195
Snow & Ferguson: 175
Socarides: 195
Social bonds: 181; created by laughter, 179, 184–185. *See also* Phatic communion
Soskin & John: 144, 147, 149
Sour: and *bitter;* personality: 195
Sparkling wine: 11, 221n
Spitzer et al.: 204, 205
Speech acts: 145–147, 177, 178. *See also* Functions of language
Spencer: 58
Standardized stimuli: for odors, 158–159; for speech sounds, 165
Stanford subjects: 63, 68, 70–85, 113, 119, 134
Strawson: 146
Stereotypes: 33 *passim*
Subjectivism: 42
Subjects in experiments: *See* Stanford subjects, Tucson subjects, Davis subjects
Suffixation: 16–17
Sugar: *See sweet*
Sullivan: 207, 208, 209
Survey data: 60
sweet: 39, 47; as a natural kind term, 52–53; as a gradable term, 53; has evaluative component, 73–74; 176–177
Sweet wine: attitudes toward, 64, 73–74
Sweetness: 6–7, measuring, 69; masked by acid, 75, 82; differences perceived, 102
Symbolic organization of language: 145
Synonymy: 19, 35, 40, 51; of words used by subjects, 78, 93, 118
Szasz: 197

Tannin: causes astringency, 20, 22, 171, 221n
Tapes: analysis of, 105–111
Taste: words for, 19–20 *passim;* blindness, 52; of sugar masked by acid, 53
Taxonomy: of illocutionary acts, 146, 177; of personality terms, 191–192
Technical terms: for wine properties, 4
Teller: 31
Temperature: affects taste discrimination, 223n
Textual function of language: 148
Texture: words for, 22–23
Thakurdas & Thakurdas: 226n
Theory-laden perception: 58, 153
Therapy: *See* Psychotherapy
Thurber, James: 3
too: 47
Touch: words for, 20
Trier: 18
Trust: 196
Truth: 30, 39–40, 44, 49–50; of illocutionary acts, 146; and definite descriptions, 169; of aesthetic judgments, 223n
Tucson subjects: 65–66, 68, 86–112, 115–117, 135, 170–173, 179–181, 182–184
Tumors: 161–163

Unusual wine words: 106. *See also* Rejected words
Urmson: 42, 43–44

Vandyke Price: 9, 13–14, 24, 128, 221n
Variability, among speakers: in describing feelings, 208; in describing people, 216
Variations: in semantic interpretation, 30; in naming, 165–167
Varietals: for classifying California wines, 4; as natural kinds, 32; stereotypic properties, 33; premium, 126–127
Vendler: 224n
vegy: 116, 126
very: 45–47
Vocabulary: learning new items, 87, 105–112
Vowels: cardinal, 163; Gaelic, 164

Weinreich: 106
Wheeler: 46
Whitman & Alexander: 196
Williams: 20, 155–156

Williams & Carter: 155

Wilson: 226n

World Health Organization: 197, 200–201

Word-circling task: 71–79, 87, 92–94, 115–120

Word clusters: 136–140, 224n

Words for wine: *See* Descriptors

Zigler & Phillips: 197, 201

Zilboorg: 195